AN UNBROKEN THREAD

AN
UNBROKEN
THREAD

Celebrating 150 Years of the
Royal School of Needlework

SUSAN KAY-WILLIAMS

ACC ART BOOKS

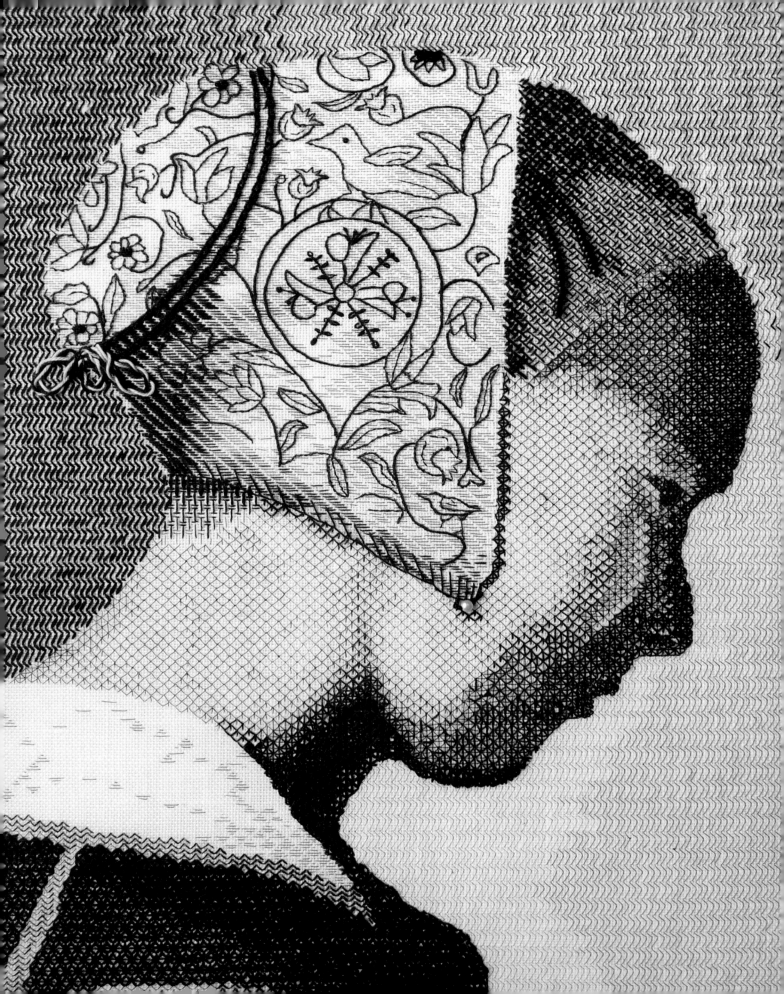

This book is dedicated to all those connected with the Royal School of Needlework who have been determined to keep it going; from Princess Helena to the team in 2020 who pivoted the RSN to an online organisation in a remarkably short space of time in order to meet the needs of our supporters.

Dr Susan Kay-Williams
Chief Executive of the RSN

Contents

CLARENCE HOUSE

In 2017, I was delighted to become Patron of the Royal School of Needlework. Although not personally blessed with many sewing skills, I have always been deeply impressed by the incredible abilities of its students and teachers.

I know that the work of the School has been dear to the hearts of several generations of the Royal Family, who have successively held the role of Patron: Queen Victoria (who apparently liked peering into cupboards and workbaskets, to see what had been concealed from her!), Queen Mary, Queen Elizabeth The Queen Mother and Her Majesty Queen Elizabeth II.

Throughout its 150 years, the Royal School of Needlework has combined traditional skills with an innovative spirit. In its earliest days, it gave vital employment to women who would otherwise have been destitute. It also offered an outlet for its members' artistic tendencies, working closely with the leaders of the Arts and Crafts movement, and creating exquisite pieces for a huge variety of occasions: military, ecclesiastical, fashion, weddings and funerals, often at nail-bitingly short notice… It is quite astonishing what can be achieved, and expressed, through the medium of hand sewing.

I saw this for myself in May 2023, when a brilliant team of members did so much for the Coronation: conserving The King's Robe of Estate, sewing the Anointing Screen and designing and hand embroidering my magnificent Robe of Estate, which features bees, butterflies, a beetle, a caterpillar and twenty-four different plants (including, appropriately for the RSN, Scabiosa – pincushion flowers).

I do hope that you will enjoy this history of the Royal School of Needlework as much as I did, and that the School will go from strength to strength in the next 150 years …

Camilla R

CHAPTER I

1872–1903

'The idea of reviving secular needlework for domestic decoration was suggested in conversation between two friends in the autumn of '72. One (whom I need not name,) had the courage, and energy to break ground alone. The few who knew and appreciated what she was undertaking soon turned their sympathy into action, and with the fostering aid of the Royal Lady who does us the honour to preside over us, the scheme took form, and the framework of the present Society was gradually developed.'

So spoke Vice President Lady Marian Alford at the opening of what were the School of Art Needlework's third premises, on Exhibition Road, South Kensington, on 22 June 1875.

The lady whom Alford considered she did not need to name was Lady Victoria Welby Gregory, founder of the School of Art Needlework.[1] The school first occupied premises above a bonnet shop on Sloane Street, Kensington, London. The title School of Art Needlework was selected because Lady Welby believed that embroidery should not just be small pieces worked at home for domestic purposes, but large significant works which should be seen alongside fine art in galleries. She also wanted to reintroduce all the techniques of fine hand embroidery that had almost been lost in the 19th century to the craze of Berlin wool work, a form of canvaswork that could be achieved with just one stitch.

Lady Marian Alford was a friend of Lady Welby; both had houses in Lincolnshire,[2] and Lady Marian was a designer and lover of historical needlework.

The third key player in the creation of the school was Princess Helena,[3] Queen Victoria's third daughter. In 1893, Helena wrote an article as part of a report on women's philanthropy in England for the Chicago World's Fair[4] to accompany the exhibits which were being sent from the RSN. In the article she confirmed Alford's narrative on the origin and founder of the school:

'As I have said, [RSN] sprang from nothing. Some friends of mine, Lady Welby Gregory in particular, first suggested the idea, and spoke to me about it. I was at once greatly struck by and interested in the scheme and asked her to let me help her in carrying it out.

'The idea was this: first of all to restore the nearly lost art of ornamental needlework to its high place among decorative arts, and in the second place to provide suitable employment for gentlewomen who, through loss of fortune or other reverses are obliged to earn their own livelihood.'[5]

This agreement as to the founding of the school is important; decades later, even the school's own publications cited Princess Helena as the founder.

While Lady Welby planned to oversee the school, from the beginning she engaged Mrs Anastasia Dolby as Superintendent to manage the tuition and the work. Dolby had been an embroiderer to Queen Victoria and was the author of two books on ecclesiastical embroidery,[6] although this is slightly ironic as it was not the initial intention of the school to undertake ecclesiastical embroidery, as Lady Welby made clear to an enquiring Mother Superior.[7] Nevertheless, regardless of the application of the embroidery, Mrs Dolby clearly had skills across all the embroidery techniques. However, the enterprise did not get off to the best of starts as Mrs Dolby died in February 1873, leading to the first crisis.[8]

At the inaugural meeting of Council, the governing body,[9] on 2 May 1873, with Princess Helena in the Chair, it was Lady Welby who gave the report and who put forward proposals for how the school was going to operate. The first need was a move to bigger premises. Council approved this, if suitable accommodation could be found on economic terms. Premises were located and the school moved from 130 Sloane Street to 31 Sloane Street in July 1873, but not without financial support from the Duke of Northumberland who put up £250 to help keep the organisation afloat, but business was beginning to come. At the Council meeting of 4 July 1873, Lady Welby announced that commissions valued at £300 were 'quite or nearly completed'.

Lady Welby took on the day-to-day management of the school for 1873 but clearly, as she lived in Lincolnshire outside the Season, this was too onerous an undertaking and in February 1874 Lady Welby became Honorary Manager and Council appointed Miss Louisa Wade as Lady Assistant Manager, initially for a limited engagement to ensure she would carry out the objects of Council, at a salary of £150 per annum. One meeting later, Miss Wade was appointed Superintendent/Manager.[10]

The idea of the school was to attract young women who had some experience of hand embroidery but who had fallen on hard times. From the initial leaflet about terms of admission the fee was 3 gns but quickly rose to £5.[11] Pupils were given nine days of lessons, described as 'absolutely necessary', although any young woman showing no promise at all after two days (later three) would be let go and her fee returned to her. Pupils and workers also had to live 'in town', that is, around the Kensington area ideally, but certainly in London.

The first students are recorded as joining on 5 November 1872. As part of the registration process they were expected to explain their personal circumstances. For first student Miss Martha Lee the register reveals that she was 'the daughter of a surveyor, of repute, who died unexpectedly in Rome leaving a widow and four daughters wholly unprovided for.'

Example of Berlin wool work border

[RSN Collection. Photograph: John Chase]

The candidates needed two referees to prove they were of good character and in some cases to provide or underwrite the fees as a loan. Once the students were earning money, the loan would be repaid in instalments from their wages. Lessons for the new entrants took place from 10 am to 4 pm.[12]

After successful completion of the lessons, the students would move into the workroom, although press reports still referred to the workers as students, as they were being taught embroidery techniques which had fallen out of use. The Register also records some of the students' abilities and shortcomings. The best one could hope for was 'good general worker' which meant they could be put to work on anything. However, for one student it says 'good general worker but do not allow her to choose her colours'.

For these women, this was their first paid work and the first annual report noted:

'There was the difficulty — a very real one — of training in regular, careful, and accurate habits of work, ladies accustomed to easy leisure rather than professional work: the difficulty of admitting all without distinction of creed (which without great and patient care might have led to painful discord); the difficulty of organizing a staff among the ladies themselves, ignorant of business and with only a few months' of experience of art-work, while there was none to lead them but an amateur with only an amateur's experience, and a complete stranger to commercial affairs.'

As a result, a set of rules was needed for the workers, beginning with:

'… it is desirable that she should regard her occupation as a profession to which she is bound to give the utmost of their time and attention, and this is not only for her own interests, but those of the school which can only prosper, or indeed continue in existence by the steady co-operation of all those concerned in it.'

The rules set out how and when workers acquired work, how and when they were to complete it, the penalties and rewards for tardiness/speed and underlined that workers were paid by the piece as well as emphasising the standards expected. The initial advertisement of the Terms of Admission stated that 'Ordinary workers may earn from 20s to 30s a week: first-rate workers considerably more'. The annual report confirms that the workers were paid by the piece 'so that the most skilful and rapid worker earns the largest sums' and by October 1873, 43 ladies were on the books.

By 1875 there were further rules to be observed: on the hours of work (9 am to 6 pm on weekdays and 9 am to 1 pm on Saturdays); on the practicalities of handing in work and being paid; and on the

One example of the several Supplements to *The Queen*, 11 June 1887 in which the RSN advertised its wares

[RSN Archive. Photograph: John Chase]

SUGGESTIONS FOR DECORATIVE APPLICATIONS OF EMBROIDERY.

DESIGNS BY THE ROYAL SCHOOL OF ART NEEDLEWORK.

1.—FRAME FOR HER MAJESTY'S PHOTOGRAPH

2.—ORNAMENTAL WALL POCKET.

3.—FRAME FOR ENGAGEMENT CARDS

4.—DIPLOMA OF THE PRIMROSE LEAGUE.

6.—NEWSPAPER OR MUSIC RACK

5.—MEMORIAL BOOK COVER.

7.—MEMORIAL BOOK COVER.

8.—DIPLOMA OF THE PRIMROSE LEAGUE.

9.—STOOL AND COVER.

10.—COVER FOR BRADSHAW.

A. COATES, PRINTER, NOTTINGHAM.

management of embroidery frames and the requisites of the workers. They were to supply their own scissors, needles, and protective aprons and sleeves. The rules continued to be reviewed and periodically updated. In 1883 it was felt necessary to insist that if workers wanted work, they had to attend the full hours each day until the order was completed. If the person was not willing to do the hours, she would have to take her chances with what work might be available, because although the aim of the school was to offer work to all, the workers had to be dependable and from their next move, in attendance.

In the workroom, if a worker was not on a specific commission, they were to copy designs from historical pieces of embroidery. They had plenty of opportunities to see examples from the South Kensington Museum[13] and from a series of exhibitions that the RSN mounted to provide this inspiration. The first exhibition was held at the South Kensington Museum but from 1875 these were held at the RSN itself. The exhibitions often featured historical pieces of needlework which were loaned from the South Kensington Museum, from supporters of the project, and from those members of the nobility (later to become Associates) who had historical pieces of embroidery in their family homes. From this inspiration they were to devise designs that could be worked on items such as blotters, Bradshaw[14] covers and other small items which could be sold at the annual sales.

As an enterprise that was never meant to make a profit but rather to support its workers and be self-supporting, the school wanted to promote its work, so from the earliest time it took every opportunity to exhibit its commissions. The first occasion was in 1874 when it exhibited at the International Exhibition, the last of four annual exhibitions to be held in and around Exhibition Road, South Kensington, London. *The Times* commented on the RSN's items:

'The large pair of cases filled with tapestries and curtain borders designed and executed at the School of Art Needlework under the special patronage of her Royal Highness the Princess Christian, display some really beautiful samples of what female fingers can achieve even in these modern and degenerate days ... There is a portière border of honeysuckle worked in feather stitch on white satin which deserves special mention, so graceful and exquisite are the flower curves, with their borders of a golden gimp. This design was furnished by Lady Marian Alford and is beautifully executed.'[15]

Behind the scenes, the fledgling organisation was having a number of issues. Lady Welby had officially stood down as Honorary Manager, there were staff disputes that needed to go to Council for resolution, the organisation was growing, there were 76 workers, and they needed bigger premises. However, Council held its nerve and within six months things had moved on.

At the Council meeting on 23 March 1875, Princess Helena began by announcing that Queen Victoria had agreed to become Patron. Miss Wade took over working out the distribution of the workload and overseeing the production of commissions. The area around Exhibition Road, South Kensington was owned and managed by the 1851 Commissioners, the body arising out of the financial success of the Great Exhibition. Following discussion with them[16] the school moved into what was known as the Belgian annexe on Exhibition Road. The move required additional staff – a Watcher (nightwatchman), a boy to run errands, and someone who could 'furnish Financial Reports as from time to time may be required'.

The first published mention of the Royal School of Art Needlework appeared in *The Globe* in a short report which also highlighted the move from Sloane Street to Exhibition Road:

> 'Princess Christian President, yesterday afternoon at a meeting held at Alford House of the council of the Royal School of Art Needlework of which Her Majesty has become patron. The school is now removing to its new premises in the International Exhibition buildings at South Kensington.'[17]

The *Windsor and Eton Express* added further that once in the new premises there would be an exhibition of some of the recent work by the school, ending with the comments that 'the work of which has done much to promote the improvement of modern needlework'.[18]

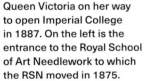

Queen Victoria on her way to open Imperial College in 1887. On the left is the entrance to the Royal School of Art Needlework to which the RSN moved in 1875.

[Royal Collection Trust/© His Majesty Charles III 2023]

Design card from early days of the RSN, showing a tree-of-life design, created by the RSN paint room

[RSN Archive. Photograph: John Chase]

The school moved in June with the official opening by Princess Helena on 22 June. In three short years, this small, still embryonic organisation had become a significant entity. With the Queen as Patron, it had the right to be called the Royal School of Art Needlework. Council was led by the very active royal President, Princess Helena, and comprised members of the aristocracy. The RSN was now located in one of the most prestigious and growing areas of new London (what has been referred to as Albertopolis, running from Hyde Park and the Albert Memorial to Gloucester Road), an area which was becoming home to many of the main London museums plus the Royal Albert Hall,[19] the Royal College of Music,[20] and later to Imperial College and from 1875 the Royal School of Art Needlework. To cement the move and the bona fides of the organisation, a new prospectus was published. The front cover listed the key supporters, from Her Majesty The Queen as Patron, through Council, the Trustees and the Art Committee. Inside it set out the full range of the school's activities: restoring ornamental needlework for secular purposes, carrying out the designs and instructions of artists, as well as offering lessons, prepared work and materials for sale. In the new space they created three workrooms, an upholstery department, a paint room and a showroom. With the increased space it was agreed that one day a week should be considered a visiting day, generally between 11 am and 1 pm, when Council members could visit as well as Associates and their guests.

Art and Design

Art and design were important to Princess Helena, the founding members believed that design was a very important part of the creation of splendid embroidery, and Lady Welby and Lady Marian Alford were both active designers and so they determined the need for an Art Committee to oversee the commissioning of designs. Following discussion at Council in March 1875, the committee was finally established in June,[21] the founding members of which were indeed prestigious: the artist Sir Frederic Leighton, with fellow artist Val Prinsep and architect G.F. Bodley.[22] This trio appear only to have attended three committee meetings, but they set down the principles on which the school should develop its approach to art and design. They suggested that old works of good design be collected and made visible to the workers, be studied and copied by the workers, as both scale drawings and a portion of the whole, and drawn to size, and finally a sample should be worked showing colouring and stitch choices, and these be collected into sample books for future reference. Furthermore, they demanded that 'no design to be worked for sale or order that has not been passed by the Art Committee', and that yarn choices should also be viewed by the Art Committee so that they could choose the colours. Finally, recognising that the school also sought to work contemporary pieces, the president and Council were informed they 'should commission certain artists to

contribute designs and that the under mentioned be at once invited
so to do: Mr Bodley, Mr Aitcheson [*sic*], Mr Morris, Mr Burne-Jones,
Mr Walter Crane.'

At the second meeting there is a minute to say that Mr Morris should
be asked to be on the committee.[23] Further they discussed Mr Arthur's
proposal of hangings for a room at the Philadelphia Exhibition, for
which Mr Bodley promised some designs, and Miss Wade informed
the committee that all the above, except Burne-Jones, had already been
contacted about designs. Their submissions were then reviewed by the
committee and passed for working.

In the minutes of what was the sub-committee relating to the
Centennial International Exhibition in Philadelphia, chaired by Lady
Marian Alford, it was noted that 'Mrs Percy Wyndham reported a
long and favourable interview (at the school) with Mr Morris who
had promised designs which could be proceeded with at once'.

Although a meeting of the Art Committee was scheduled for August
1875, there are no minutes and the next minuted meeting of the committee

Juno from the four goddesses screen designed by Selwyn Image and made by the RSN. One approach of art embroidery was to cover large areas in a single colour of thread and often a single stitch, which was a quicker and cheaper approach than shading.

[RSN Collection. Photograph: John Chase]

is March 1879 when the Hon. Mrs Percy Wyndham[24] was in the Chair with Lady Marian Alford and Miss Mary Stuart Wortley. Hereafter, the committee retained female leadership and membership.[25] With the principles set down, perhaps the gentlemen considered their work done.

Over the next quarter of a century the RSN worked with all the above designers; one name not on the list with whom the organisation had a long-term link was Selwyn Image.[26] Image is little recognised today and indeed may be considered the forgotten man of the Arts and Crafts movement, not least as several of his works have been attributed to other designers, especially Edward Burne-Jones and Walter Crane.[27]

The first works by many of these designers went to Philadelphia and/or featured in the 1880 *Handbook of Embroidery*, including *Musica* and *Poesis* designed by Burne-Jones, an embroidered version of *Trellis* and *Vine* by Morris, a series of screens and panels by Selwyn Image including *Juno* (left), *Venus, Minerva* and *Proserpine, The Four Seasons* and *The Musicians*.[28]

Of all of them, it was Walter Crane with whom the RSN had the longest relationship. Beginning in 1875 it continued to the end of the century. Crane designed whole ensembles, screens and panels through to curtain borders.

To pay for designs from these gentlemen and indeed to be able to prepare pieces of work for exhibitions, the RSN needed to raise funds. However, they made it clear in the prospectus that this was neither a charitable donation, nor a standard investment but that rather HRH Princess Helena and Council were seeking people who would render material assistance either by lending a sum of money without or at minimal interest, or by becoming a guarantor of the school. The prospectus then sets out those who have already contributed, and the amounts donated. They sought to raise a sum of £5,000 as capital to underpin the organisation and given their next activity it is easy to see why.

The Centennial International Exhibition, Philadelphia, 1876

Exhibiting at the Centennial International Exhibition in Philadelphia first appeared on the Council agenda in May 1875: 'The Manager read her monthly report … and letters were read relating to exhibitions at Enfield and Philadelphia.' This immediately necessitated a sub-committee. From their meeting on 22 July, Lady Marian Alford, Lady Charlotte Schreiber and the Hon. Mrs Percy Wyndham referred to Mr Arthur's plans for work to be done for the Philadelphia exhibition which had been sent to the Art Committee. The list of items to be made for Philadelphia was signed off by the committee on 4 September 1875, although no list was attached to the minutes. Interestingly, the RSN was probably the only organisation that exhibited in both the main pavilion and the women's pavilion. The latter by direct invitation of the Chairman of the Women's section.[29]

The RSN made a stupendous effort in their preparations for Philadelphia. They brought in additional stitchers, in particular Elizabeth (Bessie) Burden. Bessie was an excellent embroiderer of great skill, and she made a significant contribution to the works that went to the United States. The stitch formerly known as *opus plumarium* was used extensively by her and the RSN renamed it Burden stitch. It was first written about in the *Handbook of Embroidery* and is well shown in the image of *Angel with Cymbals*. Even after the work had gone to America, Bessie Burden gave lessons to workers at the RSN: 'Monday 26th Inst was fixed for Miss Burden to commence her lessons.'

It was also at this time that a core RSN skill was established. With large pieces there would be several people working on each one and it was important that the finished items looked like the work of one person, so the practical aspects of stitching, such as stitch length and size, and the approach to shading, all had to match. This concept of multiple people working on a piece, but it looking as if it is the work of an individual stitcher remains a quintessential hallmark of the RSN and has been a fundamental part of all the large-scale projects that the RSN has completed across the 150 years.

Philadelphia was the RSN's great opportunity to reach an American audience and there were big plans. The school prepared more than 160 pieces with a combined value of £2,000[30] and held an exhibition of the work at the RSN in March 1876. A catalogue listed all the pieces. In addition, the RSN shipped pieces worked by members of the royal family, including the Queen which, with some of the RSN pieces, were specifically destined for the Women's Pavilion. Originally this pre-departure exhibition was scheduled for four days but proved so popular the *London Evening Standard* reported that it was to be extended for two more days.

The Philadelphia Centennial International Exhibition opened on 10 May and ran until 10 November. At the time this must have been the most photographed event in the world as there are over 3,000 photographs – out of those, the main RSN stand appears clearly in just one. Described as a tent structure it had work hung all-round the outside. There were also freestanding pieces between the 'wall' of the display and the outer barrier. It can be seen from the images on the opposite page that on one side there was an entrance, and there were also pieces hung on the inside. Although there were overhead lamps, it is hard to know how easy it would have been to see the work inside the tent area. The front of the display was designed by Walter Crane as *Complete Design for Decorating a Room with Hangings*. In the centre are *Salve* and *Vale*, then to the right and left are two further panels of grotesques and pillars on each side, then three further hangings above.

Altogether, Crane supplied designs for 17 pieces including *Vain Jackdaw* (see page 24), and William Morris four including *Peacock and Vine* (see page 20), Fairfax Wade, George Aitchison, G.F. Bodley and

Angel with Cymbals. Bessie Burden, after whom the RSN named Burden stitch, worked and later taught at the RSN in the 1870s and early 1880s. This minstrel figure features Burden stitch.

[© William Morris Gallery]

(above) **The RSN stand in the main hall at the 1876 Philadelphia Centennial International Exhibition**
[Image courtesy of the Library Company of Philadelphia]

(right) Walter Crane's seven hangings for a room, worked by the RSN, were the centrepiece of the RSN stand in Philadelphia.
[Image courtesy of the Hathi Trust]

Owen Jones were also among those who contributed designs, and there were designs from women too, notably from Princess Helena herself, her sister Princess Louise, Lady Marian Alford and Mrs Percy Wyndham whose works included 'Velveteen curtains and Valance with sunflower Borders, designed for Her Majesty the Queen'. There were also some from members of staff, including named designs by Miss Gemmell, Miss Cresswell and Miss Philips.

The RSN stand introduced art embroidery to the United States, but very little of the work sold. For a start, the Crane pieces made a huge statement – one would need a sizeable room in which to display the whole, otherwise it would be too overwhelming. In that respect it looks much more like a promotional set than something one might take home. Secondly, the price was prohibitive. Added to the cost of making was the cost of shipping, and while import duties were suspended for the exhibition, if a piece were sold, it incurred the full weight of tariffs which were 35 per cent for textiles, and as the dollar to pound rate was not favourable to the Americans, this would have made the pieces extortionate. However, it did not mean that nothing succeeded. William Morris saw the opportunity to introduce his work to the American market at very little cost. He subsequently received good feedback and went on to sell in America.

One person who was inspired was Candace Wheeler[31] not just by some of the designs for interiors, but that they had been produced by

Vain Jackdaw is a four-panel screen designed by Walter Crane and first exhibited in Philadelphia. The RSN went on to make several more copies for customers.

[RSN Archive. Photograph: John Chase]

Gemmell Rose.

Painting Room.

Chair Back.

Scotch Daisy

5.—CHAIR BACK.

KINDLY RETURN AS SOON AS POSSIBLE.

Design by Miss Gemmell of the RSN in the 1870s. Designs were presented on cards which could be sent to potential clients, and from which they could place orders. These pieces could be used for chair backs or as decorative panels.

[RSN Archive. Photograph: John Chase]

women, and women making their own living. Such an impact did it have on her that the following year she established the Decorative Arts Society in New York and introduced art embroidery to America.[32] The exhibition also led to the first teacher being sent out to America by the RSN in 1878.

As photography was so new, reproduction of objects was expensive, so the main reviews of the exhibition featured line drawings and engravings of the objects on display. For a small, still new organisation it is remarkable how many of the RSN's pieces are illustrated in print.[33]

In the end, most of the works had to be returned to the RSN and a selling Special Exhibition was held comprising both the Philadelphia pieces and more recent work from the school. The items ranged in price from 2gns for a cushion to £310 for *Curtains and valance in red Utrecht velvet with Goldwork and Appliquéd velvet*, designed by J.H. Pollen. The Crane set would have cost £370 for all seven pieces but they were listed and priced individually. It was noted in the Finance Committee minutes that the items were at reduced prices. Admission prices were fixed for the exhibition to at least raise some funds from those who might come to see, rather than to buy.

The new pieces would have been those worked by staff in the intervening time since the previous sale, comprising domestic pieces such as chair backs,[34] table covers, screens and cushions. However, not all the Philadelphia pieces sold, so in 1878 Council resolved to send the remaining pieces to auctioneers for them to sell.

It was to see this exhibition of the returned work from Philadelphia that Queen Victoria made the first of her visits to the RSN. It was reported that 'the Queen remained in the workroom some time and besides buying several articles, gave orders for some screens'.[35]

By 1878 the RSN had become better established and with a growing reputation, royal patronage and larger premises, or to put it another way, the experiment was working. However, the method of paying staff weekly, often months before the item was sold, had become financially challenging. This was then compounded by the vast expenses of the

Philadelphia exhibition. Council member Sir William Drake reviewed
the cash position and set down his belief that the school could not be
viable without a capital investment of £10,000. Further, he stated that
all future members of the General Council of the school should make a
personal donation to the school of not less than £50, to be represented
by a non-transferable and non-dividend bearing share.[36] The debt was
already more than £6,500 excluding the Philadelphia amount, and Sir
William felt the proposed Articles of Association drawn up by the RSN's
solicitor, Curtis Hayward, really needed this financial aspect added
to them. He wanted to see the school free from debt, with stock and
a way forward. However, on a further examination of the figures he
considered £12,000 was needed. Sir William's proposal was accepted by
the Finance Committee and prepared for the General Council. Princess
Helena later wrote:

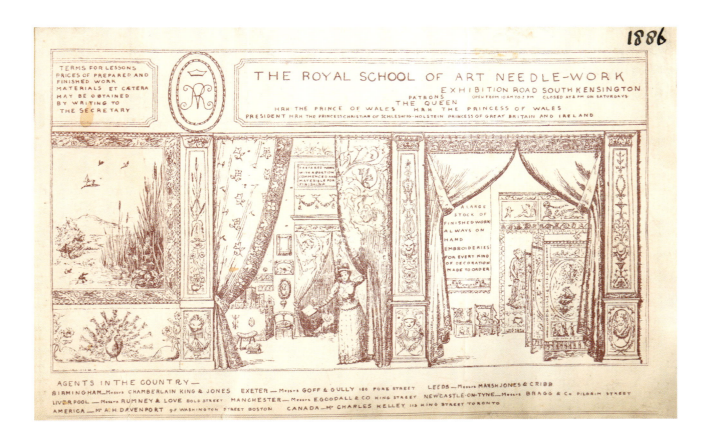

1886

THE ROYAL SCHOOL OF ART NEEDLE-WORK

EXHIBITION ROAD SOUTH KENSINGTON

PATRONS   OPEN FROM 10 AM TO 5 PM   CLOSED AT 2 PM ON SATURDAYS

THE QUEEN

HRH THE PRINCE OF WALES   HRH THE PRINCESS OF WALES

PRESIDENT HRH THE PRINCESS CHRISTIAN OF SCHLESWIG-HOLSTEIN PRINCESS OF GREAT BRITAIN AND IRELAND

TERMS FOR LESSONS PRICES OF PREPARED AND FINISHED WORK MATERIALS ET CÆTERA MAY BE OBTAINED BY WRITING TO THE SECRETARY

A LARGE STOCK OF FINISHED WORK ALWAYS ON HAND EMBROIDERIES FOR EVERY KIND OF DECORATION MADE TO ORDER

AGENTS IN THE COUNTRY—

BIRMINGHAM—Messrs CHAMBERLAIN KING & JONES   EXETER—Messrs GOFF & GULLY 180 FORE STREET   LEEDS—Messrs MARSH JONES & CRIBB

LIVERPOOL—Messrs RUMNEY & LOVE BOLD STREET   MANCHESTER—Messrs E. GOODALL & CO KING STREET   NEWCASTLE-ON-TYNE—Messrs BRAGG & Cº PILGRIM STREET

AMERICA—Mr A. H. DAVENPORT 95 WASHINGTON STREET BOSTON   CANADA—Mr CHARLES KELLEY 113 KING STREET TORONTO

Brochure promoting the sale room of the RSN as well as lessons and commissions

[RSN Archive. Photograph: John Chase]

'In 1878, experience having shown that the objects for which the school has been founded were appreciated by the public, it was determined to establish it on a more permanent basis. The school was accordingly incorporated under the Corporation Acts and received the licence of the Board of Trade applicable to associations not constituted for purposes of profit. By the terms of which the income and property of the school, whencesoever derived, must be applied solely to the promotion of the object of the school.'[37]

The aim was to provide the workers with steady employment; between commissions it was decided that they could work on a range of smaller pieces which could be sold throughout the year from the showroom, or at what became the annual Summer Sale. The Sale became a major event. It was part of the London Season and Princess Helena would personally become a saleswoman for the entire two or three days of the event. Usually, it was held at the RSN premises but in 1883 it was held at the Mansion House at the invitation of the Lord Mayor. Notice of the Sales was announced in the press and taken up enthusiastically by the regional press, especially in county areas where they might have residents who would move to London for the Season. 'Princess Christian, president of the Royal School of Art Needlework at South Kensington has appointed the 4th, 5th, and 6th of June for the annual summer sale which will be opened and presided over by Her Royal Highness'.[38]

From early on, the RSN partnered with furniture companies such as Gillow, which meant that the RSN showroom and Sale sold furniture and accessories as well as embroideries. Over time, they became particularly known for antique furniture. 'The school is now recognised as one of the best places in London to buy good old furniture. Prices are moderate and clearly labelled.'[39] The furniture department remained until 1915.

The Winter Sales started a little later but over the years became perhaps more important as they could last longer. In 1880, for example, the Sale took place on 1 December, but, as the flyer stated, it would continue through December for people to purchase Christmas presents. The further iteration of this was when Princess Helena and the Associates instituted the idea of 'At Homes'. The Associates were ladies from Helena's social circle, from the world of theatre and even some of the newly arriving Americans, for example the Bonynges, who lived in Prince's Gate. The Associates would assist Princess Helena in manning the sales tables on the opening days of the Sale. They are first mentioned as having a constitution in 1878, though it is not until 1888 that we see a printed list of criteria for the Associates and the duties they were signing up for. Associates paid an annual subscription to belong. For five shillings they could show friends around the workroom, and for a guinea they could also gain a discount of 5 per cent on any items purchased.

The winter At Homes took place usually on Thursdays between mid-November and Christmas. Two of the Associates would host the event each week and invite their friends to attend. Refreshments would be served, at the cost of the Associates, and sometimes musicians would play, and the assembled masses would be encouraged to purchase items from the school. The *Sheffield Daily Telegraph* set out the requirements on those who offered to host these occasions: 'Tea at small tables in the pretty sale room is always provided by the ladies of the committee who provide their own silver, dainty flower decorations and their own man-servants to wait, so giving the affair the charm of a private entertainment.'[40]

These events were very successful, bringing in different groups of people, and continued into the 20th century. The largest crowds, however, came out when they knew that Princess Helena would be in attendance, whether as principal host or guest. In 1895 *The Queen* noted that at the last At Home of the winter, Princess Helena herself presided and 'hundreds of ladies availed themselves'.[41]

The Associates played a hugely important support role. By 1896 there were 464 of them, and in the days before paid holiday was introduced it is noted that the subscriptions of the Associates had helped the workers to have a summer holiday period. As ever, Princess Helena personally thanked those of the Associates who never failed to attend events – especially the At Homes – and support the school.

Notice of Winter Sales at the RSN. Unlike the Summer Sale, the Winter Sales ran over weeks in November and December with Thursday At Homes hosted by the Associates.

[RSN Archive. Photograph: John Chase]

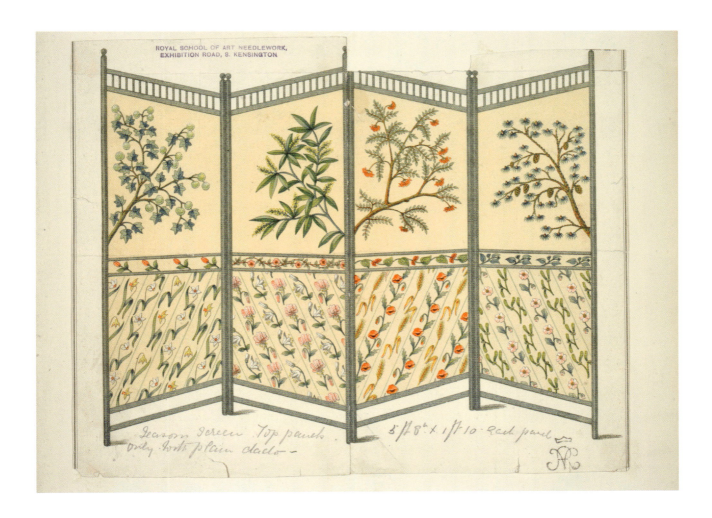

ROYAL SCHOOL OF ART NEEDLEWORK,
EXHIBITION ROAD, S. KENSINGTON

**Screen designed by the
RSN paint room, clearly
influenced by the new trend
for Japonisme.**

[RSN Archive. Photograph: John Chase]

With the formal documents of incorporation in 1878, the RSN
also formalised the terms with agents.[42] Agents had been contacting
the school since the beginning and the display of furniture in the
showroom was due to these links, but each relationship differed.
Every item produced by the school displayed a tag to say that it had
been produced by the RSN, complete with special logo[43] as proof of
origin and authenticity. This was important because once items could
be found around the country, they noticed incidents of fraud. In 1877
the RSN had to take out advertisements to protect themselves against
people purporting to sell items from the school which did not have the
authenticity stamp.

Agents were first appointed in Manchester, Birmingham and
Newcastle. When Rumney & Love (upholsterers in Liverpool)
asked to become agents, this was agreed provided that they paid for
transportation and insurance. They would get 10 per cent of the sales
price or 15 per cent if they sold more than £100 of goods. The RSN was
even contacted by a company in Rome but thought the items would be
too expensive once transport costs and tariffs had been added.

At times (for example, in 1877), so desperate was the school for cash that it kept reducing the prices – something previously reduced would be reduced by a further 15 per cent and something not previously reduced, by 30 per cent – really just paying for the cost of materials and labour, and hardly covering overheads. It was also stated that they would send items to anyone to sell anywhere so long as the minimum item was £5 and that linen items were taken in half-dozens.

Early Royal Commissions

The RSN does not have any workbooks from their early years, so the only source for information about the commissions from this period is press coverage, but as there were few photographs in newspapers the information about the commissions is purely narrative.

We first read of royal commissions in 1874: 'The school has received large orders from her Majesty and their Royal Highnesses the Princess of Wales and the Duchess of Edinburgh.'[44] Princess Helena and Lady Marian Alford had previously made the point that art needlework was not specifically for dress and costume but was more for the adornment of interiors. However, that did not stop Her Majesty from placing dress commissions. The *Illustrated London News* informed its readers that the 'dress worn by the Queen at the last Drawing Room was embroidered by the RSN as was also the new frontal to her Majesty's box in the Royal Albert Hall, which was ordered by the Duke of Edinburgh for the occasion of the Queen's last visit there'.[45] At the Drawing Room, as well as a dress embroidered by the RSN, the Queen also wore the Koh-i-Noor diamond as a brooch. The Royal Albert Hall frontal is known as the Hammer Cloth; it still exists and is used whenever the monarch attends an event at the Royal Albert Hall. The RSN has had it back to replace the letters for each new monarch.

In 1877 the Prince of Wales participated in a tournament and the *Dublin Evening Telegraph* gave a full description of the outfit: 'The date and costume of the tournament belong to the time of the Crusades. The costume of the Saracens will be furnished by the South Kensington Museum – that of the Prince of Wales to be imitated with the greatest care from the traditional attire worn by Soliman himself. The School of Art Needlework is busily employed in the embroidery and the embossing of the rich stuff of which the overshirt is composed.'[46]

Some non-royal commissions have also been recorded; one was the curtains for the newly built Manchester Town Hall in the 1870s.

Exhibitions in Paris and the British Isles

The RSN did not stop exhibiting after Philadelphia, it took every opportunity to show their work. Commissions were frequently displayed at Sales before they were despatched to their clients, and external opportunities were sought, too. In 1878 there was an International Exhibition in Paris. The RSN was asked to furnish the drawing room of the British pavilion, under the overall direction of Mr Henry of the Windsor Tapestry School. The *Belfast News Letter* wrote glowingly:

'For this drawing room the hangings will be of pale blue satin with a border and ends laid on in a cream satin with embroidery in gold thread, to describe this embroidery would require both pencil and pen for it would be impossible to give an idea of the beauty of the design, the perfection of the needlework or the grand general effect.'[47]

For those not able to get to Paris, the curtains were first displayed at the RSN, and this was followed by an exhibition of ancient needlework in the run-up to the Summer Sale.

A couple of years later, the RSN was exhibiting some even more exotic work: interior decorations for the Imperial Russian Yacht *Livadia*. One correspondent wrote that, 'The furnishing of the magnificent vessel is now completed and as the work is both artistic and costly the specimens will form an interesting exhibition of imperial splendour.'[48]

In 1880, the RSN staged an immense exhibition comprising a range of loaned articles. There were more than 200 from the South Kensington Museum alone, plus a display of modern embroidery by RSN workers which comprised more than 550

In 1883 the RSN held its Sale and AGM at the Mansion House, courtesy of the Lord Mayor, and the Lady Mayoress held an At Home.

[RSN Archive. Photograph: John Chase]

items. These included a screen worked for the Queen, the Selwyn Image *Venus*, *Juno* screen, designs by Miss Gemmell and Miss Burnside, and works designed by Crane, Morris, Burne-Jones, Fairfax Wade and even Lord Leighton, who had donated a design based on an old work, used for a blotter and casket.

The RSN also sent work around the country to be displayed as part of county art exhibitions and sometimes for joint exhibitions. Leek (in Staffordshire) embroidery was established by Lady Wardle, wife of Sir Thomas Wardle, using tussar silks that he had dyed. Leek embroidery used a small range of stitches and the loosely twisted tussar silk to work secular and ecclesiastical pieces. The often Indian-themed designs and use of the dyed silk had a particular style.[49] In November 1881, the RSN loaned more than 40 pieces to a joint exhibition in Leek, with Morris & Co. also lending eight pieces.

Ecclesiastical Embroidery

While the RSN was founded specifically for secular embroidery, Council was pragmatic enough to realise that there was both money and opportunity in ecclesiastical embroidery, the idea possibly presented to them by G.F. Bodley, member of the original Art Committee and the architect responsible for several churches at this time. In May 1881, it was announced that the RSN was prepared to start making altar frontals

When encouraged to start offering ecclesiastical work the RSN produced a promotional brochure.

[RSN Archive. Photograph: John Chase]

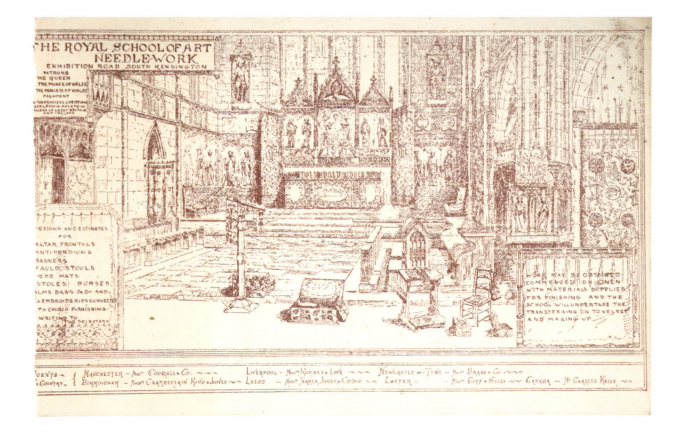

The RSN also worked for synagogues, creating lectern falls, curtains and Torah covers.

[RSN Archive. Photograph: William Gray]

and vestments. This *volte-face* was squarely positioned as responding to the needs of architects in being able to meet their exacting standards in translating design into embroidery.[50] The first ecclesiastical commission recorded in the press was commissioned by Princess Helena herself for the English Church at Pontresina, Switzerland in remembrance of her stay there in the autumn of 1880.

By 1883 the RSN was seeing the potential for ecclesiastical work. They published a price list for everything from altar frontals to kneelers and offered their services to both churches and synagogues: 'Having recently executed work for Synagogues, the school is prepared to supply all Embroideries required in the Jewish Service.' Since then, the RSN has made curtains, Torah covers and other accoutrements for synagogues.

To help advertise to potential new clients, in 1884 the RSN held an exhibition of ancient ecclesiastical embroidery and the RSN Archive contains a handwritten letter from Princess Helena to be sent to those from whom the school wished to be loaned pieces. In all, almost 200 pieces were on show including funeral palls loaned by four of the City Livery Companies.

Princess Helena

Princess Helena adopted a philanthropic role early on. Inspired by Florence Nightingale, she founded the Royal British Nurses Association, which became part of the Royal College of Nursing in the 20th century. She was also a founding member of the British Red Cross and the driving force behind the Royal School of Needlework for 50 years.

Princess Helena attended Council meetings and even held some at Cumberland Lodge, her home in Windsor Great Park. She was the catalyst for the Sales; even when family tragedy struck or she was ill, she would draft in others to ensure the Sales could be held, as they were such a vital source of income to the running of the RSN. For example, in 1901 when Queen Victoria died the royal family was in mourning, but the Sale continued in June with day one being presided over by the Lady Mayoress, and day two by the Duchess of Marlborough.

Princess Helena also took the lead in fundraising, sending personal letters, and getting support from the 1851 Commissioners; even when the new building was occupied, she did not stop fundraising until the mortgage was paid off.

Press reports described her as 'the constant Patroness'[51] and 'indefatigable', and she was. For her, the Sale was not about gracing the occasion for an hour or two, but being on duty from noon or 2 pm to 7 pm, two or three days running. The Sale started when she arrived, and she stayed at her post the whole afternoon. She took charge and people responded to her. While there were many difficulties in the first 50 years she was committed, tenacious and determined to keep the RSN going. After her death in 1923, the RSN put up a memorial plaque to her (see page 71). It was the least they could do for this woman who gave so much time and energy to the school. In turn, both her daughters continued to support the RSN throughout their lives, and Princess Helena Victoria attended many, many Sales, assisting the next generation of RSN royal saleswomen: the Duchess of York, the Princess Royal, Countess of Harewood, and the Duchess of Kent.

Schools in Scotland

By 1879, the Council minutes were full of requests for agency links (from both companies and individuals) for teachers worldwide (to New Zealand, for example), and for branches to be established (Oxford is one suggested). The RSN was always seen as the model for others to follow. The Dublin Royal School of Needlework began in 1877 as a separate entity but followed the model of the London school, even bringing over teachers from London to start it. Then came a request from a company based in Glasgow. Messrs Alexander and Howell desired to establish a branch office of the school, paying all expenses, defraying costs, and sharing profits. Given the favourable terms to the school, it was not surprising that they asked for the proposal in writing and on receiving that, established a sub-committee to review it. At that meeting it was considered that the only way in which Council could understand the terms was for Miss Higgin, the RSN Secretary, to pay a visit to Scotland. In particular, she was to investigate whether the branch was just to teach or to prepare embroidery to sell, as this would have different implications. By the next Council meeting Miss Higgin had returned and reported, the result of which was that the RSN asked its solicitor, Curtis Hayward, to draw up an agreement for Glasgow.

The final terms for the branch school in Glasgow were signed off at a Special Meeting of Council on 7 August 1879. A sub-committee under Princess Helena was appointed to keep a watching brief over the branch. The Glasgow school had commenced by the start of 1880 with one of those being sent from London to lead the teaching being none other than the first student, Miss Martha Lee, and the branch was considered satisfactory at the following RSN Council meeting. However, not six months later, a paper was received reviewing the terms of the agreement. In the Council meeting of 19 June 1880, it is minuted that a letter is to be sent from Princess Helena to the patronesses of the Glasgow branch urging them to take a personal interest in the branch school. By 19 July the issue had escalated further as the company Alexander and Howell had pulled out, so now Council needed to see if the patronesses and other supporters would advance £250 to buy back stock held by the company.

Before telephones were installed, Princess Helena was a prodigious correspondent, sending notes to say when she would and would not be coming, but also to commission pieces. This letter from 1891 refers to the Court train she ordered for her daughter Marie Louise when she was married: 'Dear Miss Ffennell I return the trial pieces for the train which I think beautiful. Please let the train be put in hand.'

[RSN Archive. Photograph: John Chase]

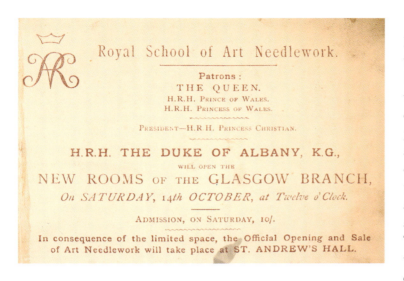

Royal School of Art Needlework.

Patrons:
THE QUEEN.
H.R.H. PRINCE OF WALES.
H.R.H. PRINCESS OF WALES.

PRESIDENT—H.R.H. PRINCESS CHRISTIAN.

H.R.H. THE DUKE OF ALBANY, K.G.,

WILL OPEN THE

NEW ROOMS OF THE GLASGOW BRANCH,

On SATURDAY, 14th OCTOBER, at Twelve o'Clock.

ADMISSION, ON SATURDAY, 10/.

In consequence of the limited space, the Official Opening and Sale
of Art Needlework will take place at ST. ANDREW'S HALL.

For a very brief time the RSN had branches in Edinburgh (mostly for teaching) and Glasgow (for working and teaching). However, they were shown not to be viable, and both were closed by 1884.

[RSN Archive. Photograph: John Chase]

Matters improved a bit, so Princess Helena sent her brother the Duke of Albany to open new rooms for the Glasgow school, but such was the number of people wanting to attend that the formal opening was held elsewhere so nullifying the effect of more people visiting the workroom. Meanwhile a branch had opened in Edinburgh also offering teaching, although Glasgow would undertake any commissions. In 1883 both advertised classes and Edinburgh opened a loan exhibition of historical embroidery. This was another extensive undertaking with more than 350 items listed in the catalogue, many of which had been loaned by estate owners in Scotland.

However, things did not improve financially and in 1884 Princess Helena called an end to the Scottish branches. The Edinburgh branch was never heard of again, but the Glasgow branch clung on, rebranding itself in December 1884 as 'the Glasgow School of Art Needlework, formerly the Glasgow Branch of the RSN'.[52]

Lessons and Prepared Work

As early as 1874, Council agreed that workers of the school could give lessons to amateurs even in their own homes. Of course, the price of the lessons meant that they would only be going to the more well-to-do homes but there continued to be interest, so in 1878 the Council of Management announced classes in ornamental needlework at Exhibition Road. The lessons were to offer 'every kind of stitch in Crewel, Silk and Gold' with 'Gold' really meaning ecclesiastical embroidery.

There was detailed instruction for the teachers who conducted the lessons in private homes. They were to take the linen and threads required for teaching, but these remained the property of the school and had to be brought back at the end of the lesson. However, the pupil could purchase a piece of linen or silk to keep at home and the teachers were also encouraged to take with them cushions and chair backs for pupils to purchase if they wished to work their embroidery on something other than a sampler. In terms of the lessons at Exhibition Road the maximum class size would be 12. Where the classes continued from term to term there would be a reduction in the fees.

At the same time, the RSN formalised what they could offer for what was called 'Prepared Work' and 'Finished Work'. Prepared Work was a bespoke kit. These were individually made, the customer could choose the design and its purpose (cushion, chair back, curtains, etc.) and the colours they wished to work it in. Then the RSN paint room would design it, paint the canvas for canvaswork,[53] or prick and pounce the design onto linen for crewelwork[54] or damask, velvet or other fabric for goldwork,[55] provide a guide image and all the matched threads in wool, silk, cotton or metal, while the workroom would provide a stitch guide for completing the project. The school would even make a start on the project, if desired, before handing it over. The range of pieces for which the RSN could supply designs included domestic items such as chair backs and table covers but also included children's dresses, baby blankets and even aprons and pockets for the new-fangled game of lawn tennis. Many patterns were available, but once commissioned the materials could not be returned as they were made as bespoke kits.

'Finished Work' was the term used for complete items. The school published a list of the range of objects it could make (though not limited only to these) and the price bands. Curtain borders on serge could be from £2 10s to 10gns for about 3½ yards (approx. 3 metres). Sofa backs on linen or silk could be from 2gns to £10. Children's dresses could be from 1gn to 3gns and a completed Lady's Lawn Tennis Apron could be from £1 5s to £3 10s. There were also accessories which were one of the mainstays of the Summer and Winter Sales as gift items: blotters, photograph frames, book covers, envelope boxes and handkerchief sachets.

By the issue of the Prospectus of June 1879, the school was sending out teachers anywhere in the country if there was a minimum grouping of 12 ladies (two classes of six) to teach.

The Handbook of Embroidery

There was also interest in developing a book of embroidery which would show how to work the different stitches. There was much talk about this, and in the Council Minutes of 1879 it was agreed that 'a handbook of Embroidery be produced for publication under the superintendence of Lady Marion [sic] Alford'. However, as little seemed to be happening it was compiled by the Secretary, Miss Laetitia Higgin. When she heard of this, Lady Marian insisted on editing it. All the parts about the history of needlework and its role as an artform can be said to be by her. Finally, the *Handbook of Embroidery* was published in 1880. It did not, however, just comprise details of how to work certain stitches but also included designs by the likes of Burne-Jones, Morris, Image and Crane, and from Miss Gemmell and Gertrude Jekyll.[56] These designs were not there as 'designs to have a go at' but rather to give people the idea of what art embroidery was and to encourage readers of the book that, if they wanted these large pieces then they needed to commission the RSN to do the work.

The book was a bestseller. Interestingly, it was printed with two different covers (illustrated opposite), that featuring a Selwyn Image design was the version for general sale while the cover featuring women at home and work was reputedly for the RSN workers, although there is no written evidence of this. To Lady Marian, this book did only half the job. She wanted to show the scope and scale of needlework as art. She gave

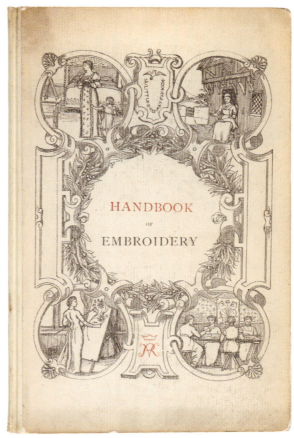

(left) **Front cover design by Selwyn Image for the 1880** *Handbook of Embroidery*

[RSN Archive. Photograph: John Chase]

(right) **Although there was only ever one edition of the Handbook, unusually, there were two covers. It was said that this was the cover for the workroom.**

[RSN Archive. Photograph: John Chase]

two lectures about needlework and design at the RSN in December 1880, which proved so popular that they had to be repeated the following year.[57]

Despite the success of the book there was only one edition because of a dispute between Miss Higgin and Lady Alford as to the copyright. Eventually taken to law, in the end both ceded their rights to the RSN[58] but it also led to Lady Marian standing down as Vice President. She now wanted to write what she had originally seen as the companion book to the practical handbook, about the history of needlework. *Needlework as Art*, her *magnum opus*, was finally published in 1886. She died unexpectedly in 1888.[59]

Visitors

Princess Helena was always keen to promote the work of the school, so she brought many guests to visit, and hopefully to buy or commission the RSN to create work for them. Looking at the press reports it is notable that all Helena's brothers and sisters visited, some regularly, including her sister Vicky, by now Crown Princess of Germany. Princess Alexandra, the Princess of Wales brought her mother, the Queen of Denmark, and sister. Another time the Princess of Wales visited accompanied by the Duchess of Edinburgh, and again with the Dowager

Empress of Russia. The Duchess of Teck was also a frequent visitor while others were more occasional, such as the Queen of Norway.

Perhaps the most exotic of visitors in the early days was the wife of the Chinese Envoy. The press informed its readers that 'The chief wife of the Envoy did not come to England but the favourite one did, a young lady of two and twenty who has been married about six years.' The paper went on to inform its readers that the lady could not be received at Court as polygamy was against the law and furthermore that the lady, known as the Tottering Lily of Fascination, was not to be looked upon by men. However, she did visit the RSN, and the paper commented, 'The Tottering Lily was quite incredulous that English ladies could embroider as well as the Chinese and insisted on proof of the fact, she afterwards sitting down at a frame and doing some inches of embroidery in a very artistic manner.'[60]

Gifts

The tradition of giving gifts to the RSN's Patrons and Presidents began very early. The first recorded special gift was to Queen Victoria for her Golden Jubilee in 1887:

'The quilt which her Majesty was graciously pleased to accept just recently from the Royal School of Art Needlework is really a most beautiful specimen both of taste and workmanship. It is made of white satin, richly embroidered in a conventional design with old thread. It has a crown and the monogram VR with a scroll bearing the dates 1837 and 1887 in the centre. The quilt is lined with crimson satin, while two of the corners are each quilted into the form of a crown. The two opposite corners have the monogram. The Queen was evidently much pleased with the gift.'[61]

The following year the RSN made a banner for the silver wedding anniversary of the Prince and Princess of Wales, and possibly an embroidered casket – the RSN still holds drawings of the designs but there is no evidence of this being made or given. For the Queen's Diamond Jubilee, the RSN made Victoria a white circular embroidered cloak.

Tableaux Vivants

Although the RSN aimed to be self-sufficient, there was always need for further funds for new activities. In 1891 and again in 1892 the RSN held two fundraising events which involved many of the Associates and other supporters of the school: tableaux vivants. These were terribly fashionable, and the press noted for the first of these that it was under the direct patronage of the Queen and Princess Helena. As the *Manchester Courier* put it:

Section of an embroidered hanging made by the RSN for the silver wedding anniversary of the Prince and Princess of Wales (later Edward VII and Queen Alexandra)

[RSN Collection. Photograph: John Chase]

'Many members of the haute monde are amongst the company whom Mrs Bancroft has to drill. The RSN suffers, like many similar institutions, from a want of funds, and it is hoped that this effort pioneered, as it will be, by royalty, will do something towards retrieving the fortunes of the Kensington Penelopes.'[62]

Tableaux vivants were events where ladies and gentlemen dressed up to portray a particular scene. They struck a pose as the curtains opened. People looked, oohed and aahed, and clapped, and then the curtains closed. When scenery was involved, the change between scenes could take longer than the scenes themselves, so musical interludes were a key part of the event.

The first one, in 1891, was under the direction of Mrs Bancroft, a notable actress and theatre manager who would later commission the RSN for theatre curtains. As such, the press felt that the event was in safe hands. The brief programme simply lists the participants, so we must leave it to the press to know something of the content: that it included *The Farewell of Charles I* and a scene from *Masks and Faces* in which Mrs Bancroft herself took part. Royalty attended all three performances, which took place at the home of Mrs Frederick Beer in Chesterfield Gardens. On the first evening, Princess Mary Adelaide, Duchess of Teck and the Duke of Teck attended and the following evening Princess Helena with her husband and daughter joined the Prince of Wales for supper before accompanying him to the event.

The first tableau was a great success and so a second was mooted, but with a more embroidery-related theme and to be held in a theatre to accommodate a larger audience. It was organised by Mrs Tyssen-Amherst and Lady William Cecil and her sisters, under the artistic direction of Mr Hermann Schmiechen. This time the nine scenes depicted embroidery from different periods: Egyptian, Greek, Roman, Tudor, with the final scene featuring Lady Dallas as the Goddess of Industry. The Tudor scene is of the Prioress of the Syon Convent refusing to let Henry VIII's soldiers take the Syon Cope. The RSN still has several drawings of the scenes, costumes and the design for the mock Syon Cope.[63] The ladies who participated in this event were featured in the magazines and newspapers of the day in their costumes.

Meanwhile workers at the school were preparing items to go over to the World's Fair in Chicago in 1893. There is no complete list of the items but from press reports *Pomona* (see page 42; a large embroidery designed by Edward Burne-Jones and William Morris and worked by the RSN, reputedly under the guidance of May Morris)[64] and a Bible cover worked for Princess Helena for her 25th wedding anniversary, designed from one in the collection at the Bodleian, were among the items. So, too, was a screen embroidered in the Louis Seize style, along with a Louis Quinze screen and a piano cover. It was stated in the

Morning Post that some 400 objects were going which had been made by women, but not all of those were from the RSN.

The Launch of the Training School

The RSN first started certificating people in the late 1870s, though this was for workers rather than students and initially focused on efficiency not technical skill. The first Certificates of Efficiency were awarded in 1879, with one going to first student Martha Lee.

In the 1890s there was a new thrust in public life in relation to technical teaching. Technical colleges were being established to teach practical skills, aimed at achieving a better qualified workforce. It was a theme taken up by the press, and Princess Helena and the RSN were not oblivious to this. In June 1893 a pamphlet was printed in which Princess Helena set out the plans for the future which included:

1. The erection of a permanent building as headquarters of the school.

2. The creation of a fund for the permanent endowment of the school, so that a properly trained and efficient staff may always be available.

(left) **Some of the ladies who participated in the 1892 Tableaux Vivants fundraising event to raise money for the new building**
[RSN Archive. Photograph: John Chase]

(right) **A selection of the tableaux as displayed in the *Illustrated London News***
[RSN Archive. Photograph: John Chase]

3. Training of pupils, who would afterwards earn their own livelihood by their work.

4. Training of teachers, who would in their turn be sent to different parts of the country to train others and who would therefore earn their own livelihood by teaching.

Alongside the above were also proposals for a School of Applied Design, which would be run by women in parallel with the embroidery school; its prospectus outlined that this school was to be an institution where women would learn from practicing teachers to design for various branches of the decorative arts. The idea was endorsed by Walter Crane who wrote in support of not only the idea but also the basis of the curriculum.

So, it was decided in 1895 that the RSN would establish a formal training school. The offering was a two-year certificate or a three-year diploma course, the latter fully equipping the graduate to teach hand embroidery and sewing at a school or one of the new technical institutes.

The programme comprised City and Guilds qualifications in basic sewing as well as experience in art and design (which would be taught at the RSN), and three years of hand embroidery teaching to cover all the major Western techniques. Students were also expected to make regular visits to the South Kensington Museum to look at historical embroideries. Classes began with six pupils on 1 October 1895 in a classroom borrowed from the Imperial Institute.

Surprisingly, given the absence of records in other areas, there survive details of the first students and their outcomes. The students were Miss Lydia Reynolds of Putney, Miss Mary How of London, Miss Price of Newport Pagnell, Miss Maud Hewitt of Ipswich, Miss Cussande of London and Miss Clairellen Shaw of Jamaica. Awarded their diplomas in 1899, the inaugural students had varied careers. Miss Reynolds had a portfolio career of working for the RSN and teaching elsewhere, including the Norwood Art School. Miss How did not achieve her diploma as she failed plain sewing and drawing, but the RSN twice helped her to find employment. Miss Price remained for two years and gained the certificate. She found a situation immediately, but it did not suit her, and she resumed her old occupation. Miss Hewitt had entered the school in the hope of completing the three-year course but had to leave at the end of the first year to find employment. She went on to teach at Battersea Polytechnic and later Camberwell Polytechnic and was eventually awarded an RSN certificate in consideration of her good reputation as a teacher in 1901. Miss Cussande entered the school with the aim of completing three years but became 'eccentric'; she could only work in the workroom, as opposed to the classroom, but eventually left, finding a situation as a nursery governess. Miss Shaw gained the

i am the ancient apple-queen · as once i was so am i now ·
for evermore a hope unseen · betwixt the blossom and the bough ·
ah where's the river's hidden gold · and where the windy grave of troy
yet come i as i came of old · from out the heart of summers joy ·

Pomona, designed by Edward Burne-Jones and William Morris. It was embroidered by the RSN and was the centrepiece of the work exhibited at the World's Fair in Chicago in 1893.

[Private collection. Photograph: Bridgeman Images]

diploma after three years and then worked in the workroom for a year until her sisters were ready to return to Jamaica. The first American student arrived in 1896 staying for less than a year, but she went on to teach at the Municipal Art School of Leicester for seven years before returning home to Philadelphia for her health, where she undertook private teaching.

The first recorded financial support for students came from the Worshipful Company of Broderers, the City Livery Company of embroiderers. Originally established to maintain standards in embroidery, the company can be dated back to at least 1561 when it received its royal charter. In 1899 they awarded a scholarship to pay the course fees for one student.

The Evening School

Although the RSN had introduced the Training School, Council was also aware that there were instructors who were teaching at schools and the new technical institutions who were self-taught. This was not considered good practice, so they decided to establish evening classes, enabling people to study without giving up their work, and applied to the London County Council (LCC) for a grant to support payment of the teachers. Eventually, in December 1896, the LCC agreed to pay the RSN not exceeding £150 per annum to provide suitable teachers. Classes would run five nights a week, two focussing on design, two on embroidery, and Friday night was untutored but the classroom was open so students could come and study in an appropriate space if they did not have such at home. Seemingly, there was some delay in appointing a design master and the LCC official became very irritated with Miss Wade, reporting inertia on the matter until the next meeting of the committee. Only three days after the letter confirming the grant is one asking, 'Do you not think that some progress might be made towards securing teachers of design and towards the further development of the school as an art [school] without waiting for a formal meeting of your committee!'[65]

To launch the evening classes, Walter Crane agreed to give a lecture on 'Needlework as a Mode of Artistic Expression' at the Imperial Institute, for which he was paid 10gns. At first the RSN demurred at the cost, but the LCC pushed for it because although his fee was high, they believed at least half of the cost would be covered by ticket sales. At the same Council meeting Mr William Paulson Townsend was approved as the teacher of design and Miss Scott, from the workroom, as the teacher of embroidery for the evening school. The lecture was widely advertised, and tickets were free for apprentices and students. More than 300 people attended.

A press release was prepared, and 18 samples of work were laid out for the reporters to understand 'the least course which a pupil should pass through before she may be considered to be equipped as a

'Teacher'. The 18 samples were then listed in the book as a programme of study over three years, though without visual examples:

Year one

Stitches: crewel on linen

Shading: crewel on linen

Drawn work with linen thread

Two samplers: appliqué

Laid work: crewel on linen

Smocking

Year two

Shading: crewel on linen

Group of naturally treated flowers

Conventional design silk and gold

Drawn work: silk on linen

Appliqué: fine linen on silk

Ecclesiastical embroidery

Tapestry work on canvas

Year three

Sampler: crewel on linen

Two samplers: initials, monograms

Appliqué – advanced

Ecclesiastical embroidery

Conventional design

Princess Helena was keen to include design in the curriculum generally. William Paulson Townsend worked as the Master of Design for the RSN for many years and in 1899 published a book on design for embroidery in which he featured not only the designs of the leading lights of the Arts and Crafts movement but also the work of students.[66]

Administratively, it was determined that the evening classes should have their own accounts and reporting line, to be kept separate from the general activities of the RSN, not least to protect the money that was being contributed by the LCC. This was approved by the

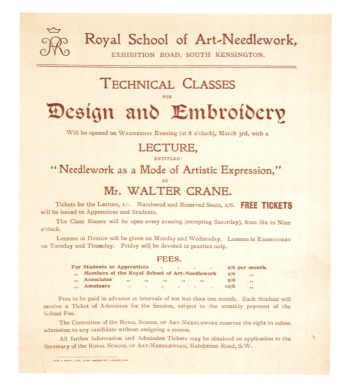

ROYAL SCHOOL of ART-NEEDLEWORK.

Needlework Show Rooms.

Furniture Show Rooms.

* Christmas Presents. *

(above) **Crane's shepherd design, used by the RSN for a brochure on Christmas gifts in the 1890s**
[RSN Archive. Photograph: John Chase]

(opposite left) **Poster/invitation to the lecture given by Walter Crane in 1897 to launch the evening classes which the RSN ran continually through to the 1980s (except during the Second World War). The classes included design as well as embroidery.**
[RSN Archive. Photograph: John Chase]

(opposite right) **Of all the designers and artists of the Arts and Crafts movement, the RSN worked most often with Walter Crane – for a quarter of a century.**
[Photograph: Heritage Image Partnership Ltd, Alamy]

Executive Committee and the LCC in June 1898 and became known as the Teaching Branch. The Teaching Branch Committee held at least one meeting a year to which a member of the LCC was invited. The Training School, which taught the RSN certificate and teacher's diploma, was separate.

The third part of the organisation was that for the workers, and it was still possible to enter the workroom without attending either the Training School or the evening classes. However, workers remained on piece work. It was not until 1899 that Miss Wade requested of the Executive Committee that those members of staff who had been working for 20 years or more be paid a fixed salary based on hours of attendance rather than by the piece.

CHAPTER 2

The Dawn of a New Century

In 1900 the RSN continued its promotional activities by exhibiting at the Paris Exposition. The British had a pavilion at the fair, designed by Edward Lutyens in the Elizabethan style and so the decorations had to be in keeping. Prior to going to Paris, the RSN exhibited the work. The *Evening Standard* informed its readers that the school had made curtains, valances and quilts with the curtains 12½ feet (3.8 metres) high. In total, 56 embroiderers had worked on the pieces designed by Miss Whichelo, which had been completed in just two months. The *Dundee Evening Telegraph* stated that they were worked on cream Kirriemuir linen and that 8olbs (36.8kg) weight of wool had been used in the decoration. Miss Whichelo and the RSN won a gold medal for their work exhibited in Paris.

The design was of interlaced trees (variously described as magnolia, medlar or pomegranate) with roses and convolvulus and at ground level, daffodils. Nellie Whichelo joined the RSN in 1879. She rose to be head of the paint room and was responsible for many designs.

Then, on 22 January 1901, Queen Victoria died. The royal family wanted to commission a pall for the hearse, but the time was very short, and no commercial company would take on the work. Princess Helena stepped in and said that her school would do it. From the moment the order was given to when the finished pall left Exhibition Road, the job had been with the RSN for 48 hours. As repeated commentary would confirm, the embroidery was undertaken in just 21 continuous hours of stitching. This commission not only cemented the RSN's reputation for exquisite work but also its ability to undertake work at speed, something which would be called on again before long. It reinforced two mantras which run through the entire history of the RSN. First, as originally seen in the work for Philadelphia, that because of the way that RSN students have been taught, when completed, no matter how many people have worked on it, the finished piece will look like the work of a single person. Second, for rush jobs, defined as any job whereby working only standard working hours would not see it completed in time, the approach is 'never a seat shall go cold' – if one person gets up (because at the RSN there is always a team) another can sit down and carry on. These principles remain true today.

The pall was much described in the press; they tell us that 45 women were engaged in the work. 'All night on Friday they sat up to complete the pall, and they deemed the sacrifice small for the honour of paying

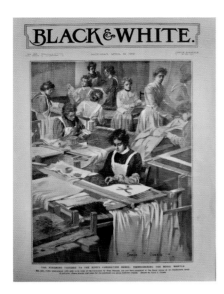

(above) **The front cover of Black & White magazine depicting the RSN 'embroidering the royal mantle' for the coronation**

[RSN Archive]

(top left) **This hanging was part of the display designed by Nellie Whichelo for the Paris International Exhibition. It won a gold medal.**

[RSN Archive]

(top right) **This is the only extant image of Nellie Whichelo, who worked at the RSN from 1879 to 1939 mostly as a designer in the paint room.**

[RSN Archive]

(below left) **The funeral pall with the embroidered corners clearly visible as the hearse is pulled through the streets of Windsor**

[Royal Collection Trust/© His Majesty Charles III 2023. Photograph: Croydon: Bender & Lewis]

(below right) **From the Illustrated London News, 2 February 1901. Some of the 45 members of the RSN team who stitched for 21 continuous hours to create Queen Victoria's funeral pall.**

[Drawing by W.L. Bruckman and Van Anrudy. Photograph: Look and Learn]

this last loving tribute to their Queen.'[1] Many of the newspapers reported that the finished piece was exceedingly beautiful. It bore the royal crest at each of the corners, and at the centre was a cross worked in cloth of gold with surface embroidery. The following year as part of a Festival of Needlework, the *Nottingham Journal* recalled this work from 'the most important school of art needlework', concluding: 'In gold and silks of many colours, the arms of the Empire were the single bright spot in that solemn pageant.'[2]

A New Era

With the coming to the throne of Edward VII it was to be anticipated that there would be much to do for the coronation, but even before that, the authorities turned once again to the RSN when Edward immediately wanted to make changes in time for the State Opening of Parliament which was going to be held on 14 February. Queen Victoria's Chair in the House of Lords had to be updated with the insignia of Edward, but he wanted to be accompanied by his wife Alexandra and there was no chair for her. At the beginning of February, the RSN was 'preparing new cushions of crimson velvet heavily embroidered in gold',[3] not only for the King's throne but also for the Queen's Chair of State in the House of Lords, both of which were completed in time for the State Opening.

The changing of a monarch, especially after such a long time, meant that there was much to be prepared and the RSN was asked to work on many elements, starting with monograms. From the Hammer Cloth at the Royal Albert Hall to the King's horse guard, all needed to have insignia changed from V to E. Estimates of the number of new monograms created by the RSN ranged from 170, just for the King's stables at Buckingham Palace and Windsor, to well over 200.

Interest in the coronation began from the middle of 1901, as plans became more fixed. The *Sphere* newspaper reported that the Queen herself 'was anxious that commissions be given to the RSN'.[4] Many of the gowns were going to be made in Paris, but from the RSN Archive we know that the Duchess of Portland's gown was designed by the House of Worth and that it was sent to the RSN to be embroidered. The most prestigious of the gowns worked by the RSN was for Her Grace the Duchess of Somerset who was considered the first among the female nobility as the wife of the Duke of Norfolk had already died.

The coronation was set for 26 June 1902 and the RSN had been 'entrusted with embroidering the King's mantle'.[5] Princess Helena had persuaded her brother that his mantle should not, like Victoria's, have the heraldic symbols woven into it, but rather that only a plain cloth of gold should be woven and the workers of the RSN would stitch the heraldic designs. The layout of the motifs was left to Miss Whichelo. The *Daily Telegraph* commented, 'To Miss Whichelo was entrusted the extremely difficult task of drawing a design adaptable to the shape of the mantle and introducing at proper intervals the necessary devices …

down the front on either side the Rose of England alternates with the Imperial Eagle and the Irish shamrock. In the next line are the crown, thistle of Scotland and the lotus.'[6] The mantle would be worn during the most sacred part of the ceremony, the anointing, which takes place under the canopy, also made by the RSN. The *Daily Chronicle* described the canopy as 'made of cloth of gold adorned with heraldic eagles, executed in silver silks'. The paper went on to say: 'The splendour of the combination of gold and silver is most majestic, and the embroideries are exquisitely fine and lovely.'[7] Not that the RSN did all the work for the coronation. Queen Alexandra's train was worked at the School of Art Needlework in Sloane Square and many of the royal family had their dress embroidery undertaken at the Royal Irish School of Art Needlework in Dublin, as a way of sharing out the work.

The RSN was also engaged in embroidering uniforms for the Beefeaters and the Yeoman Guard, the King and Queen's Garter banners for St George's Chapel, Windsor and commissions from the Empire. One was for a tablecloth of gold embroidery for the banquet hosted by the Viceroy at the coronation celebrations in India.

Coronations take place in Westminster Abbey, and it is a tradition that the new monarch presents an altar frontal for the chapel of Edward the Confessor. The RSN prepared this for the King comprising an altar frontal of crowned *E*s on crimson velvet embossed with the favourite rose and crown design plus a super frontal, and reredos with the Latin message *Cor Regis in Manu Domini* meaning 'the heart of the King in the hand of the Lord'.[8]

The coronation was scheduled for 26 June, but Edward developed appendicitis just before and had to have an operation, so the coronation

The Queen's Coronation Robe.

finally took place on 9 August. After the coronation Princess Helena persuaded her brother to allow the RSN to mount an exhibition of the coronation regalia for three weeks in October as a fundraiser for the building fund.

On seeing the mantle at the exhibition, the *Brighton Gazette* commented that 'to the really artistic mind this vestment is less a work of beauty than one of brazen magnificence and overwhelming, almost blinding gorgeousness'.[9]

However, work was not limited to only that which would be part of the coronation itself. Madame Tussaud's waxworks was a popular attraction for visitors to London, especially in an era before television and when the number of people who would see the royal family on coronation day was only a tiny fraction of the British public. Tussaud's asked the House of Worth for copies of some of the dresses to be worn by the royal family at the coronation and asked the RSN to undertake the embroidery along with copies of the King's and Queen's robes.

While Queen Victoria was alive, Edward and Alexandra as Prince and Princess of Wales had both become Patrons of the RSN. Now, as Queen, Alexandra chose to remain Patron and she was joined in 1902 by the new Prince and Princess of Wales (George and Mary).

The coronation of Edward VII: when he is wearing the mantle

[Painting: Edwin Austin Abbey, 1902. Photograph: incamerastock/Alamy]

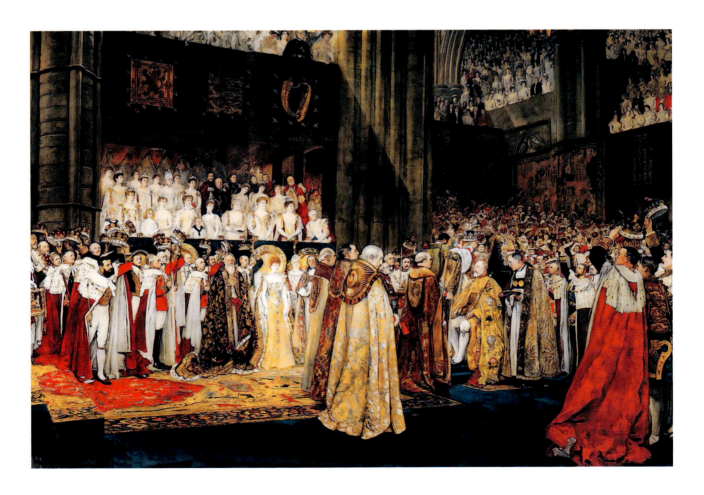

At the end of such a year it would be forgiven if the work of the Training School was almost completely forgotten, but no, the Duchess of Somerset, as Princess Helena was unwell, presented the awards and diplomas on 12 December, including to Marguerite Randell. Miss Randell, armed with her teaching diploma and with lace-making skills (enhanced by a month in Bruges), went initially to teach in South Africa. When ill health prevailed, however, she had to return, the RSN sending another teacher. She came back to the RSN in 1911 to be awarded a gold seal to her diploma, the highest mark of distinction that the RSN awarded for teaching and only given to those who had completed the diploma and gone on to give a high standard of teaching endorsed by references and testimonials. Miss Randell was only the third graduate to receive the gold seal, the two previous were already working at the RSN. Miss Randell began teaching at the RSN in 1913 and went on to head the Training School until 1951. She wrote two books on hand embroidery. By the end of 1902 there were 18 students on the training programme and 107 enrolled on night school classes.

Cuttings from the coronation robes of King Edward and Queen Alexandra kept by Rosina Smith, a worker at the RSN

[RSN Archive. Photograph: John Chase]

The New Building

Moving to a purposely constructed building was talked about as early as 1888 when a letter was received from the 1851 Commissioners informing the RSN that they were going to give the area the school was occupying to the Royal College of Music. The Commissioners proposed to build new premises for the RSN at the end of the South Kensington Museum. However, Princess Helena did not think they should be housed within the museum. Instead, she began to think about a whole new building and negotiated space with the Commissioners. Fundraising for the new building began in earnest from 1893 when Princess Helena distributed embroidered purses to some of the Associates and hoped they would be returned filled with donations. The total amount raised was over £150. While this was a lot at the time, the building was going to cost considerably more. Fairfax Wade was engaged as the architect. He was already known to the RSN as he had provided designs for Philadelphia and the *Handbook of Embroidery*. There is little information on the brief that was given but it was to comprise significant display and sales areas on the ground floor, plenty of space for workrooms with as much natural light as possible, as well as the new electric light, and at the very top of the building, accommodation to be used by students and staff. In 1893 an image of the proposed building appeared in *The Builder* magazine[10] but this design was superseded by the requirement of the 1851 Commissioners, who wanted a building

The
Royal Box
at the
Imperial
Theatre,
Westminster,
S.W.

*By Bedford,
Lemere, & Co.*

**Lillie Langtry's Imperial
Theatre with drapes
embroidered by the RSN**

[Image courtesy of Matthew Lloyd,
www.arthurlloyd.co.uk, originally
published in *The Playgoer*, 1901]

that was going to be in keeping with the rest of the area, albeit smaller than the two museums and the Imperial Institute.

By 1898 Princess Helena was exhorting the Executive Committee that she wanted to make a start on the building. Construction was put out to tender; costs were going to be around £30,000. The Executive Committee also started looking for organisations to share the building with, to help them cover costs. The first was the School of Art Wood Carving which went on to occupy an area on the top floor. City and Guilds sought out the RSN with regard to sharing the building but was initially turned down on the basis that the use they were proposing was not connected with artistic design, but when costs rose this was rescinded and the school was actively encouraged by the 1851 Commissioners to take the offer of occupation, for a term of five years initially.

Before work started, Princess Helena had raised £11,000 towards the building. Of the early donors the largest sum came from a legacy donation from the Pfeiffer Trust whose aims were specifically to support the education and employment of women.[11] Other donors included four City Livery Companies: Clothworkers, Mercers, Skinners and Merchant Taylors, as well as many individual donations.

Amongst those who assisted at the Sales and held the At Homes at the RSN were several ladies from the theatre. Mrs Bancroft, who had assisted with fundraising since the first tableaux vivant in 1891; Lady Alexander, wife of the theatre impresario Sir George Alexander; and perhaps most famous of all Mrs Lillie Langtry who had the RSN execute curtains for her new theatre, the Imperial, in 1901. Designed by Miss Whichelo and overseen by Miss Wade, the principal, and stitched in gold thread, they cost more than £200 and some said the price was as high as £400. The *Northern Whig* newspaper described them as an artistic triumph.[12] But they were not merely clients, they all held theatrical benefit performances for the new building, raising between them nearly £1,000.

The laying of the foundation stone was undertaken in 1899 by the Prince of Wales. During the ceremony, Princess Helena allowed herself to reflect on what had been achieved in the almost 30 years since the founding: '... working with Leighton, Morris, Burne-Jones and Crane – I am sure I would meet with no contradiction were I to say that the way in which our teachers and workers have executed the ideas of

these eminent gentlemen had not been unworthy of
the taste and genius of their originators.'[13] She went
on to note that the school had welcomed visitors
from around the world: the Americas, Europe and
the colonies, and its model had been copied by
institutions in a number of countries.

By the foundation-laying, the Princess had raised
£14,000, still well short of the £30,000 needed, so
she made a further appeal in person and via a slip of
paper in the programme, so those attending could not
fail to notice. However, as is frequently the way with
building projects, there were unforeseen elements
which increased the costs from the original £30,000
to £50,000. With only small donations coming in,
it was all looking a bit precarious. In January 1901
a note printed in red ink was sent to the members
of the General Committee and the Associates to say
that work was at a standstill and additional funds
to the tune of £6,000 were needed urgently. The
1851 Commissioners had made a potential £20,000
available as a loan; however, they would only
make £14,000 available until such time as the RSN
raised the balance. The minutes of every Executive
Committee from 1900 through to well beyond the opening, are filled
predominantly with matters of fundraising and the building, especially
as the costs escalated. The money crept in very slowly and, due to the
royal family's mourning following the death of Queen Victoria, Princess
Helena was absent for all of 1901 returning only in March 1902. This
was the most critical time, and the building project was living hand to
mouth; only as funds dribbled in, could more be done.

The archive holds an invitation card for an At Home to meet
Princess Helena at the London home of Mr and Mrs Edward Stern on
12 May 1902. Edward Stern had served as High Sheriff of Surrey and
his country home was near Chertsey, a town for which he had made
several philanthropic donations, including the local park. Shortly after
the At Home, the press reported the donation of £10,000 to the building
fund from Mr Stern as a coronation gift to Princess Helena. The Minute
book records that 'The cordial thanks of the Committee were accorded
to Mr Stern for his handsome gift.' It was further noted that Mr Stern
wanted some of his donation used specifically to finish the outside of
the building. The architect, Fairfax Wade, was asked to get on with this
but hopefully to get the planned carving at a more economic price than
previously estimated.

This gift enabled the full loan from the 1851 Commissioners to
be released and moved the whole project to within a short hurdle of
the final goal, even allowing the RSN to have a telephone installed.

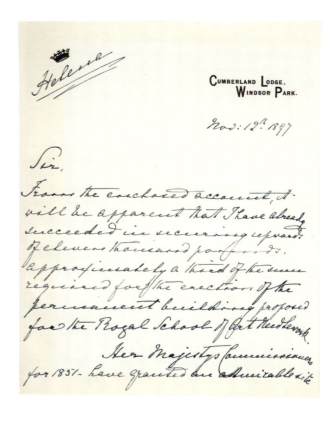

Princess Helena was the
RSN's principal fundraiser,
personally writing to anyone
whom she thought might
support the RSN's drive for a
new building. This is a copy of
the letter she first sent.

[RSN Archive. Photograph: Susan
Kay-Williams]

(left) **The new RSN building was opened amid snow in 1903 by the Prince of Wales**

[RSN Archive]

(right) **The showroom of the new building which was also used for the Summer and Winter Sales**

[RSN Archive]

However, to reach the goal the Executive Committee had to take out a loan of £3,500 for the fixtures and fittings such as counters for the showroom and linoleum for the floors. The finances were all still incredibly tight, every penny was needed. At the opening ceremony, for example, seats were sold. The cost of the event was £37 14s but ticket sales left a shortfall of £7 2s 6d. With mounting initial costs, a further loan of £2,000 was taken out in 1904.

The new building was opened by the then Prince of Wales, later George V, in 1903. In her speech one can feel some of Princess Helena's mingled stress and relief, how much of a challenge it had been. She acknowledged the gift of Mr Edward Stern: 'let me sincerely thank you, Sir for your presence here today to crown the completion of our work.'[14] Stern went on to serve on RSN committees and was knighted in the 1904 King's honours for his philanthropy. Princess Helena also acknowledged how far the RSN had come: 'No one who remembers the needlework of thirty years ago will question the progress, I might say revolution, which has occurred.' In the programme was a list of 51 projects out of 1,118 that had been completed by RSN workers in the three years 1901–1903, beginning with the King's coronation mantle.

The building was huge, too big for just the RSN at the time of the opening, but Princess Helena had high hopes of establishing a school of design for women alongside the RSN, so it was seen as a building they could grow into.

The *Gentlewoman* magazine sent a journalist round the building before it was officially opened and they wrote that while it was not on the scale of the three principal buildings of the area: the Imperial Institute, the Natural History Museum and the Victoria and Albert Museum, 'it is extraordinary how well it maintains its position as an architectural feature. This may be due in part to the fact that it is a corner building, but still more because in animation, in colour, design, and style it affords such a contrast to the adjacent buildings.'

The enthusiastic reporter continued: 'the second floor is devoted to the work department itself, with classrooms for drawing and design. On the third floor again are more workrooms beautifully lit and convenient and spacious dining-rooms and kitchens. ... The whole of the interior is lit by electricity and warmed by hot water. The RSN have now a home worthy their reputation and the objects so zealously pushed forward by Her Royal Highness Princess Christian.'[15]

However, even after the opening of the building there was still a need for funds as there were those two bank loans and a mortgage. The Princess prided herself that the school made ends meet and looked after itself. As the *Illustrated London News* wrote:

> 'Apart from the building debt, the school is quite self-supporting, the pupils' fees and the payments received for the exquisite needlework that is executed suffice to meet all liabilities ... Princess Christian has been the mainstay of the school and has probably written her name on the history of women's work by what has there been achieved under the influence of Her Royal Highness's kindness and business ability.'[16]

The loans weighed heavily on her, even though the interest was going to be covered by the fees the City and Guilds were paying as rent. Finally, resolution came in the form of a donation of the not insubstantial amount of £26,000.[17] All the newspaper reports stated it was from 'an

The workroom in the new building, showing military and other commissions in progress
[RSN Archive]

A single panel of embroidery made as a sample to indicate the type of work the RSN could undertake for evening dresses

[RSN Collection. Photograph: John Chase]

anonymous friend (whose name is understood to be well known in the commercial world)'.[18] However, the minutes reveal it to be Mr, later Sir, James Horlick. Mr and Mrs Horlick were listed in the programme at the opening as one of the 51 clients who had had work undertaken, and Mrs Horlick was already an Associate. This donation was made at the end of 1905 and covered the loan for the 1851 Commissioners and the other outstanding costs of the move. It was a huge relief to Princess Helena and the Executive Committee who recorded:

'It was moved by Her Royal Highness, the President, seconded by the Hon WFD Smith and carried unanimously that the very cordial thanks of the Committee are accorded to Mr Horlick for his most munificent donation which relieves the school from the Building debt which has hitherto seriously embarrassed its operations and prospects. It was further resolved that Mr Horlick be invited to join the Executive Committee.'

Horlick did indeed join the committee and served on it for many years, through thick and thin, alongside Stern, and such was the committee's relief that they moved from monthly to quarterly meetings.

At the first Sale in the new rooms in June 1904 the *Morning Post* noted that Princess Helena would be presiding each day of the Sale, that the spacious workroom had been transformed into a tearoom and that Mr Alfred de Rothschild's Band and the Ladies' Orchestra would be playing, now that there was more space available. Four days later the paper reported that a thousand people had attended, revealing a much higher level of interest at the first sale in the new premises and the *St James's Gazette* wrote that Princess Helena was 'most pleased with the result, the final day yesterday being the most successful of any'.[19]

In 1904 the RSN first started taking military colours for repair and conservation, and subsequently began making new colours and guidons. This work would continue for many decades.

Enabling more people to see the work of the school was a key theme that appeared repeatedly. In 1907 there was an exhibition in a Grafton Street gallery in London's West End. Princess Helena was shown round by Miss Wade and Sir Edward and Lady Stern. The centrepiece of the exhibition was *Pomona* and some of the workers were stationed there to

(left) *The Mill,* based on the Burne-Jones painting of the same name. It was made for the *Franco-British Exhibition* in London in 1908, and subsequently hung in the RSN showroom.
[RSN Archive]

(right) Burne-Jones created a number of images for the RSN. As when working with Morris, he created faces and figures for the RSN while others designed the rest of the scene, but this is a complete design.
[RSN Archive. Photograph: John Chase]

demonstrate how the work was made. Pieces had also been loaned for the exhibition. When the Prince and Princess of Wales visited, they much admired the damask curtains from Blair Castle, loaned by the Duke of Athol. In fact, so popular was the exhibition that it was continued for several more days.

Other partnerships included links with Liberty, indeed Sir Arthur Liberty served on the business committee of the RSN, and with Debenham & Freebody (D&F). This latter came about when, in 1907, Princess Helena announced that the embroidery of dresses was to become a special feature in the future, a departure from just interiors, military and ecclesiastical pieces. The idea was to work with an English-based French dress designer/maker Madame Pacard, who would design the gown and the RSN would work the embroidery, especially for single panels down the front of the garment and trains for court gowns. Only a short time later, Madame Pacard went in with Debenham & Freebody and then ladies could go to D&F and choose a gown, and have it made by Madame but with the RSN providing the embroidery.[20] This was signed by the Executive Committee but was short lived as an exclusive contract, being terminated in February 1909 because it was not delivering enough work to retain sole agency status.

While noting that the RSN might be good at working the dress panels, the *Sketch* newspaper noted that art embroidery and fashion embroidery were two quite different things: 'Dresses are for the passing hour; art embroidery is for life times and more.'[21]

The Mill

In 1908 the *Franco-British Exhibition* was held at White City/Shepherd's Bush in London. The President of France, M. Fallières, came over on a state visit. The *Daily Telegraph* noted that the King and M. Fallières visited the exhibition:

> 'One of the earliest exhibits to be inspected here was that of the RSN, the King explained that it had been established by his sister, Princess Christian. Especially noticed by the Queen, as well as the President was the magnificent panel of The Mill from designs by Burne-Jones and her Majesty remarked that she had seen it at the school when still unfinished on her last visit there. Two smaller panels of Music and Poesie, by the same artist, were also much admired, as was an enlarged reproduction in correct heraldic colouring of the Windsor Castle book plate worked to the order of her late Majesty. The Queen returned to this exhibit a second time to notice some of the beautiful and characteristic embroideries as applied to furniture.'[22]

Another report also marvelled at the 'picture in needlework of considerable dimensions, made by students at the school from a copy of one of Burne-Jones's works. The effects of the original are produced with wonderful accuracy'.[23] The finished size of the piece was 19 feet by 8 feet (580 × 240cm).

Perhaps inspired by the response to this exhibition, the RSN then rearranged the sale room at Exhibition Road to feature more hangings designed by Morris, Burne-Jones and Crane.

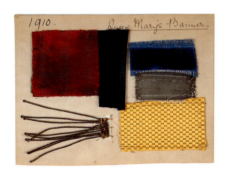

(above) **Left-over materials from the making of Queen Mary's Garter Banner**

[RSN Archive. Photograph: John Chase]

(right) **Queen Mary's Garter Banner which still hangs above her tomb in St George's Chapel at Windsor**

[Image courtesy of and © The Dean & Canon of Windsor]

Pageant of Empire

In 1910 the RSN worked six huge banners, 10 feet by 7 feet (300 × 210cm) for the colonial section of the Pageant of Empire. The banners were for South Africa, Newfoundland, Canada, India, Australia and New Zealand.

The event was meant to take place in spring that year, but then Edward VII died and the whole event was postponed for a year.

Meanwhile at the lying-in-state of King Edward, the funeral pall made by the RSN for his mother, less than a decade earlier, was reused to cover the coffin.

Coronation of George V

The ability of the press to speculate is not new. In November 1910 it was anticipated that George V would wear the same mantle as worn by Edward, made by the RSN, and as other things would be reused, such as the canopy, it was assumed that there would be a lesser role for the RSN, but not so. First, there was the making of the Garter banners for the King and Queen. A new monarch automatically becomes the head of the Order of the Garter and their banners hang in St George's Chapel, Windsor (the home chapel of the Garter order) for the duration of the monarch's reign. They used then to be taken down when the next monarch succeeded but George VI passed a decree which changed the fate of these banners. Today, those of Edward VII and Alexandra (also made by the RSN) hang still in the Windsor chapel, and those of George V and Mary hang over their tombs. They bear the coat of arms of the individual. This is always more interesting for the Queens as theirs must contain the arms of their husband as well as their own, meaning that they can be very dense with imagery on the right-hand side (see page 59).

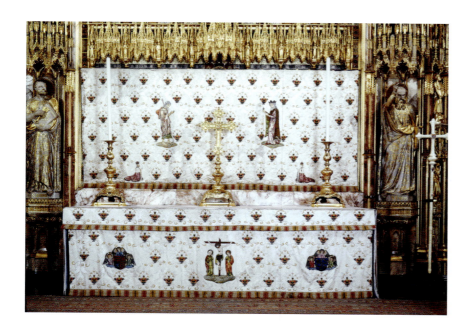

The dorsal behind the cross and candlesticks for the coronation of George V and Queen Mary in 1911, made by the RSN

[Image © Dean and Chapter Westminster]

(left) **Antependium designed by Philip Webb and worked by the RSN in the early 20th century**
[RSN Collection. Photograph: John Chase]

(right) **Altar frontal design by the RSN, early 20th century**
[RSN Archive. Photograph: John Chase]

There was also the making of the Garter which is the gift of the Worshipful Company of Girdlers to the monarch, and the embroidering of two pairs of gloves with the Queen's monogram and crown given for the coronation by the Worshipful Company of Glovers. The RSN was also charged with repairing or remaking the Heralds' outfits at a reputed cost of £30 each just for the gold embroidery. Plus, there were orders for several coronation gowns from peeresses, especially as the new Queen advocated that as many materials as possible should be British.

There was also an altar dorsal which was to be given by the King and Queen to Westminster Abbey. Designed by Rosina Smith of the RSN, it featured St Edward and St John, and at the bottom the figures of the King and Queen in coronation robes kneeling. This was used for the coronation in 1911 and subsequently for the coronations of George VI and Queen Elizabeth II. It is still used by the Abbey each Edwardtide (October), to commemorate the founding of the Abbey.

Finally, though, it was decided that George V would wear the mantle and cope of George IV, which was sent to the RSN for conservation, repair and preparation to be worn again. Meanwhile, there were other items that needed attention. At the end of May the new King was to attend a concert at the Royal Albert Hall. With the monarch present the Hammer Cloth would be displayed in front of the royal box and once again it needed its initial changed, from E to G.

Beyond the coronation the workroom was generally busy with regimental colours and ecclesiastical vestments for cathedrals, churches and priories all over the country, from Ripon to Wales.

First World War
During the First World War, the Training School and the workroom kept going but they nevertheless found a way to help. The RSN offered free lessons in sewing and darning:

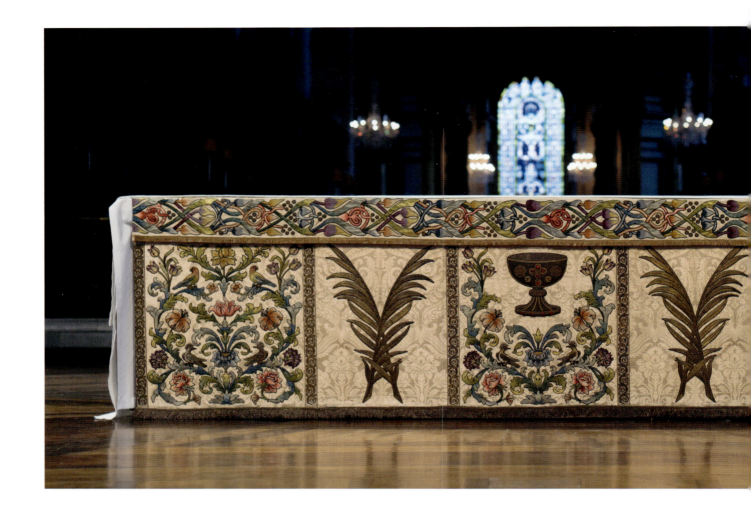

'Showing Soldiers How to Sew. The Royal School of Needlework, at South Kensington is noted far and wide for its delicate stitchery and embroidery, but, for the present, this finer work is being laid aside in its classes. The school has made a very sensible and thoughtful offer to the recruits for the New Army and will place its services at the disposal of officers and men who wish to be taught the homely and necessary arts of darning socks, mending clothes, and knitting. There has been a ready response, and many men are already acquiring dexterity with the needles. It may prove a very helpful accomplishment to them later on.'[24]

Workers were also making 'housewives' a pouch which contained all that the soldier needed to mend his uniform, comprising needles, a thimble, wool and thread. They were further encouraged to support the men at the Front by purchasing shirts, mittens and socks etc. as Christmas gifts at the Sale.

Later in the war, the RSN offered designs and stitch guides that could be worked by returning soldiers and sailors as occupational

therapy. One work of note is the altar frontal that was made by injured servicemen for St Paul's Cathedral, designed by the RSN.[25] The design was later reused by the RSN for an altar frontal for St James's Cathedral, Toronto, Canada. Using embroidery as occupational therapy was realised to be a powerful activity. In fact, even before the start of the war, the press had been talking about a rise in interest in hand embroidery, and more than that, about it being an antidote to 'brain fog' or nerves.[26] In 1916, at the Summer Sale of the RSN a collection was taken to send materials to Netley Hospital which offered stitch therapy. Stitching can be an absorbing activity and the process of stitching as a repetition, almost a meditation, means that it could help the injured men to focus on stitching and perhaps think less of the pain they were enduring, or quieten the mind from the trauma of battle and loss. At least one person connected to the RSN acted as a tutor to the injured soldiers, achieving 'wonderful successes'.[27] Miss Marjorie Naylor was a graduate of the teaching diploma and during the war taught wounded soldiers to stitch. For her work, in December 1917 she was awarded the prestigious Teachers' Gold Seal by the RSN.

The cost of running the school was £1,000 a year by 1915. By early 1916 the war was having a bad impact on business. The Executive Committee noted that the workroom needed to increase its throughput threefold to make ends meet. Work had dropped by 50 per cent in six months and the school was losing £200 per month. However, the sub-committee were very aware of their original founding purpose and that there would now be a growing number of women who, being made widows, would want to turn to the likes of the RSN for work. However, Sir Edward Stern felt that any applicants should be put to war work as there was a shortage of workers.

At the Summer Sale in 1917, with the war in its third year, even the tea was in the spirit of the times. 'Lady Robertson and Lady Strathcona were busy at the troops' stall in the tea-room, where a war rations tea was served instead of the "five-o'-clock" de luxe, customary on these occasions.'[28]

Badges for the Royal Flying Corps

At the end of 1915 there was a Christmas sale, intended to raise funds for the school and to offer items for sale for the troops. *The Gentlewoman* magazine, particularly, noted one display: 'A small cabinet contained specimens of especial interest viz, embroidered badges to be worn by members of the Flying Corps for whom the school have worked a large number. The badge is a bird with outspread wings, some being done in gold thread for special occasions, while a scarlet bird is for ordinary wear, and a blue bird on white material for summer use.'[29]

Patriotic Needlework Competition

In October 1915 the *Daily Sketch* newspaper announced a competition for Patriotic Needlework for which prizes would be given and certificates

Certificate from the second
Patriotic Needlework
Competition sponsored by
The Daily Sketch and judged
by Miss Bradshaw

[RSN Archive. Photograph: John Chase]

awarded. Judges were to come from the RSN. People were encouraged to visit the exhibition to support wounded soldiers via the Red Cross.

> 'A three-day Exhibition of Needlework will be opened at the Central Hall, Westminster, to-morrow. The exhibition, which has been organized by the Daily Sketch, will contain the work of several thousand women in every English-speaking part of the globe. As prizes, amounting to £1000, are being given by the promoters, the perfection and delicacy of the needlework is assured. The proceeds of the sale will go to the Red Cross and the Order of St. John. The personality of the stallholders will make the affair especially interesting; society and stage are joining to ensure its success.'[30]

So successful was the competition that it was re-run the following year, again with judging by RSN staff.

In 1917 the RSN was asked to make a series of banners for an event at the Royal Albert Hall on 15 December to recognise the First Seven Divisions who had borne the brunt of the early phases of the war. The banners were described by several correspondents as beautiful.

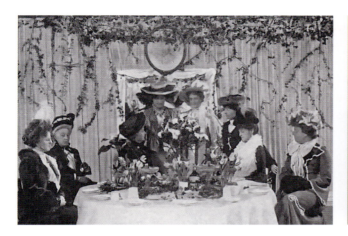

(left) **RSN Summer Sale with Principal Miss Louisa Wade second from left. Miss Wade had many titles in her 40 years, retiring as Principal in 1915.** (*The Tatler*, 22 April 1903)

(right) **Miss Bradshaw, second Principal of the RSN from 1915 to 1932**

[RSN Archive]

Eventually, as the war came to an end business did rally. By 1918 the Executive Committee was seeking new trainees for the workroom and discussing using disabled men returned from the war. In 1919 Sir Edward Stern gave Princess Helena a cheque for £2,000 for the school, to be used wherever need was most, in commemoration of the Peace. He died in 1933 after many years of service on the RSN committees.

Miss Wade

Miss Wade was appointed Superintendent in 1875, later Principal and stayed for 40 years, finally retiring at the end of March 1915. She had immense knowledge of the work of the RSN and oversaw the making of Queen Victoria's funeral pall and the coronation requirements for both Edward VII and George V. One press tribute described her as giving 'all her energies to the interests and welfare of the school'.[31] There being no government or company pension provision in place, in recognition of her length of service the Executive Committee voted to pay her an annual pension of £300. This was a large amount, as much as the salary they paid her successor initially.

She was succeeded by Miss Evelyn Bradshaw who had joined the RSN in 1911 as Miss Wade's Vice Principal to aid in the management of the school. After the short tenure of both Lady Welby and Mrs Dolby, the RSN's leadership is mostly noted for its longevity. Except for Mrs Field in the 1980s, all other principals have been with the organisation at least into double figures, though no-one has served longer in the role than Miss Wade. Miss Bradshaw was appointed as Principal in 1915 and continued in the role until 1932, giving a total of 21 years of service to the RSN.

Queen Mary

Princess Victoria May of Teck (Queen Mary) made her first recorded visit to the RSN on Tuesday 5 April 1881 aged 13. Visiting with her mother, Princess Mary Duchess of Teck, they came to see the Exhibition of Ancient Needlework, an exhibition so popular that it was being extended over the Easter holidays to accommodate the level of interest. As Princess of Wales, she became Patron with her husband and Queen Alexandra in 1902, a role she retained through to her death in 1953.

As the new Queen in 1910 she was introduced to the public as someone with a stimulating interest in embroidery. She was described as 'an expert needlewoman ... who encourages this domestic art in everyday'. In 1913 Queen Mary began a programme of at least two visits per year to the RSN, and they were often referred to as 'unexpected'. She would not visit alone, but was often accompanied by her daughter Princess Mary, later the Princess Royal, Countess of Harewood, and sometimes her sons too. Both Edward, Prince of Wales and Bertie, Duke of York visited the RSN. Given her interest she always wanted a full tour of the workrooms.

'Her Majesty made a tour of the whole building inspecting the various workrooms and conversing with the workers.'[32] It was noted that 'Queen Mary is particularly fond of paying private visits to the many philanthropic and other institutions in which she takes an interest.' She stayed an hour or more and inspected the work of the students and workroom, noting she 'seemed to be particularly pleased with a set of beautiful chair covers which were being made, and with some novel silk-embroidered pictures'.[33] These unannounced visits continued even through the war.

By the 1930s Queen Mary was taking on bigger stitching challenges. In 1932 it is recorded that the Queen was in discussions with the RSN for the design for a set of chair covers with the colours of pink, blue and beige chosen by the Queen.

Queen Mary's interest in embroidery never waned and she also encouraged her children to participate. In 1936 the newspapers wrote about the stitching royal family:

'ROYAL EMBROIDERY. Mrs. Francis Abel Smith is to hold a reception to-morrow in connection with the institution which provides the Royal Family with its chief hobby needlework. The Royal School of Needlework deserves its title, for it has not only trained members of the Royal Family to do embroidery, but it provides them with work and also sells them examples of the finished article. The King does embroidery. Queen Mary is at present making a chair cover and sofa cushion-covers for Marlborough House in a floral pattern on pale blue. The Princess Royal is copying the design of an Aubusson carpet for a chair. The Duke and Duchess of York are between them making the covers for a set of 12 chairs to be decorated with the white rose of York and their crest. The Duke of Gloucester is at work on a piece of Florentine embroidery. Indeed, the Duke of Kent is the only one of Queen Mary's children who has not followed her favourite hobby.'[34]

Churchwork triptych by one of the Misses Jones. The sisters completed the diploma in 1918 and went on to head the churchwork department until the early 1950s.

[RSN Collection. Photograph: John Chase]

The Beginning of the Lingerie Department

Despite the war, the RSN started producing lingerie in 1916, introduced with a delightful snippet in the magazine *Tatler*. The gossipy correspondent 'Eve' writes: 'Saw more clothes at Lady Deerhurst's "at home" at the RSN where Princess Marie Louise came to tea too, and we bought of all things – crepe de chine undies. But as I've said before awful nice sensation it gives you combining well, pink crepe de chine with charity.'[35]

The *Gentlewoman* reported that 'Princess Christian is greatly pleased at the immediate success of the new department at the school.'[36] Later that same month Queen Mary visited accompanied by Princess Mary and this time her second son, Prince Albert. The Press reported that this visit caused a bit of a stir. 'The Prince and Princess both interested themselves in the beautiful work of the girl students. The Queen's Sailor-boy chatted vigorously with the workers and burst into broad smiles when a lady who intended to show the Queen some blouses spread out by mistake other portions of a trousseau the college was making.'[37] (Albert would have been 20 at the time.) By December the press reported that the

RSN had already completed orders of lingerie for the Queen, Princess Mary and Princess Helena.

The latter part of 1910–1920 was also an important one in the Training School in terms of people who will play a role later in the story. In 1916 Miss Ruby Essam graduated from the diploma course after three years and went straight into the workroom. Two years later Miss Alice and Miss Jesse Jones took the same route. Miss Essam worked in the general workroom while the Misses Jones went on to run the churchwork room.

A Change of Name

The archive of the RSN contains copies of a letter which at face value seems very innocuous but which hides a great deal of activity behind the scenes. As noted in the minutes of the Executive Committee of 1922:

> 'Miss Bradshaw reported that comment had been made of late in various quarters on the use of the word "Art Needlework" in the name of the school, as inadequately expressing the wide scope of its activities in the present day. Letters on this subject from Sir Cecil Smith and others were read and it was suggested that the word "art" should be omitted, the name of the school in future to be Royal School of Needlework. HRH The President having already signified her approval of the change to Miss Bradshaw this change of name to be the subject of special business at the next Annual General Meeting according to the Articles of Association.'

The next meeting of the Executive Committee was not until 1923 and it simply records that 'the alteration in the name of the school to Royal School of Needlework had been made, the Royal Warrant granted, approved by the Board of Trade and registered under the Companies Act'. However, it was not simply a matter for the Executive Committee, as a royal organisation the request had to go to the King for approval, and that was when the issues began. The civil service was asked to investigate the whole thing and discovered that no royal charter had been granted when Queen Victoria became Patron in 1875. On this discovery, the bureaucrats were not that keen on the school retaining its royal title, notwithstanding that Princess Helena was still its active President and that both the King and the Queen were Patrons of the organisation.

In the end, this was all presented to the King for a final decision, with a strong recommendation to remove the royal title in disregard of Princess Helena, but it was the King himself who commented that he was minded to allow the RSN to keep its royal title and for it to become

Miss Ruby Essam's certificate on graduating from the diploma in 1916, signed by Princess Helena, Miss Bradshaw and Miss Randell
[RSN Archive. Photograph: John Chase]

The change of name caused
consternation among the civil
servants as to whether the
RSN should remain royal. In
the end, the King stepped in.

Transcription:
*See Correspondence with
Lord Stamfordham within.
The King approves the
change of name to "the Royal
School of Needlework".
His Majesty does not wish
the School to be asked to
discontinue the use of the
Royal Arms, & it appears that
the use of the Monogram
(which resembles[?] V.R) is to
be discontinued.*

*It is difficult to make R.S.A.N.
out of the V.R. as Princess
Christian suggests.*

*Inform the School of H.M.'s
approval of change of title
(Nothing need be said about
the RA unless they raise the
question)[!]*

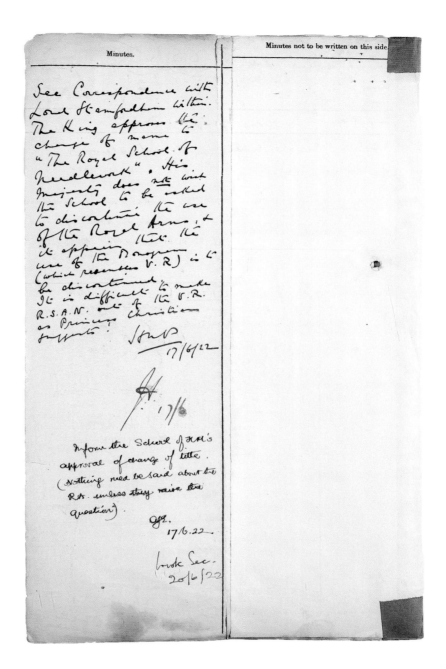

the Royal School of Needlework henceforth, as can be seen from a
scribbled note on papers now in the National Archives (see above).

Death of Princess Helena

The *Pall Mall Gazette* reported that, although in failing health, Princess
Helena had set the dates for the Summer Sale at the RSN as 12 and
13 June 1923 and that she intended to be there in person as royal
saleswoman, but it was a promise too far. She died on 9 June 1923 of
influenza and a heart attack. The periodical *The Truth* perhaps put it
most appropriately when they wrote:

'By the testimony of all who met her she had no idea of being a mere ornamental patron; she wanted to know and to work. And she did. The Royal School of Art Needlework which owed so much to her from its inception onwards, exemplifies in another direction the zeal with which she laboured when her interest was enlisted.'[38]

The Yorkshire Post[39] acknowledged, 'In no centre of her many activities is Princess Christian's loss felt more sincerely that at the Royal School of Art Needlework. At "my school" as the dead lady used to call it – for she was very fond of this centre of beauty in needlecraft.' The Sale was, of course, postponed and held later with Princess Mary presiding.

After Princess Helena's death both her daughters took a more active role at the RSN. Princess Helena Victoria officially became Vice President in 1924, and Princess Marie Louise became a member of Council in the same year. In 1925 a memorial tablet was discussed, and funds raised. It was designed by W.R.R. Blacking[40] and erected on the wall of the Exhibition Road building, but was removed before departure and has stayed with the RSN.

A new president was needed, and the archives show it was Queen Mary who suggested who should be approached. Her second son Prince Albert had just married Elizabeth Bowes-Lyon, so Queen Mary suggested the new Duchess of York be approached. There is a letter from her secretary accepting the post of President, her first official role following her marriage, although there is a postscript which says that she did not believe that she would be able to give as much time as Princess

(left) **Her Royal Highness The Duchess of York attends her first Winter Sale as the new President of the RSN, 29 November 1923; with her are the Duchess of Wellington and Lord Campbell.**
[TopFoto 0977759]

(opposite) **After her death, in honour of Princess Helena's commitment to the RSN, this plaque was commissioned. It was originally hung in the Exhibition Road building but has moved around with the RSN.**
[RSN Collection]

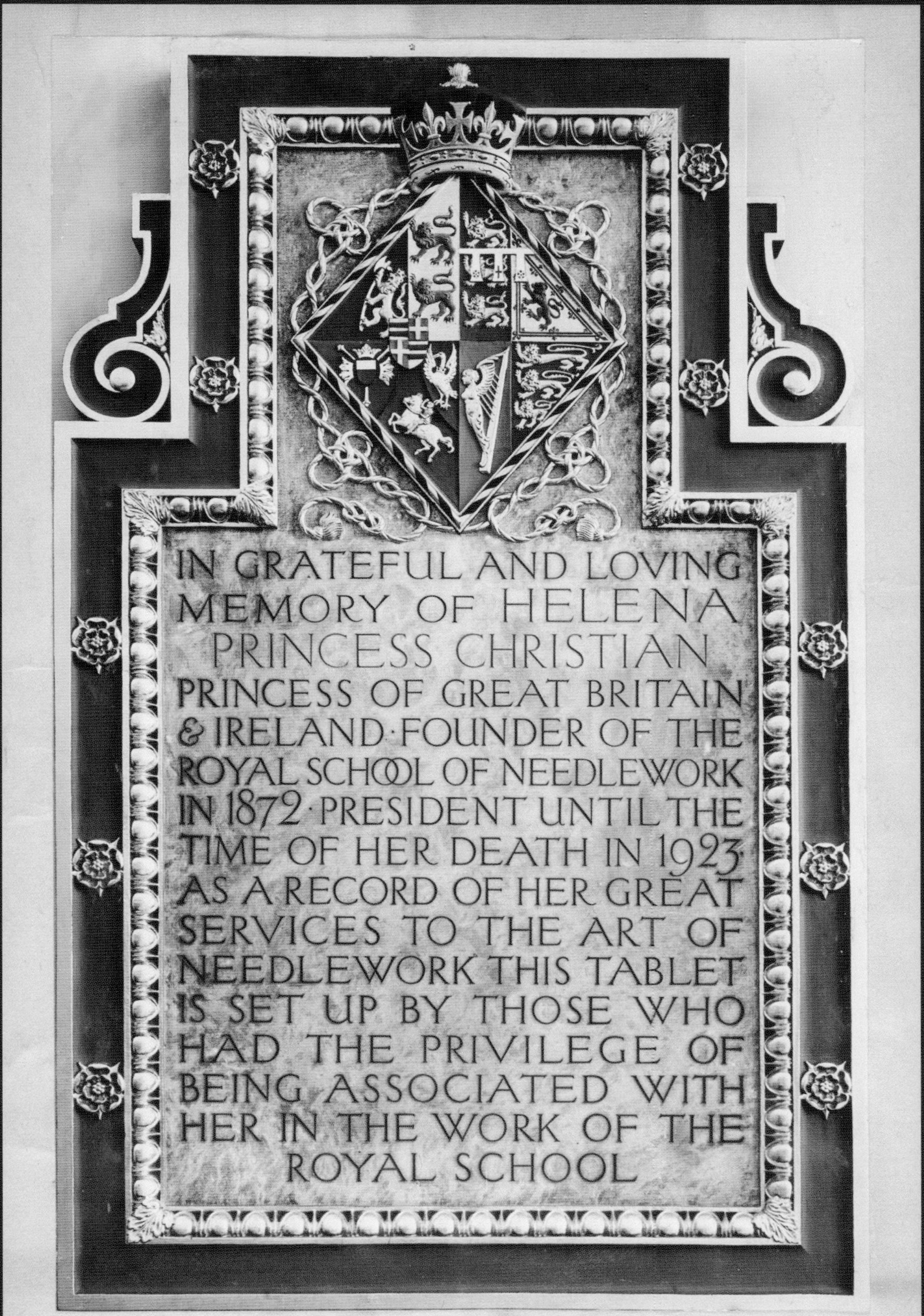

IN GRATEFUL AND LOVING
MEMORY OF HELENA
PRINCESS CHRISTIAN
PRINCESS OF GREAT BRITAIN
& IRELAND·FOUNDER OF THE
ROYAL SCHOOL OF NEEDLEWORK
IN 1872·PRESIDENT UNTIL THE
TIME OF HER DEATH IN 1923
AS A RECORD OF HER GREAT
SERVICES TO THE ART OF
NEEDLEWORK THIS TABLET
IS SET UP BY THOSE WHO
HAD THE PRIVILEGE OF
BEING ASSOCIATED WITH
HER IN THE WORK OF THE
ROYAL SCHOOL

(left) **The smaller-than-postage-stamp canvaswork picture of a kingfisher was originally made for Queen Mary's Dolls' House.**
[RSN Collection. Photograph: John Chase]

(opposite) **The miniature tester bed for the king, embroidered by the RSN for Queen Mary's Dolls' House**
[Royal Collection Trust/© His Majesty Charles III 2023]

Helena had. She attended her first Sale in winter 1923 and remained President until 1949 when she took over from the King as Patron. She remained an active supporter all her life.

Queen Mary's Dolls' House

Queen Mary's Dolls' House was the idea of Princess Marie Louise (Princess Helena's second daughter) so not surprisingly, the school was one of many organisations which contributed pieces to it. In particular, the RSN made the King's and Queen's beds. The King's tester bed has an embroidered bedhead featuring the crest and embroidered coverlet. The Queen's bed also has an embroidered crest in silver and has a part-worked small canvas over a chair. It is not known if the RSN made the part-worked canvas, but it still has in its collection a small postage stamp-sized embroidery of a kingfisher made originally for the house but not in the end required.

CHAPTER 3

Lady Smith-Dorrien

When Miss Bradshaw announced her retirement in 1932,[1] Queen Mary once again stepped in. It was she and Princess Helena Victoria who invited Lady Olive Smith-Dorrien to become Principal and it was reported that Queen Mary spent two hours with Lady Smith-Dorrien 'going personally into every detail of the re-organisation under the new Principal'.[2]

Lady Smith-Dorrien was an embroiderer and was well connected in her own right as well as through her husband's family. All of this helped the RSN to reach new customers in the 1930s, especially for the lingerie.

Leadership and Management

For the first 50 years of the RSN Princess Helena was at the helm overall. Miss Wade and Miss Bradshaw might oversee the day to day running and the management, but Helena oversaw direction, although she increasingly brought on to Council and committees, people who could help the organisation – benefactors, businesspeople and people with connections. After Princess Helena died Miss Bradshaw was more at the forefront but for the organisation overall this was one of the quietest periods. Nevertheless, as Queen Mary saw, there was a need for something new. With the appointment of Lady Smith-Dorrien it is once again back to a strong leader, and the minutes are all about what Lady Smith-Dorrien is doing or asking for. The business leaders from the turn of the century are now retiring from the committee and being replaced over time by representatives of some of the companies the

RSN uses as suppliers or partners: first Mr Hunter of William Briggs and Co. (died 1943), then Mr J. Clarke of J. & P. Coats (commenced 1946), as well as titled ladies.

Sales in the 1930s

The Sales continued for summer and Christmas throughout the 1930s. Several members of the royal family would share the duty of acting as saleswoman on one or both days. From the older generation, Princesses Helena Victoria and Marie Louise made regular appearances, and from the younger generation it was usually the President, the Duchess of York, interspersed with the Princess Royal. Their appearance certainly brought people to the events: 'When the Duchess of York took her place as saleswoman at the annual pre-Christmas display at the RSAN [*sic*], Kensington today her table was surrounded by eager buyers all anxious to have the proud memory of having been "served" by the Royal visitor. Her charm and ready smile endear the "little Duchess" as she is so affectionately called through the country, to those who have the honour to assist her by making up the parcels of goods bought, making out accounts or advising as to the history of some particular treasure.'[3]

The main items for sale, at least from the press reports, appear to have been lingerie and accoutrement: nightwear, bed linen and an item which went on to be particularly popular during the Second World War and which was always written in the workbooks as HWBC – hot water bottle covers.

It was also noted that in the display part, there were contributions from male embroiderers. The *Sheffield Independent* noted: 'There are usually contributions of Knitting and embroidery from the Prince of Wales, Lord Harewood and the Earl of Gainford who is an expert embroiderer.'[4]

Tea was also an important part of the Sale events. For the November sale in 1931, *The Times* reported that ladies had come in the morning to select items but had then requested they be put on one side so they could return in the afternoon when they could be 'sold' the item by the Duchess.[5] The accounts of that same event tell us that income from teas and donations amounted to £15 11s, expenditure amounted to £11 3s of which the largest single amount was the cost of tea for the reporters which amounted to £2 3s 6d; still there was extensive press coverage which would have been useful for the RSN in encouraging further visitors. The Summer Sale, it was recorded, earned £186 4s 6d while the November sale earned £233 2s 5d, a 25 per cent increase in takings in the winter.

Both the Principal and the royal saleswomen believed it was important to have items of different prices available to attract all manner of buyers, especially in the early years of the 1930s.

Princess Mary, the Princess Royal assisting at the RSN Sale in the 1930s
[RSN Collection]

ROYAL SCHOOL OF NEEDLEWORK
Patron: HER MAJESTY THE QUEEN

H.R.H. The Duchess of York, President
H.H. Princess Helena Victoria, Vice-President
have graciously consented to sell at an
Exhibition of Embroideries and Needlework
to be held at
45, Park Lane, W.
Wednesday, November 21st, 1934
2.30 to 6 p.m.
Thursday, November 22nd
10 a.m. to 6 p.m.

Many models, copied from the best Paris Houses by the Royal School of Needlework, will be displayed.

Admission First day 5/–
Second day 2/6

Invitation to the 1934 RSN
Sale held on Park Lane –
lingerie and tea dresses were
the main items to sell

[RSN Archive. Photograph: John Chase]

Nevertheless, there were things to celebrate; 1932 was the Diamond Jubilee of the RSN and the Princess Royal led the sales team for the annual Summer Sale. 'Wherever she went crowds of buyers came to receive their parcels wrapped up by the Princess … New washing pyjamas, suits of satin intended for dinner wear in summer, as well as tea gowns with braces of lace were on the Princess's stall.'[6]

The winter of 1932 saw the first sale at Sir Philip Sassoon's home on Park Lane. Both the Queen and the Duchess of York visited on the first day and the Queen thought it so splendid that she insisted it be open for a second day. Both the Queen and the Duchess made purchases including dresses – 'party frocks' for the young Princesses.[7] The next day the Duchess of York was royal saleswoman. Lady Smith-Dorrien reported that orders to the value of £1,100 had been taken at the event, many times more than had been the case at previous sales. By winter 1937 this was up to £1,476.

Lingerie in the 1930s

When Lady Smith-Dorrien joined the RSN in 1932 it was a difficult time for luxury items, the ramifications of the Wall Street Crash and the General Strike were still being felt, money was tight and the RSN needed to encourage people to shop again. Lady Smith-Dorrien would go on annual trips to France to see the latest Parisian designs and then bring them back to be reinterpreted for English tastes and made by English workers, in the form of the RSN team. As a result, fashionable ladies came to the RSN for everything from one-off pieces to trousseaux. 'Girls at the school are busy at the moment upon a yearly order for a Royal lady for lingerie of the finest white lawn embroidered with sprigs of roses and edged with narrow lace. Lawn lingerie is becoming almost as popular as crepe de chine with brides, especially in primrose yellow and rose pink. Dainty details for the trousseau of Lady Mary Abel Smith were selected recently in this room.'[8]

Such was the development of the lingerie department that Lady Smith-Dorrien approached the Duke of Westminster about giving them a lease on a building in the West End near the major department stores:

'Wednesday – This morning I was shown over what will be, I should imagine, one of the most fashionable shops this summer. This is the lingerie establishment, just opposite Claridge's in Brook Street, that the Royal School of Needlework is to open early in

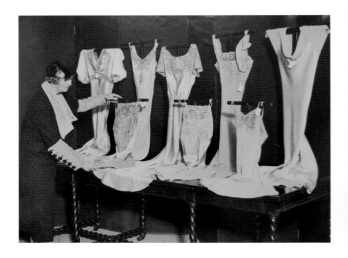

April. The Duchess of York, who is taking a great interest in all the arrangements, has been instrumental in obtaining this shop for three months, and here the skilled embroideresses of the school will be able to display examples of their handiwork. These include some really delightfully worked lingerie. Princess Helena Victoria has, I was told, promised to give tea parties to some of her friends in the salon of the little shop, where copies of lingerie chosen by ladies of the Royal Family, including the Queen, will be on view daily. The Duchess of York is planning to have some little muslin frocks made there for her daughters, and the Princess Royal, whose town house is only a short walk from the shop, is sure to be one of its first customers.'[9]

The shop turned out to be a great success and Lady Smith-Dorrien asked the Duke of Westminster to extend the lease.

The high point of the lingerie department was the making of trousseaux. The RSN worked on part of the trousseaux of several young royals – the Princess Royal, the Duchess of Kent, as well as society ladies, but the most extensive was probably for Lady Alice Montagu-Douglas-Scott's wedding to the Duke of Gloucester in November 1935. Although it was commented that a trousseau no longer comprised dozens of each item as they had in the 19th century, there was a wide-ranging set of objects. These were delivered to the palace in October, shortly before the wedding, and afterwards were put on exhibition, in the great tradition of the RSN displaying its work.

As a line of related work, the RSN also made layettes for babies, or as one paper described them 'baby trousseaux'[10] for the Princess Royal, the Duchess of Kent, and others.

Once the Sales moved to Park Lane they sold many more orders for lingerie and those customers would then go to the Brook Street shop. By 1936 Lady Smith-Dorrien was aware that Brook Street was now too

(left) **Lady Smith-Dorrien arranging lingerie for a Sale in 1935. She went to Paris twice a year to select new patterns and designs.**
[TopFoto EU043187]

(right) **Making lingerie at the RSN**
[Associated Press RID126/50/1]

Advertising image for the RSN lingerie department exhibition, 1935
[RSN Archive. Photograph: John Chase]

small and a second property round the corner, 59 Davis Street was rented
from November 1936.

Meanwhile, core embroidery custom had dwindled and the RSN
started to talk about downsizing, especially as the College of Design
never materialised and the two original tenants had moved out, as early
as 1933, only 10 years after Helena's death. Imperial College not only
started to use some of the rooms from 1934 but shortly after took over
the management of the building, making a partial payment for it to
the RSN. The RSN would now pay rent and a final payment would be
paid to the RSN by Christmas 1949, by which time they would have
departed.[11] At the same time, the pressure of work and the challenges of
evening transport meant that Lady Smith-Dorrien frequently could not
return to her apartment at Hampton Court Palace and instead slept in
an improvised bedroom at the RSN. Queen Mary came to hear about
this and promised to turn the unused rooms at the school into a little
flat for her.

Work levels were never a constant, there were always peaks and
troughs, and Lady Smith-Dorrien put out an invitation to churches and
regiments to have their laid-up colours netted to make them last longer,
thus stimulating work for the main workroom. Several regiments took
up this offer which helped to keep the core stitchers occupied.

School Needlework Certificates

From 1930 to 1960 the RSN offered certificates in needlework for pupils
who were still in school. These pupils never came to the RSN, but their
work was submitted by their teacher and then marked by the RSN.
There is little information about the scheme except that it was taken by
some schools year on year, especially Catholic schools who might send
20 or more pieces of work for assessment. A book in the archives lists all

those whose work was passed. Sometimes the entry might say something like 12 pieces submitted, 10 certificates awarded, but never give the names of the unsuccessful pupils.

The Jubilee Sampler

In the 1930s there was a definite increase in interest in home embroidery. People were buying magazines with transfers so they could work items at home. Most were practical items. Samplers were considered activities for young girls at school and there was no tradition of samplers for adults. That changed with the Jubilee of George V. To commemorate the Silver Jubilee, Lady Smith-Dorrien created a sampler for people to stitch at home. Different from samplers of old, it comprised pictures of some of the milestones of the reign, most notably the press wrote about the wireless and the King's first broadcast to the nation. There was also a poem to commemorate the reign and underline the pictures. This was a huge success.

'When the Royal School of Needlework designed a Jubilee sampler depicting some of the important events of the King's reign, it was never anticipated that more than a few of the more ardent supporters of the school would wish to work a record in stitchery of the last 25 years. When the school found that demands for the design far exceeded the supply, investigation was

Samplers designed by Lady Smith-Dorrien for (from left to right) the Silver Jubilee of George V, Edward VIII after his abdication and the coronation of George VI

[RSN Collection. Photograph: John Chase]

made which revealed that the samplers were being used, under glass, to cover coffee tables, or being turned into fire-screens or cushion covers. Thus, have samplers come back into fashion and now young and old are purchasing these samplers to work at home and during the holidays.'[12]

So, when George V died a year later, the RSN prepared ultimately two new samplers. One was for Edward VIII (extant versions show it to have been issued after abdication as the last verse refers to 'eight short months did Edward reign') and then Lady Smith-Dorrien prepared a third for George VI, in the same style, incorporating the two Princesses and the letter E and the crown cypher for Elizabeth his Queen.

From then on, the RSN often prepared samplers for special royal occasions, sometimes in connection with a newspaper or magazine, right the way through to the early 1980s with ones for the wedding of the Prince of Wales and Lady Diana Spencer, and then the birth of Prince William, although it must be said that they returned more to a style that would have been recognisable to earlier generations, worked in tent stitch or half cross stitch.

Making Connections

Meanwhile, Lady Smith-Dorrien made connections with William Briggs and Co. and decided that the RSN would supply designs to the company.[13] This really started the stronger links between many of the associated companies, with representatives from Briggs, Coats, Pearsall's, Toye Kenning and others, joining the Executive Committee or Council.

During 1936 the workbooks are full of updates to military standards and guidons as well as netting those which had been laid up. There were also new commissions such as regimental colours and King's colours for the 1st Battalion Scots Guards. Each containing their battle honours, these were expensive commissions so the estimate for the two was almost £135. There are also orders for civic colours. In 1937 the City of Bradford ordered a standard that was to be 3 feet 9½ inches by 12 feet (1.24m × 3.7m) in red and blue silk and embroidered with gold. When completed this was shown in the local paper and exhibited in the City Hall.

Above all, the workbooks reflect the popularity of canvaswork at home. Orders could range from design and preparation, through to stretching, mounting of finished pieces, and repairs. Following the lead from the Queen and the rest of the royal family, the trend was for chair seat covers on canvas whether in gros point, petit point or a combination of both. Sets of chairs were very popular, which the paint room could prepare and if working it got too much the stitcher could send it all back for the RSN to complete.

There were also the first commissions for advertising, such as the perfumery company Dubarry who wanted a design worked for a talcum powder holder.

Staff and Workers in the 1930s

In the 1930s the workers were not well paid, plus there was no national health service. The subscriptions from the Associates went towards providing a holiday period, stocking the medicine cupboard, sick pay for one member of staff and hospital expenses for two others. The Associates also gave treats by issuing provisions for a Christmas meal.

For some, the RSN had provided lifelong occupation, but it was not set up to provide for workers beyond their service. One of the outcomes of this was that people continued working. There was no state pension scheme so if they had no family, they had to keep providing for themselves, and given that wages had often been low, they probably did not have much in the way of savings. The oldest retired at 82, and this led to other issues, as the older staff worked more slowly than was accounted for when the work had been costed. In the first instance it was decided that these people, initially including Miss Whichelo, would only work on the things they were best at, taking away administrative duties, but it was this problem which led to the RSN trying to fund pensions for them. In 1937, when the coronation took place, Lady Smith-Dorrien asked to stage an exhibition of the coronation robes in aid of the pension fund of the RSN workers. In the past only those with extreme long service had been offered something.

(left) **Miss Evans working on the 1935 Lord Chancellor's Purse, which was based on the one created by the RSN in 1929**

(above) **Lord Hailsham and members of the RSN, including Mrs Field (far left) and Miss Bartlett (far right), with three of the Lord Chancellor's Purses**

[RSN Archive]

Miss Wise working on the coronation chair for Queen Elizabeth, which features the Bowes-Lyon crest, 1937

[LNA © TopFoto]

The Lord Chancellor's Purse

It is not known exactly when the RSN worked its first Lord Chancellor's Purse but the first recorded in the press is that for 1929; since then, the RSN has made new ones in 1935, 1937, 1948 and the current one in 1984.[14] Historically the purses were made for each Lord Chancellor to hold the Great Seal and became their property when they stood down. During the 20th century the role and ownership changed. For example, it is now used for carrying the King's Speech at the State Opening of Parliament, and retiring Lord Chancellors are no longer allowed to keep theirs. The current one came back to the RSN for repairs in 2010 and is still in use.

Coronation of George VI and Queen Elizabeth

Work on the 1937 coronation took place in stages. What had been needed for Edward changed on 11 December 1936 with the Abdication. When it was clear that the Duke of York would become King, the magnitude of work increased significantly for the RSN. In 2011 the great-nephew of Miss Essam brought in a list of the major items that the RSN made for the 1937 coronation along with details of some of the accompanying media activity, including radio broadcasts to the Empire.

The first order in the workbook was for the embroidery of seven chairs; these were the Chairs of Recognition for the King and Queen (in which they sit before they are crowned), the thrones (for after they are crowned) and the chairs for the Duke of Kent, Duke of Gloucester and HRH Prince Arthur of Connaught. There is a pencil note on the bottom of the order which shows the speed of working. It says, 'The 3 in four weeks. Re Lady Smith-Dorrien, the 4 to follow in three weeks.'

The organisers considered the Robe of Estate used by Edward VII and George V was looking worn, so the RSN instead repaired the robe of George IV, which was in better condition and needed little work. The RSN then made the trains for the two Princesses who were to be included in the day. The largest piece was the Robe of Her Majesty Queen Elizabeth. Lady Smith-Dorrien worked on designs for both the Robe and the Dress but in the end Madame Handley-Seymour made the dress with RSN working the embroidery, and both took the theme of the emblems of the Empire including as well as the rose, thistle, shamrock and daffodil, the lotus of India, the protea of South Africa, the maple leaf of Canada, the wattle of Australia and the fern of New Zealand.

In all, 35 women from the RSN worked on the coronation regalia, some of whom had been working for the RSN for more than 50 years. Work on the new canopy required separately worked eagles which would later be applied onto the cloth of gold material, reputedly costing £14 a yard. Once the Queen had agreed the design for the Robe work could begin in earnest.

By March the press was printing teaser photographs of many aspects of the work: the coronation robe, the thrones – each with their respective coats of arms – and the chairs, although they had only been allowed in on one day. In addition to all the above, the RSN made model copies which would be used around the Empire, after being checked by Queen Mary and Queen Elizabeth.

(left) **Miss Girdlestone working on the canopy for the coronation in 1937. She also worked on the canopy for the coronation in 1902.**
[Central Press Photos/Getty]

(right) **Preparing the cope which was to be worn by George VI. It had previously been worn by George V and George IV.**
[© TopFoto EU047735]

(below) **Working on the coronation Robe of Estate for Queen Elizabeth in 1937**
[The Times/News Licensing]

During all this work Lady Smith-Dorrien negotiated holding an exhibition of the coronation robes and some of the peeresses' gowns at the RSN for two weeks after the ceremony. It was pre-advertised extensively in the newspapers as early as February, even though it would not start until 17 May. It was to be open seven days a week and until 8 pm during the week so that working Londoners would have an opportunity to see it. The presentation of the robes was under the supervision of Mr E.H. Symonds of Reville Ltd, and the company marketed butterflies made from the purple and red coronation velvet by wounded ex-servicemen for 5s and 2s, respectively.

It was on Tuesdays, when the entry price was higher, that special visitors came. First among them were Queen Ena of Spain and Princess Helena Victoria who paid a surprise visit the day after the exhibition opened and 'found it hard to tear themselves away from the main item there – the robes of the King and Queen'.[15] On the first Sunday Queen Mary arrived for a private visit with her daughter Princess Mary and son-in-law Viscount Lascelles, Princess Helena Victoria and Princess Marie Louise. On the following Tuesday the Duke and Duchess of Kent visited, mingling with a large crowd. Then the Queen herself paid an informal visit, also mingling with the general public.

The exhibition caught the attention of the public and visitors came from all over, singly or in groups. All the workers of Messrs F.C. Martin of Tewkesbury had a works outing to come and see London, including the coronation robes, returning home at 2 am after a 20-hour trip. A few days later, 800 ladies of the Bilson Unionists came to London by train and were met at Paddington by coaches which took them to Westminster Abbey, Hampton Court Palace, the coronation exhibition at the RSN and finished with the Royal Tournament at Olympia before returning home.

(left) **The royal family on coronation day in the Throne Room at Buckingham Palace. The RSN made the robes for the Queen and the Princesses, while the King reused that of previous monarchs.**

[RSN Archive. SZ Photo – Scherl]

(right) **Coronation souvenirs made from the velvets used by Reville's for the robes of some of the principal figures. The company helped the RSN stage the coronation exhibition.**

[RSN Collection. Photograph: John Chase]

The exhibition was an immense success, 50,000 people visited in the first two weeks, so it was kept open, ultimately for six weeks attracting 141,000 people. It then went to Edinburgh where a further 100,000 people saw it. The money raised from the London exhibition was to fund the pension scheme of the workers of the RSN. At the end of the exhibition Lady Smith-Dorrien had £11,000 for the workers' pensions. However, while the money was undoubtedly needed for pensions, it was needed for funding the RSN as a whole, too. The auditors allowed Council to take payments for slow workers to cover 1936, 1937 and 1938, as if part payment of a pension, while the rest was invested for future pension payments, although Council did insist that both capital and dividends could be taken as needed. It was named the Coronation Fund.

Following the coronation, it was back to everything else, though it was noted that 'the exquisite handwork on the Coronation Robes seems to have given a fillip to appreciation of fine needlework. That at any rate was my impression when I visited the RSN branch at Brook Street to look at the latest designs in lingerie.'[16] Meanwhile Lady Smith-Dorrien was kept busy giving talks around the country, showing images of the work of the RSN and recent commissions.

(top) **A display from the coronation exhibition at the RSN**

[Halogene images, RSN Collection]

(left) **London Underground poster for the *Exhibition of Coronation Robes* at the RSN**

[© TfL from the London Transport Museum collection]

(above) **Exhibition catalogue for the coronation exhibition – the dates of which were extended into July**

[RSN Collection. Photograph: John Chase]

(left) **Certificate of exhibition for the RSN from the 1938 Empire Exhibition in Glasgow**

[RSN Archive. Photograph: John Chase]

(right) **The RSN stand at the Empire Exhibition, Glasgow**

[RSN Collection]

The publicity over the coronation robes was also a good opportunity to promote the wider work of the RSN and the idea that women could make a profession of needlework, through the Training School diploma. On the back of this publicity, there was of course a Winter Sale, again at the home of Sir Philip Sassoon where the Queen, Queen Mary and Queen Ena of Spain visited in advance of the public attending, and the Duchess of Kent agreed to be the royal saleswoman for the first time.

By 1938 the RSN had returned to some semblance of normality with three areas of work: lingerie and interiors, military work of standards and guidons, and ecclesiastical work of altar frontals and banners, as well as the Training School and evening classes. There were also two exhibitions of which the main one was the Empire Exhibition in Glasgow where the RSN took a stand at the centre of the commercial section of the Women's Pavilion to exhibit some of the coronation regalia and household items including a replica set of the quilt and accessories that the Queen and Queen Mary had given to Prince Paul and Princess Frederika of Greece on their wedding in 1936, made by the RSN.

Second World War

In preparation for the war, the RSN made arrangements for a shelter nearby and installed fire extinguishers in the building while an early casualty was the loss of the school's Drawing and Design Master, who was called up for camouflage work for the Royal Air Force in May 1939.

Before the start of the war the Executive Committee had said that strict economy was essential. Lady Smith-Dorrien took swift action. All the younger workers were dismissed (as there would be plenty of war work). The Training School and evening classes were temporarily closed while awaiting inspection to see if the classes could continue. Blackout arrangements had been made and Lady Smith-Dorrien proposed moving all the remaining workers/departments into one room. The remaining staff all had at least 18 years of service.

Subsequently, it was announced that the Training School and the evening classes had reopened in November 1939 with 20 day pupils and 37 evening students. However, by 1940 only three students remained in the Training School and the two evening classes were being held on Saturdays, due to the air raids.

In 1939 Miss Whichelo retired after 60 years and Miss Isabel Rogers after 54 years. However, the state of the pension finances was such that the Chairman asked that all those in receipt of funds be written to asking if they had other means, so that the RSN could reduce payments to others to make some money available for the two new retirees.

The Davis Street shop was closed. Lord Ebbisham, Chairman of the Executive Committee managed to secure a reduction on the rent for the period of the war, providing the rent was paid promptly. The following year, however, the lease on the Brook Street property finished so it was agreed to move everything to Davis Street.

In 1940 the RSN sent out an appeal for funds to Friends and Supporters. Some 70 orders were received in response. Mr T.J. Hunter, Managing Director of William Briggs contacted suppliers on behalf of the school and raised £934.

Pensions were reviewed and modified, all being reduced to make capacity for the new retirees. However, not much later Miss Whichelo complained that she could not live on her pension; the Executive Committee was told that it had been supplemented temporarily by 5 shillings a week from the Associates' fund. It was agreed that Miss Whichelo's money should be increased to £2 per week in the light of her 60 years of service. However, the raise did not last long. At the very next meeting all the allowances were reviewed again and all but one reduced. Alongside this was need for further retrenchment. However, Queen Mary visited in December 1940 just before Christmas and on being told that there had had to be a reduction in the pensions agreed to make up the difference for one year. It was later reported that cheques had been received from both Queen Mary and Her Majesty Queen Elizabeth. There was, fortunately, some respite on the fund when Miss Ffennell (Secretary for 54 years) died in 1941 having received one of the larger amounts from the fund.

At the end of 1940 Davis Street was bombed twice and burgled, and was in a very bad state. All remaining stock had been returned to the main building (although it is not clear what state it was in) and the Davis Street shop was closed. Work in hand was announced at each meeting, dropping as low as £370. This necessitated a further reduction of nine staff to save nearly £200 per annum and the Misses Jones (joint heads of the churchwork department) were asked to forego a salary and instead take the project money less an agreed percentage. The lingerie department was finally closed in 1942 as it was impossible to make it pay.

Needlework in War-time

With the experience of the First World War still comparatively recent, it was assumed there would be shortages. Briggs, publishers of the two leading magazines *Needlewoman* and *Needlecraft* merged them, titles and all, but reduced the size of the publication. The first edition of the new title carried an introduction from Lady Smith-Dorrien and featured six of the regimental insignia that the RSN and Briggs had worked on with the War Office.[17] These kits were being made for male or female stitchers to work either on the front line or at home where it was a way for people to choose the insignia of their loved ones' regiments. That first edition explained how the badges might be used, for example to decorate a *Radio Times* cover. Briggs produced a transfer of the insignia in two sizes. The RSN had worked a sample which was shown on the cover, and then provided the instructions. These kits were later used to be sent to prisoners of war. The RSN was encouraged to raise funds

Launch of the regimental badges, worked by the RSN in conjunction with Wm Briggs and the War Office. Appeared in the first edition of *Needlewoman and Needlecraft* magazine.

[RSN Archive. Photograph: John Chase]

CRESTS OF H.M. SERVICES

DESIGNED BY THE ROYAL SCHOOL OF NEEDLEWORK AND APPROVED BY H.M. WAR OFFICE

ROYAL NAVY

THE ROYAL AIR FORCE

THE CRESTS ILLUSTRATED HAVE ALL BEEN WORKED ON A FINE BUT HEAVY QUALITY CREAM LINEN IN CLARK'S "ANCHOR" STRANDED COTTON WITH MILWARD'S "GOLD SEAL" CREWEL NEEDLE NO. 8. IN ADDITION TO THOSE ON THE FREE TRANSFER A LIST OF CRESTS AVAILABLE IS GIVEN ON PAGE 28 TOGETHER WITH ADDRESSES FROM WHERE THEY CAN BE OBTAINED.

THE SEAFORTH HIGHLANDERS

COLDSTREAM GUARDS

ALL WHO ARE INTERESTED IN THE SERVICES WILL DERIVE MUCH PLEASURE FROM EMBROIDERING THESE CRESTS. THEY MAKE LOVELY LITTLE WALL PLAQUES WHEN FRAMED AND CAN ALSO BE USED AS MOTIFS ON "RADIO TIMES" COVERS, BLOTTERS, ETC., AS ILLUSTRATED ON PAGE 13.

THE ROYAL NORTHUMBERLAND FUSILIERS

ROYAL ENGINEERS

Page Fourteen

Page Fifteen

for more to be sent out as the kit with all materials cost 7/- each to be dispatched through the International Red Cross. In 1948 the Red Cross Welfare section said that they wanted to raise the standard of work of their patients in the BAOR Hospitals: 'In future all designs and colourings for these patients were to be supplied by Messrs Briggs from the Royal School of Needlework. Workers of higher standards could, on application by the matron, be supplied with designs and materials direct from the RSN.'

By the end of the war the RSN and Briggs had produced embroidery kits for all the allied regiments. The RSN has several of the transfers and instructions but no actual examples of worked badges in its Collection.

Lady Smith-Dorrien believed that a positive approach to facing hardships and restrictions would also be needed, so the RSN launched a series of booklets called *Needlework in War-time*. Each booklet cost three shillings but it was more of a correspondence course. At the launch tea party in June 1941, they invited the editors of women's magazines and the Directors of Education of the Women's Auxiliary Service, the Federation of Women's Institutes and the Red Cross, and it was agreed that headmistresses of all schools should be sent a copy of the first booklet to interest them in the scheme with a specimen lesson.

By the following meeting it was reported that the Board of Trade had requested two additional lessons: Remodelling and Dressmaking. By February 1942 there were 930 subscribers.

(below) **Lady Smith-Dorrien developed** *Needlework in War-time* **as a correspondence course to encourage the making and remodelling of clothes at home.**

[RSN Archive. Photograph: John Chase]

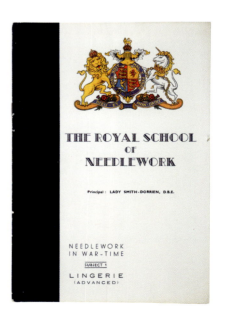

(opposite) **Briggs transfers for the first seven badges**

[RSN Archive. Photograph: John Chase]

(left) **One volume actively promoted the therapeutic aspect of stitching.**

[RSN Archive. Photograph: John Chase]

(right) **Most of *Needlework in War-time* was printed in black and white but occasionally there was a splash of colour.**

[RSN Archive. Photograph: John Chase]

In the preface to the first volume, Lady Smith-Dorrien puts forward one of her main beliefs, that knitting, though necessary, became mechanical. She continued, 'we need some occupation that temporarily absorbs our minds entirely and this we find in needlework of all kinds. I have the entire medical profession with me, I believe, when I say that working out an intricate design is the best possible remedy for over-strained nerves – for it is literally fascinating and all worries are forgotten for the time being.'[18] This theme was one she elaborated on in a press release that went out across all allied countries. Press cuttings in the RSN Archive show it being picked up by newspapers in New Zealand, Australia, South Africa, Southern Rhodesia[19] but above all in Canada where it was featured in papers from Newfoundland to Vancouver[20] under the heading 'Sick Soldiers Embroider their way back to health'.

Needlework in War-time comprised 11 volumes, although in a typical RSN twist, volume 1 was Lingerie which came in two levels: an elementary version and an advanced version.[21] Lady Smith-Dorrien said that the purpose of these booklets was to create a band of members who were able to make their own underwear and to transform and reuse materials so that nothing went to waste, and to avoid having to buy new clothes. However, it was an eclectic range of titles and projects.

Volume 1: Elementary Lingerie featured a slip and basic vest and knickers; Advanced Lingerie featured how to make a nightdress and what was described as 'vest and knickers' which today we might describe as camisole and knickers/underskirt.

Volume 2 was Children's Clothes, volume 3 was Embroidery on Canvas, complete with two colour images. Volume 4 was Patchwork and Quilting with the emphasis on quilting not, as might be expected, the

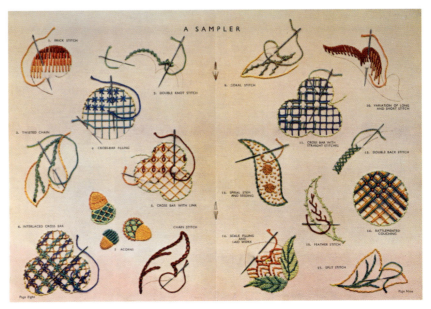

patchworking of pre-used fabrics. Volume 5 was Ecclesiastical Embroidery because many churches had been damaged in the war and church members might wish to occupy themselves by making new pieces. Although Lady Smith-Dorrien noted that a full altar frontal and super frontal might be too much for many to tackle, she encouraged them to start with something smaller such as stoles, burses, chalice veils and alms bags.

Volume 6 was Whitework. The technique could be used for tablecloths, tray covers and for linens for church. This volume has the least by way of pattern and mostly concentrates on stitches. On the back cover is a work by a student of the RSN Training school under the heading Advanced Whitework so this was not for the faint-hearted. Volume 7 was about embroidery other than canvaswork, which focused on crewel embroidery with wool on linen twill and uses a great variety of stitches.

Volume 8 was perhaps the most purposeful. It tackled the teaching of stitching to beginners and returning servicemen who needed stitching for convalescence and possibly for a future income. Lady Smith-Dorrien was aware of what had been done by the RSN and service personnel during and after the First World War and wanted to ensure that it could be offered again. The booklet featured a variety of techniques as she considered men might find some techniques more interesting than others.

The final three booklets really reflected the impact of rationing. Volume 9 was Darning and Patching. Volume 10 was about remodelling an old garment, and Volume 11 was Dressmaking, to make new clothes with the utmost economy.

Lace

Lady Smith-Dorrien had one further idea during the war and that was to collect lace in the hope of selling it, especially to Americans to raise funds

(left) **Lady Smith-Dorrien suggested collecting lace for the war effort, with the best being sold at the Dorchester.**
[RSN Archive]

(right) **Buyers at the RSN Lace Sale at the Dorchester, all proceeds from which went to the war effort**
[RSN Archive]

for the war effort. Initially some striking pieces of lace were given and there was a feature in British *Vogue* showing Lady Louis Mountbatten and Mrs William Rhinelander Stewart wearing two of the pieces, and a sale at the Dorchester. Money from sales went to the British War Relief Society. However, much of the lace that was donated was small pieces removed from garments rather than stand-alone lace veils and other items, so it did not sell. Some of it remains at the RSN today and is occasionally sold off to support RSN projects.

Insignia Badges

In March 1941 the Executive Committee minutes record that HM The King had sent over a naval officer's cap badge with a view to the school reproducing them. By Wednesday 30 April Lady Smith-Dorrien had received an order for 250 of these at 25 shillings each.

The workbooks show that Lady Smith-Dorrien was first contacted about insignia for the new Army Air Corps (AAC) in 1941, a badge was designed, and a prototype was commissioned. However, this was turned down by the War Office who then came up with their own design. In order to get as many men qualified as soon as possible, they were trained in groups and on completion of the course were awarded their wings. We see from the RSN workbooks that at times AAC pilots were ordering their own wings and at other times, especially as those first qualified graduated to become trainers, they would order bulk supplies. The RSN was also providing wings for the Army Observer Corps (AOC). From the workbook entries it would seem as though the RSN always had badges on standby as sometimes enquiries would come in, and there is a note on the file saying how many were sent by return, with the remainder to follow and an idea of when. These were always wanted 'urgently'.

(left) **While the Training School was closed during the war, Miss Randell went into the workroom. The RSN made hundreds of badges during the war, especially for the Army Air Corps (Gliders) and the Army Observer Corps.**

[RSN Archive. Photograph: LNA]

(right) **One of the many pages of AAC and AOC wings orders in 1942**

[RSN Archive. Photograph: Susan Kay-Williams]

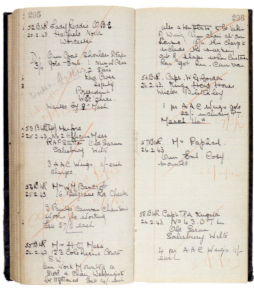

These, however, were not the only badges that were made; there are orders in the workbooks for a range of insignia including Red Cross epaulets.

The Executive Committee started discussing the future of the school after the war in 1943, especially the building and enhancing the educational side of the organisation. One idea was to create a panel of teachers for lectures and demonstrations in needlework around the country, which Lady Smith-Dorrien had drawn up in consultation with Mr Clarke of J. & P. Coats Ltd.

With the war concluded, work in hand rose quickly to £1,500 by the end of 1945, but the overall financial position was somewhat perilous.

RSN Embroidery in the Movies

Marguerite Randell wrote about the inclusion of a panel of embroidery in a film. The Board of Trade picture *Border Weave* featuring the Empire wool industry showed a map of the world with floral border, complete with trade routes. It was embroidered in petit point by the RSN, as was the old-fashioned style of sampler used in *The Gentle Sex* propaganda film of the ATS, showing the lines, 'O Woman in our hours of ease ...'

In the 1940s the RSN was contacted by the designer for one of the Powell and Pressburger films about a piece to go behind the opening credits of a film. As their film company was called The Archers the central tree of the picture had to feature an archery target in the company's colours. The film was *The Life and Death of Colonel Blimp* and the canvas showed the hero on horseback against a background of wartime activity with his family tree and heraldic device included.

Powell and Pressburger returned to the RSN for the film *Black Narcissus* in 1947, this time an actress would be seen stitching, so its

Work in progress on the image seen behind the opening credits of *The Life and Death of Colonel Blimp*

[RSN Archive. Photograph: John Chase]

Deborah Kerr in *Black Narcissus* – the main part of the embroidery was worked by the RSN. This scene is certainly set up for the camera as the piece would not be worked from where Kerr is sitting.

[© Mary Evans/AF Archive]

star Deborah Kerr came to the RSN for stitch lessons. The brief this time was for the RSN to produce three canvases of the same design, one just started, one halfway through and one nearly completed.

Queen Mary's Wartime Stitch Projects

Throughout the war, Queen Mary occupied herself by stitching, and continually sent missives to Lady Smith-Dorrien for additional materials. Despite now being in her 70s she stitched with prodigious speed although, as she aged, she asked for fewer colours and shades, and always wanted her canvas softened because she stitched in the hand. Her major project during the war was a carpet, designed and made up by the RSN. When eventually finished, the carpet went on tour in Canada raising $100,000.[22]

Handwritten note from Queen Mary requesting threads for the carpet panels

[RSN Archive. Photograph: John Chase]

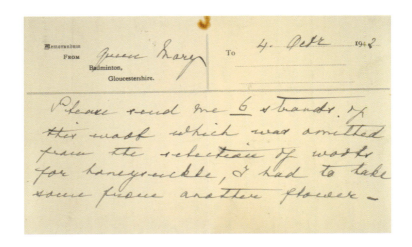

CHAPTER 4

The Move to Prince's Gate

After the war big changes were needed, reorganisation of the workroom departments, assessing what was viable, restarting the classes and as the RSN had already sold its current building to Imperial College, a move was imminent. The remaining lease ran out in 1949. Lady Smith-Dorrien wrote to Imperial College asking to have the lease extended due to the difficulty of finding premises after the war, but the request was turned down.

By autumn 1945 the training programme of the RSN was restarted but shortened so that students could complete it in two years, although it was still recommended that those suitably qualified stayed on for a third year to undertake the finer forms of work.[1] Jean Millwood was a student at the RSN from 1945 to 1947 and recipient of a Broderers' scholarship of 10 guineas. She wrote: 'When I started in September, aged 17 and straight from school, there were not so many of us so we each had a window to work at. But we soon had to close ranks as our numbers increased when girls were demobbed from the Forces and came, either to resume their disrupted studies or to start afresh.'[2] Jean was presented with her certificate by the Queen in 1947 and returned again in 1951 for the send-off to Miss Randell.

The whole landscape of education was changing and this threw up a new issue for RSN diploma holders. Until now, the diploma had been accepted as a teaching qualification, even though the students did not take any classes in teaching. After discussion with the Ministry of Education the Ministry accepted that, for the time being, diploma students would be granted the status of qualified teachers if, as part of the diploma, they passed the City and Guilds Ordinary Certificate in

Plain Needlework (which had always been part of the course) and a City and Guilds Teacher's Certificate in some other needlecraft subject, for example Dressmaking, Millinery, Ladies and Children's Tailoring or Home Upholstery.[3] They also needed two years' satisfactory teaching or 'other suitable experience', and the diploma of the RSN would be accepted as 'other suitable experience'.

With these qualifications, they could teach in primary and secondary schools. However, the letter went on:

> 'As regards establishments for further education (which broadly speaking can be defined as technical, commercial and art colleges and day continuation schools), the Minister lays down no requirements regarding the exact qualifications to be held by a teacher. That is left to the employing authorities.'

More, significant changes would be coming for the Training School in the 1950s but for now it could continue; the Ministry of Education approved the modification, and the RSN increased their fees, which had not been raised for 20 years. Erica Wilson was one of the students in the first postwar cohort; she graduated in 1948 and then went on to teach RSN evening classes and to work in the showroom before emigrating to the United States in the mid-1950s. After the publication of her first book *Crewel Embroidery* the publishers Faber and Faber contacted the Principal about Erica, and a warm invitation was extended to her to come and give a lecture at the RSN and sign copies of her book.

Another event that returned as soon as possible was the annual show and award ceremonies for the Training School. Queen Mary had been a regular visitor to this event and continued to support it until shortly before her death in 1953.

The war had taken its toll and in 1947 Lady Smith-Dorrien asked to stand down from what she described as the business side of her role, while

(left) **Miss Randell in the Training Room**
[RSN Archive. Photograph: William Gray]

(right) **Queen Mary inspecting work at the RSN, with Lady Smith-Dorrien**
[RSN Collection. Unknown photographer/ Keystone]

Queen Mary inspecting students' work at the annual display, with Chairman, Earl Spencer in the background

[The Times/News Licensing]

retaining the role of Principal. The Executive Committee's response was for them all to resign and they decided to ask the Queen what they should do now. The Queen appointed Earl Spencer as Chairman though it would be some months before any of the committees met again. When they did, the key issue was pay levels for workers because with the RSN's low pay they could not attract enough new or returning workers to undertake the jobs they had on the books. Then there was availability of materials. Lady Smith-Dorrien made her first trip to Paris in 1947 to acquire canvas and threads, being careful that the amount she brought back was under the licence level and, finally, the search began for new premises.

Lady Smith-Dorrien was keen to keep the Jones sisters at this time as there were many new orders from all those churches which had been destroyed in the war. It was agreed that they should be offered free accommodation (board and lodging) in the present school building and later in the new building, which was yet to be acquired, and that as a further inducement they both be paid an extra 10 shillings weekly.

New Premises

At the end of the war there were few buildings available that were large enough to accommodate the RSN. Through connections, they were pointed to a house on Prince's Gate, just round the corner. The owner had turned down £30,000 for it and wanted £35,000 but the survey showed that it was in need of so much work that he eventually accepted £27,500. It was very dilapidated but there was nothing else available. Payment terms were one third in cash and two thirds by mortgage, but the RSN had to take out a loan for the cash and they still had to find funds to undertake the required work. The building needed everything to be updated: rewiring, new heating and lighting. Estimates came in at £14,000. Council was horrified and asked that this be brought nearer to £9,000. The lowest tender received was £12,000, and J. & P. Coats donated towards the mortgage with Pearsall's contributing to the removal costs. As a result of the move, however, the RSN no longer had the large showroom space that had been used for sales and exhibitions. From now on, it was not possible to hold the regular sales or exhibitions of any size at the RSN, external premises would have to be used.

In 1948 Princess Helena Victoria died and Council asked both Princess Marie Louise and Princess Alice, Countess of Athlone[4] to become Vice Presidents. The following year the RSN was informed that the King was going to stand down as Patron and that Queen Elizabeth would replace him and join Queen Mary as Patrons. Princess Alice became President. Like Princess Helena before her, she was an active President and served on Council for many years.

In 1949 the Teaching Branch Committee started meeting again after the resumption of evening classes following the move to Prince's Gate. Evening classes were now predominantly for embroidery and were still supported by the London County Council.

Lady Smith-Dorrien partially tendered her resignation again in May 1949 but agreed to work three days a week and leave Miss Bromley, the Vice Principal, to develop her skills and broaden her experience the rest of the time. Council accepted the part-time working as they were trying to fend off the thought of her leaving. She had been a strong Principal who brought a lot of business through her connections before the war. When she finally gave her full resignation in 1950 it triggered an Extraordinary General Meeting while they decided what to do. Lady Smith-Dorrien had been at the RSN for 18 years. She died in 1951.

One of the last things that Lady Smith-Dorrien did was to take out a one-year contract for a showcase on the *Queen Mary* ship. The cost was £200, and it was to be paid for by Lady Smith-Dorrien's Lace Fund and would exhibit articles of lace, along with finished goods to buy such as evening bags and nightdress cases, but also kits which people might purchase to work on the journey from Great Britain to the United States. Although it did not make a profit in the first year, it was kept on, with a similar booth later being taken on the *Queen Elizabeth* until both ships were retired. These were used to promote the RSN and to try to encourage Americans on the ships to come and visit the RSN when they reached London.

Diploma graduates of 1949 included Barbara Dawson who worked for several years at the RSN and later went on to write several books, and Marjorie Wilson whose work has now been donated back to the RSN. In total there were 17 who received the diploma and six received awards of merit. The Queen had consented to present the diplomas. From the following year it was agreed that, in order for students to take their full training at the RSN and obtain Qualified Teacher status the course should be extended to three years. Meanwhile the evening classes restarted as well. It is worth noting that men as well as women, and not just those using it as occupational therapy, were stitching commercially.

To appoint a replacement for Lady Smith-Dorrien there was an open advertisement. Three candidates were interviewed including Dorothea Nield, one of the teachers in the Training School. The post went to Mrs Grace Hamilton-King. Princess Alice welcomed her by saying how pleased she was that Mrs Hamilton-King was prepared to undertake the direction of the complex work of the RSN. Given what was to come, that was a greeting of some understatement.

One of Mrs Hamilton-King's first meetings was with the Ministry of Education. They were seeking a stronger design element to the RSN course. The diploma course had reverted to being a three-year course

Illustration of the RSN's home at Prince's Gate. This image was used to promote the launch of the Friends in 1976.
[RSN Archive. Photograph: John Chase]

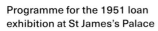

so that students could incorporate more design and aspects of teaching in order for them to gain Qualified Teacher status. Mrs Hamilton-King stated that in future she hoped the RSN would become a centre for training students for the National Diploma in Design. This was discussed by Council and their primary concern was that 'as long as the standard of the RSN and its diploma were maintained they were happy with the addition of the design scheme'. By mid-1951 the Ministry of Education agreed that the course of study in hand embroidery at the RSN was a special subject leading to the examination for the National Diploma in Design and they approved the course for that examination.

One of the ways out of the financial problems of the early 1950s was through expansion, so Miss Fenn and the Misses Jones were given notice to quit their apartments in Prince's Gate. They would each be paid a higher weekly wage to help pay for external accommodation. However, the plans had to be put on hold due to cashflow issues when the bank refused to honour cheques for some of the remedial work on the building. The Chairman notified Queen Mary and the Queen of their predicament. In response, Lord Claud Hamilton, comptroller to Queen Mary responded that the Queen 'has graciously promised herself to guarantee the sum required'. The RSN breathed again.

Loan Exhibition at St James's Palace, 1951

Further support came from the royal family in 1951. An exhibition was first mooted in 1950 as simply an 'autumn exhibition', one of three the RSN was considering during 1951, including a presence at the Festival of Britain. It was the Chairman, Earl Spencer, who said he would investigate whether it would be possible to hold it at St James's Palace, and in the programme it was announced that it was held 'by generous permission of His Majesty the King'.

By February 1951 the RSN did not know if they would be allowed to include coronation robes from 1937 and they were still asking others to lend works so, as the programme had to be printed it was simply called 'Loan Exhibition'. Harrods Ltd had 'undertaken without any liability to the Royal School of Needlework the whole of the planning, erection and decoration of the Exhibition'. Objects were lent by private owners and other museums. Pieces dated from the 16th century to the 20th and covered all styles of embroidery. The majority were worked in Great Britain. The centrepiece was the Throne Room in which the Robes of Estate for the King and Queen and the gowns of the Queen and other members of the royal family were on show. Following this room were the Royal Exhibits in the Picture Gallery, many of which were worked by members of the royal family headed by Queen Mary. The exhibition continued with a series of altar frontals made for Westminster Abbey by the RSN, including Queen Mary's offering to the chapel of Edward the Confessor at the time of her coronation. In total there were some 270 pieces.

Queen Mary officially opened the 1951 exhibition.

[The Times/News Licensing]

Queen Mary had agreed to open the event at noon, and in the evening there was to be a reception which the Queen was going to attend, as were the television cameras. All television was live at that time, and this would be the first time Her Majesty had been seen on television.

The Daily Mail recorded the event:

'Televiewers last night saw the most charming and intimate pictures of the Queen ever screened. They watched her as she visited St James's Palace to see an exhibition in aid of the Royal School of Needlework.

'Long focus views seemed to take watchers almost to the Queen's side, as she moved smiling through the throne room.

'Guests unaccustomed to the cameras bowed and curtsied awkwardly; footmen bobbed or shuffled out of the way, but the Queen moved gracefully through the crowded rooms.

'As the Queen entered the throne room, she gave a gesture of greeting and a smile directly to the camera.

'On TV screens in thousands of homes she stood in the entrance to the throne room wearing a crinoline with diamonds sparkling in her hair and at her throat.'[5]

The exhibition was a great success with 63,000 people attending and the RSN made over £12,000. In addition, afterwards Harrods had put the coronation robes and a small part of the exhibition on display at their department store and paid the RSN 500 guineas and met the cost of an RSN member of staff being on duty throughout the opening hours.

So successful was it that Council 'unanimously agreed that in view of the financial success of the Exhibition the Chairman should ask Her

Majesty Queen Mary graciously to accept repayment [of the loan] so generously given by Her Majesty in October 1950 to assist the Royal School when in financial difficulties.' It was later reported that when Earl Spencer spoke to Queen Mary about the return of the loan, Her Majesty wished to convert the loan into a gift.

Sampler for the Festival of Britain

In the tradition that the school had re-established for samplers, they created one for the Festival of Britain featuring symbols of the two different periods, the original 1851 Great Exhibition and the new era of postwar Britain. Two versions were offered: one in Pearsall's silks[6] and one in wools from Briggs.

Miss Randell, Head of the Training School decided to leave at the end of 1951 after 40 years at the RSN. It was agreed that the party for her would be part of Diploma Day, and for that the Queen had consented to award the diplomas and certificates. So many people were expected that they needed a large venue and this they found at 23 Knightsbridge which could accommodate 300 guests, allowing all the returning students to pay tribute to Miss Randell. She died in 1955.

Appointing Miss Randell's successor was something Mrs Hamilton-King took seriously. There were 14 applicants; after review she interviewed three but only one, she considered, was really up to the post although she was 'worried about the applicant's personality. Her credentials were first class'. Miss Beryl Dean,[7] graduate of the RSN Training School in the 1930s was appointed for the September term with the idea of shadowing Miss Randell.

Miss Dean had been in charge of the Training School only since January but by the committee meeting at the beginning of May 1952 there was great disquiet about standards of teaching. 'Several members of the Committee had recently inspected the work that was being done and considerable dissatisfaction was expressed. After discussion it was decided that a member of the Committee together with the Principal should interview Miss Dean and explain to her the views of the Committee and their decision as to the methods which they wished to be employed.' The meeting was held, the matters discussed, and the resolution was Miss Dean leaving at the end of the summer term. Mrs Dorothea Nield was then made Head of the Training School, working part-time, and a lecturer was brought in for Principles of Teaching.

Mrs Hamilton-King had come in with ideas of expansion but even after the money from the exhibition, by the end of the year there was little capital, and their debt was growing. The bank asked the RSN to stabilise it at £33,000, requiring that £250 be paid off quarterly.

For 1952 entry there were 21 students, all interviewed by Mrs Hamilton-King herself and it was reported that the school had returned to its usual high standards. However, during 1953 new rules were being introduced regarding teacher training. It was also noted that at some schools and colleges the technical excellence of the RSN graduates was not what the schools wanted. It was time to review the training on offer. In 1954 some graduates of the RSN diploma went to St Osyth's – a teacher training college – to take a one-year course after their RSN graduation. The Ministry of Education approved and recommended that all the RSN graduates take the same route. Meanwhile the curriculum was tweaked to offer something

(left) **A worked version of the Festival of Britain sampler which contrasted the world of 1851 with that of 1951**
[RSN Collection. Photograph: John Chase]

(right) **As Patron of the RSN, Queen Elizabeth attended the annual prize-giving and awarded the certificates.**
[RSN Archive. Photograph: Graphic Photo Union]

(below) **Jean Millwood's invitation to the 1951 Diploma Day**
[RSN Archive. Photograph: John Chase]

slightly more contemporary. Several of the individual units had design changes, some by the students. By 1953 the syllabus of the Training School comprised:

Stitches Sampler – line and filling stitches

Stitches Sampler – more contemporary design of above, design changed every year.

Simple appliqué sampler begun after two weeks of training

Simple Appliqué Sampler, method as above but more contemporary design, changed every year

Old English Sampler

Jacobean, reinforcing Old English but using a design from the V&A

Subsequent pieces could all be designed by the students.

Simple (or coarse) white sampler

Direction of stitches sampler (long and short on plants)

Canvas sampler

Blackwork with gold sampler

Silk laid and tapestry shading sampler

Churchwork sampler

Fine white

Own design

In addition, students had to put together small samplers for teaching, notebooks on the stitch techniques, heraldry and the history of the craft, and undertake design.[8]

Coronation of Queen Elizabeth II

In 1952 Mrs Hamilton-King was contacted about the RSN making the coronation Robe of Estate, and chairs for Her Majesty, the Duke of Edinburgh and the Dukes of Gloucester and Kent. Fewer items than previous coronations, as several items would be reused: the altar dorsal made by the RSN in 1911 for the coronation of George V and Queen Mary and the canopy from 1937 made by the RSN for George VI and Queen Elizabeth among them.

Principal of these was the Robe of Estate and the RSN was asked to develop three designs from which the Queen chose. The theme for the coronation was peace and prosperity during her reign and on the selected design this was depicted by an intertwining decoration called Olives and Wheatsheafs (although from time to time the press got this confused and the plants were referred to as laurel and corn ears).[9] Some of the longer

(left) **Miss Essam working the crown for Queen Elizabeth II's Robe of Estate.** *The Sphere*, 21 February 1943

[© Illustrated London News Ltd/ Mary Evans]

(right) **Working the coronation Robe of Estate at the RSN in 1953, with Miss Wise (left), Miss Evans and Miss Bartlett (right), and Miss Rasey (standing)**

[Photograph: PA Images/Alamy]

standing newspapers expected this work to go to the RSN and as usual were full of speculation before the event. 'Whenever there is a royal occasion calling for ceremonial robes the name of the Royal School of Needlework is certain to figure.'[10]

The embroidery could only happen once the cloth had been woven. This took a comparatively long time for Warner's, working with the silk from Lullingstone Castle produced by Lady Zoe Hart Dyke. The press announced that the Queen had chosen the design by mid-November, but it was February before the velvet cloth arrived at the RSN. Mrs Hamilton-King noted to Council that there would not be much profit from the making of the robe because of the overtime, since the material had been so late arriving. Contrary to popular opinion, only 12 women worked on the robe, one of whom was Miss Ruby Essam who worked the crown as part of the royal cypher which appears at the bottom of the robe. This was worked as a slip and applied afterwards, not least because of the time constraints. In total the robe took 3,500 hours.

At the beginning of her reign, the Queen chose to use the Imperial crown with her cypher rather than that which had been used previously by her father. This meant that where regiments and others featured the monarch's crown, they all had to be changed. There are notes scribbled over RSN workbooks at this time saying 'NEW CROWN' as a reminder to everyone.

For security, the RSN had consulted Scotland Yard and they were given a police guard complete with police dog. Photographers and television cameras were allowed in on 12 and 13 February only and advance photographs showed only two or three people working on the train, usually Miss Evans, Miss Bartlett and Miss Wise, and left much to the imagination. Some images also included Miss Rasey, Head of Workroom or Mrs Hamilton-King. It was noted in the *Illustrated London News*, which ran a full-page image of Miss Evans and Miss Bartlett, that Miss Evans had been with the school for 40 years and had worked on the 1937 coronation robe of Queen Elizabeth.[11]

As a thank you to the team who worked on the robe, they received an invitation to go and stand inside the gates of Buckingham Palace to see the Queen on her return from the Abbey. This was a great honour and would have given a much greater vantage point than in the huge crowd that gathered outside the gates of the Palace.

Coronation Exhibition, 1953

As previously, following the coronation there was an exhibition of the regalia, again in aid of the Royal School of Needlework but no longer at its premises. Instead, permission was given by the Queen for it to take place in four rooms at St James's Palace. The catalogue at first glance resembles that of 1951 but this time it was the new Queen who was centre stage with the revised crown motif and a strong EIIR in the centre. The Patron (the Queen Mother), the President (Princess Alice) and the Chairman (Earl Spencer) were all featured, as was the coronation sampler that the RSN created for sale. This was one of many the RSN designed for the coronation, most for third parties such as women's magazines, newspapers and even W.D. & H.O. Wills, the cigarette company.

Many of the items worn by the key participants were included in the exhibition, plus examples of peers' and peeresses' robes. Harrods agreed to set up the exhibition again even though on this occasion there would be no opportunity for it to go to the Harrods department store. News of the coronation and the RSN's part in it spread round the world, starting with the Commonwealth countries, then on through Europe and especially Malta, but was also reported in *The New York Times, The*

(left) **Catalogue for the coronation robes exhibition held at St James's Palace in aid of the RSN**

[RSN Archive. Photograph: John Chase]

(right) **Cover of the exhibition catalogue from the Leeds exhibition, overseen by Mrs Hamilton-King**

[RSN Archive. Photograph: John Chase]

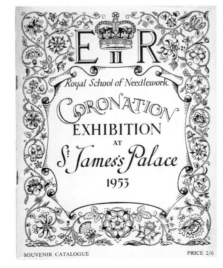

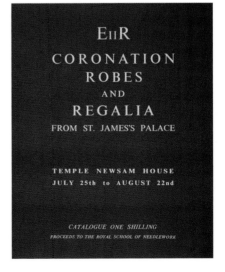

Iraq Times from Baghdad, *Japan News* from Tokyo and even the *North Borneo News* where mention was made of the replica crowns that were being made to be displayed in some Commonwealth countries. Queen Mary had apparently asked that one of them went to the RSN exhibition prior to going to a museum in New Zealand.

At various points the catalogue highlights that pieces were designed and made by the RSN. At the end of the exhibition was a display of work by students from the RSN and the catalogue included information on the Training School course.

The opening day, 10 June, was followed by an evening reception at 10.30 pm[12] which was attended by Her Majesty Queen Elizabeth the Queen Mother and 600 guests, and which welcomed BBC television cameras. It was commented that the royal family was thrilled with the reception of the coronation on television and so were more than willing to invite them to other planned activities such as the opening of the coronation exhibition.

After London, Mrs Hamilton-King had arranged for most of the exhibition to go to Birmingham and Leeds at a fee of £500 each, payable

(left) **The Robe of Estate, showing the entire embroidery designed and worked by the RSN**
[Royal Collection Trust/All Rights Reserved]

(right) **The coronation sampler was made for the exhibitions in Birmingham and Leeds as the robe itself had been loaned elsewhere. The sampler shows the design and the 18 varieties of gold thread used in the work.**
[RSN Collection. Photograph: John Chase]

The RSN made coronation souvenirs from some of the left-over purple velvet. They were edged with gold thread and filled with emery powder for cleaning needles.

[RSN Collection. Photograph: John Chase]

to the RSN, although the Queen's robes were not able to go as they went to the United States. Because of the absence of the robe, the RSN decided to make the sampler, still in the possession of the RSN, which showed visitors the 18 varieties of gold thread which had been used in the work and a section of the pattern on the purple silk velvet.

The souvenir for the coronation, which was also available on the *Queen Mary* ship as well as at the exhibition, was a small emery needle-cleaner cushion made from the coronation silk velvet, edged with gold cord and packaged in a special box confirming its origin and authenticity. It was agreed that this would be sold at 17/6 or $2.50 on the *Queen Mary*.

The exhibition was a success, with 70,000 people visiting it in London before it went to Leeds and Birmingham, but this time the RSN did not specify what the money would be used for because the restricted money of the Coronation Pension Fund had not helped the organisation. Profits were in excess of £10,000 and the school used £5,000 to pay down the loan at the bank, so that it became less than £15,000, and the remainder of the monies raised were put aside for use, while earning interest.

At the AGM in 1954 it was also agreed to place on record the grateful thanks of the committee to His Late Majesty King George VI and to HM The Queen for so graciously allowing the school to hold exhibitions in 1951 and 1953, respectively, at St James's Palace – the outcome of both of which had proved very successful.

After the coronation Mrs Hamilton-King was invited to visit the United States on a lecture trip. She visited New York, Washington, Chicago, Kansas City and New Orleans, in which cities she appeared on television and radio programmes in addition to giving lectures in person to audiences of all kinds. She made many contacts with people interested in taking links further.

The Workroom

In a review just after the war it was noted that 16 members of staff had 20 or more years of service, headed by Miss Winifrede Jones who started at the RSN in 1901. The list included Miss Randell (1906), Miss Evans (1910), Miss Essam (1916), the Misses Jones sisters (1918) and Miss Rasey (1924).

Until 1954, the churchwork department had been separate from the main workroom. It was run by the Misses Jones who had gained their diplomas in 1918 and had become something of a personal fiefdom, run on less and less business-like methods. Mrs Hamilton-King complained she did not know what was going on in there. Council agreed that small churchwork commissions should go to the main workroom under Miss Rasey and that the principal should have a formal meeting with the sisters.

At the meeting, the principal spelled out that the Misses Jones needed to comply with the rules of the school, especially regarding hours of work, answering of letters and charging of accounts. The Misses Jones replied that they could not work under those conditions and decided to depart. They felt that the work they had in hand would take until September, but Council wanted them out by the end of July. The churchwork department was then incorporated within the main workroom and the churchwork room was made the paint room, but not before being completely cleared, cleaned and painted.

The Patron, Queen Elizabeth The Queen Mother returned again to award the diplomas and certificates in 1955. One of the recipients that year was Joyce Ackroyd. Over the entirety of her course, she scored 149¾ out of 150. It was noted that this was a record. It was not noted for what she lost the quarter mark.

Marlborough House Exhibition, 1956

After the success of the 1951 and 1953 exhibitions, the school was keen to organise another one, despite all the work involved. Her Majesty The Queen had placed Marlborough House at the disposal of the RSN. It was agreed that the Chairman, Earl Spencer should organise it with the help of the Principal. It was to run for six weeks in summer 1956 and pre-publicity had resulted in good advance sales and group bookings. Harrods would again construct the exhibition. There would be a large section devoted to contemporary as well as period works of embroidery, including a display of ecclesiastical vestments and church furnishings, a number of particularly beautiful and interesting specimens of which had been lent by the Dean and Chapter of Westminster Abbey and the Rector of Stonyhurst College as well as a group of royal exhibits.

Mrs Hamilton-King, Principal of the RSN from 1950 to 1966

[RSN Archive. Photograph: Desmond O'Neill]

(right) **The two Misses Jones (right, second on the right) headed the churchwork department but by the early 1950s it had become something of a personal territory.**

[RSN Archive. Photograph: Central Office of Information]

(below) **The Queen Mother examining a whitework cap by Joyce Ackroyd (left). Joyce was probably the highest-scoring student, losing only a quarter of a mark over the three years of her course.**

[Photograph: Fox (Getty)]

It was hoped that a carpet worked by the late Queen Mary would be displayed, and a settee and chairs were lent by the Queen Mother. There was also to be a student exhibition. The Queen Mother agreed to come to an evening party at Marlborough House in association with the exhibition on Tuesday 8 May. HRH Princess Alice agreed to receive the guests and it was hoped television would come too. In total 34,000 visitors attended, of whom nearly 6,000 were part of organised groups. Final profit was lower than previously at £3,035; the principal noted that the costs had increased significantly since 1953, but it had led to an increase in business and the workroom was now completely occupied after a slow period.

Following the Marlborough House exhibition Earl Spencer retired as Chairman, he had worked very hard in supporting three major exhibitions, and the Queen Mother considered who might replace him. It later transpired that the patron offered the role to two others. They had each taken the opportunity to discuss the position of the school with Earl Spencer and subsequently turned it down. The Dowager Countess of Bessborough did not take that route, though may well have regretted it by the end of her appointment. The least problematic thing was an overhaul and updating of the Memorandum and Articles of Association in 1958. To comply with charity legislation, the principal was removed as a share-owning member of Council, instead reporting to it. Also, henceforth the chairman would be appointed by Council and notified to the patron.

At the beginning of her tenure Mrs Hamilton-King had been all for expansion, seeking more space and potentially moving, but by the end of the decade it was a very different picture. During the 1950s education changed. There was a greater focus on art and design. The RSN tried to incorporate some of this in the Training School curriculum and there is some evidence in the finished work from the end of the 1950s. Basic stitches now gave a more '50s brutalist feel to the pieces. In crewelwork the four squares were replaced by a monochrome and polychrome piece. The churchwork piece was changed, removing the gold symbols for a separate technical class, and replacing them with a piece known as 'two saints and a cross' which incorporated work in three techniques, and the laid work piece could be a design of the student's own choosing. But it was not enough.

The Diploma

The RSN was losing money at a prodigious rate. In the workrooms, the older stitchers remained but the school seemed unable to attract and retain younger staff, just as they accomplished some good skills, they left to get married. Any donations that were given were for the Training School aspect of the work. Even the money raised from the exhibitions was quickly swallowed up. In the academic year 1958–59 Mrs Hamilton-King and Council invited the Ministry of Education to advise them on a way forward, although the visit had to be postponed after a serious flooding occurred at Prince's Gate.

The Ministry's recommendations were that the course had to be for three years, so dropping the two-year certificate completely. The Ministry agreed the RSN needed to incorporate the National Diploma in Design, doing this would give the students greater skills and enable them to earn higher salaries as teachers. There should be a full-time head of the Training School – Mrs Nield was only part-time, at a salary level higher than Mrs Hamilton-King herself.

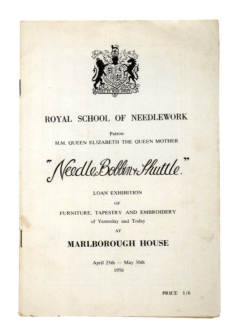

(above) **Catalogue for the 1956 exhibition at Marlborough House**
[RSN Archive. Photograph: John Chase]

(top left) **Basic stitches**
[RSN Collection. Photograph: John Chase]

(top right) **Basic stitches adapted to the design style of the 1950s**
[RSN Collection. Photograph: John Chase]

(centre left) **Basic stitches – crewelwork**
[RSN Collection. Photograph: John Chase]

(centre right) **Basic stitches – crewelwork motifs**
[RSN Collection. Photograph: John Chase]

(bottom left) **Basic stitches in crewelwork motifs – 1950s version**
[RSN Collection. Photograph: John Chase]

(bottom right) **Blackwork and goldwork by Dorothy Abnett**
[RSN Collection. Photograph: John Chase]

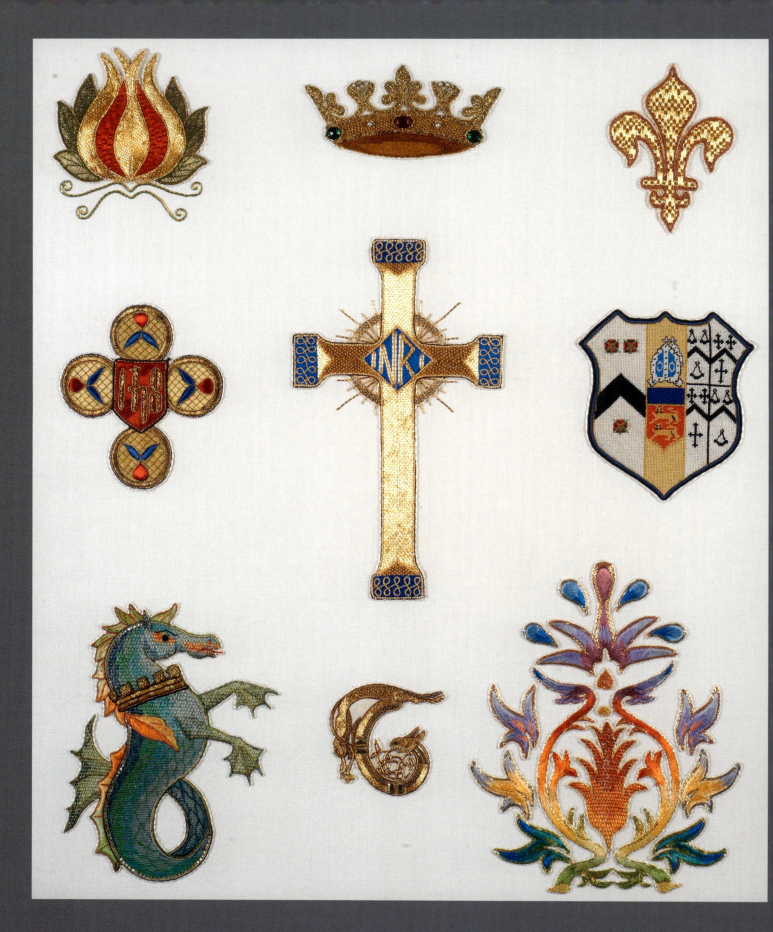

(opposite) **Goldwork and churchwork by Margaret Bartlett**

[RSN Collection. Photograph: John Chase]

(right) **Basic appliqué by Margaret Bartlett**

[RSN Collection. Photograph: John Chase]

The cost of all these amendments was going to be something of the order of £12,000, but the sources of income would only be the three-year students. Mrs Hamilton-King approached the Ministry for more financial help, but they would only pay a portion of the £12,000 required. There was some willingness to change at the RSN, the school took steps in developing the art and design curriculum, appointing a new Design Mistress, Constance Howard,[13] and they approached the Royal College of Art (RCA) about enabling RSN students to receive some training there. Initial discussions were encouraging but at the beginning of 1961 the Council of the RCA turned down future collaboration. Furthermore, the Ministry of Education was unable to offer further assistance, especially as they had not seen the magnitude of change they wanted.

This forced the hand of Council. The future for students was brutal. On 3 March 1961 the Chairman, the Dowager Countess of Bessborough and Mrs Hamilton-King held a meeting with the parents of current students. The Countess set out the issue that they had wanted to enhance the course but the report by the National Advisory Council on Art

Education of October 1960 wanted more than the RSN could offer, and then came the body blow.

Parents and students were informed that the Training School would close at the end of the summer term. It was suggested that current second and first years might look to go to Hammersmith where Beryl Dean was now teaching, or Goldsmiths where Constance Howard remained. The alternative was for students to go to St Osyth's to both study embroidery and take the teacher training certificate. Parents and students were up in arms, they were well aware that the technical teaching at these other places was not what it was at the RSN, and for those who did not want to teach at the end, it seemed particularly hard.

A press statement was put out on 21 March 1961 which talked about what had happened, contextualised it in the scope of the recent education report and also talked about the rest of the RSN although the best it could say was that 'the remaining activities of the Royal School will be continued for the time being'. This was picked up by newspapers across the country and interpreted as the closure of the RSN, not just the Training School. The students, led by Major Strange who took evening classes, set up a Save Our School protest group and Earl Spencer wrote a

Whitework by Kathleen Barnard
[RSN Collection. Photograph: John Chase]

(top) **Laid work by Marjorie Wilson**
[RSN Collection. Photograph: John Chase]

(below left) **Reverse appliqué**
[RSN Collection. Photograph: John Chase]

(below right) **Reverse appliqué – 1950s version**
[RSN Collection. Photograph: John Chase]

letter to *The Times*. As a result of this, Council met with Earl Spencer in a very fractious meeting but their position was unchanged, the Training School would close.

The tutors at the Training School headed by Dorothea Nield had been let go with a testimonial, which was presented by HRH Princess Alice at the general awards ceremony on 20 October 1961, and a cash sum. After the lavish events for the presentation of certificates in the early years of the 1950s, the final presentation of certificates in 1961 was a very simple affair just for the students and tutors at the home of Princess Alice at Kensington Palace.

The evening classes did continue for the '61–'62 season. There was capacity for 144 students, and by the start of term, 87 previous attendees and 50 newcomers were registered so only seven places remained unfilled.

This left the workroom. This was both an asset and a problem child as quantities of work ranged enormously and so sometimes it contributed and sometimes it did not. For many it was the heart of the RSN. However, the administration costs of the workroom were far higher than it could bear and in 1961 there were only six full-time embroiderers, one of whom was in her 80s and not up to achieving the required productivity. A lot of the predicament was due to low pay.

Financially the RSN was in a very bad way; money in the bank was down to £1,000 in the deposit account plus an overdraft. It was now proposed that the top three floors of Prince's Gate should be made into flats and sold with the workroom, paint room, saleroom and upholstery departments occupying just the bottom three floors with the workroom doubling as an evening classroom. It was alternatively suggested that they should move to a warehouse, a proposal that one Council member referred to as 'not consonant with the dignity of the RSN'. Some Council members did not want to become property investors, but others thought it was the only way to bring in any sizeable income. However, to transform the space into apartments meant using money they did not have so they had to take out more loans. They also needed to clear the rooms and in doing so found the 19-feet-by-8-feet (580 × 240cm) embroidered version of Burne-Jones' *The Mill* made in 1908, still rolled up after the move from Exhibition Road. Following consultation with the V&A it was offered to Wightwick Manor as a gift by Council in 1959 where it was 'requested that, the gift having been originally embroidered in the school workrooms from the Burne-Jones design, [that] some recognition to this effect should be displayed with the panel'. Other, smaller pieces of the RSN Textile Collection were also disposed of. A gift of more than 110 samplers had been made to the RSN back in the 1930s, some supposedly dating back 200 years. Already they were listed as only 'about 70' and on the basis that some were described as deteriorating they sought to sell them in 1957.

It was an immense retrenchment to the role, purpose and scope of the RSN and took away a huge part of its activities. Mrs Hamilton-King had been interviewing students for the Training School prior to March but was unsure what to say to them. One person, interviewed with her mother in January 1961 persevered, she had wanted to study embroidery since being taken as a child to an exhibition at which the RSN had exhibited. When the stories of the RSN's closure hit the press in April she wrote to Mrs Hamilton-King.

A reply came stating that given the uncertain circumstances she could still come in September but only to the workroom and Mrs Hamilton-King could only guarantee a position until the end of December. Even Mrs Hamilton-King did not know what would happen to the RSN after that and the Queen Mother was asking to be kept informed. Elizabeth Wailes accepted, as she felt she would gain valuable experience even in that short time and she wanted to be an embroideress, rather than a teacher. She joined the RSN on 4 September 1961.

However, things stabilised and in October Mrs Hamilton-King wrote to Elizabeth's mother to say that the workroom was going to be continuing in situ and that she had spoken with Elizabeth who was very happy there and wished to stay. As a result, she was going to give her a raise in December and another in March and she hoped she would be with the RSN for 'many a long day'.

Here she received two types of training – on the job, which she experienced every day and could learn directly from the likes of Miss Essam and Miss Wise. She also took evening classes from the RSN. In addition, as if in the Training School, she took City and Guilds and took the opportunity to learn from both Constance Howard at Goldsmiths and from Beryl Dean at Hammersmith, with the latter building a professional relationship which was to continue for the next 40 years.

At first, she was put to work in the whitework department of the RSN, but this was not her best technique, that was goldwork. Meanwhile the

(above) **Churchwork by Jane Page**
[RSN Collection. Photograph: John Chase]

(below) **Canvaswork by Dora Matthias**
[RSN Collection. Photograph: John Chase]

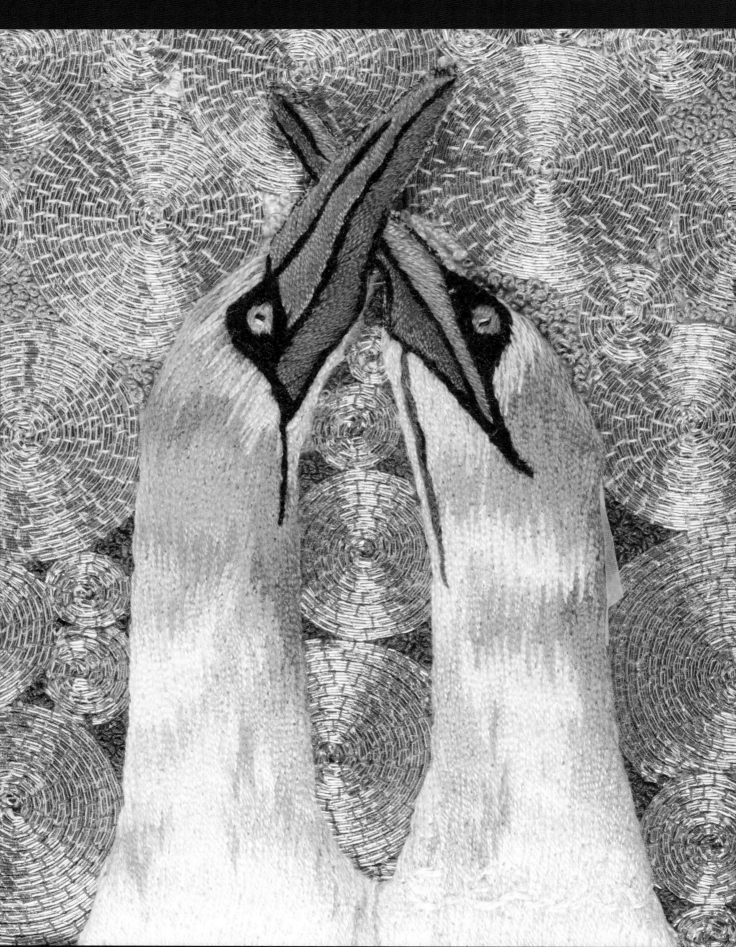

**Goldwork and silk shading
worked by Elizabeth Elvin**
[Photograph: John Chase]

newly Elizabeth Elvin, despite originally saying that she did not want to be a teacher jumped at the chance when asked to lead her first classes in churchwork during the academic year 1964–65. While at the RSN, before she left to have her children, she worked on the Hastings Embroidery and a number of churchwork pieces. Once a mother, she focused on teaching, not returning to the workroom until the later 1980s.

Meanwhile, one Council member held a meeting with representatives of eight of the City Livery Companies to discuss possible ways forward. The livery representatives said they were primarily interested in the training aspects of the RSN as they felt that the workroom was a commercial undertaking and should be run on commercial lines and be self-financing.

During a visit to Toye Kenning, a company that made gold thread and undertook military goldwork, Mrs Hamilton-King first asked about apprenticeships. She was informed that an apprentice was 'given instruction in her craft, sufficient to ensure that she could earn a living wage and be of use in the workroom. An apprenticeship would be 2–5 years depending on what had to be learned from a senior staff member, who would get extra pay for the work and the apprentice would need to be under constant supervision.' It was the City Liveries that wanted to see the launch of an apprenticeship scheme.

The Training School already had a set curriculum. While some changes were made at different times, and mostly in the final decade of the diploma programme, it had recognisable elements that would have been as familiar to Miss Ruby Essam in 1916 as they were to Miss Bartlett in the 1930s, Erica Wilson in the 1940s and 1950s student Marion Scoular.

However, looking through the list of techniques, the ones that do not appear are those which might be considered the techniques of the workroom: both sides alike, military goldwork, conservation and cleaning, tassel making, braids and cords, skills that one would learn on the job rather than through the classes, because teachers would not be teaching them in schools and polytechnics.

The other key element of being in the workroom was speed. In the classroom or at home, working on a project, time was relatively unimportant; in a commercial environment, matching the expected speed was vital if the work was to be done within the allocated time. Even today, the time the Future Tutors spend in the studio is partially to increase their speed of work, as much as to introduce them to the techniques of conservation.

CHAPTER 5

A Change of Approach

Apprenticeship

As part of the discussion on the future, two livery companies accepted the invitation to have seats on Council: the Broderers and the Gold and Silver Wyre Drawers. The Broderers' representative, Wing Commander Page requested that a minute be added at the AGM regarding the establishment of the apprenticeship, requesting a resolution be passed to encourage other livery companies to assist in the development of the programme for the training of young embroideresses and preserving the craft. It was agreed the programme should be for two years and the idea was for the trainees to have 2–3 hours of tuition a day and then to work the rest of the day in the workroom. As there was a former Training School graduate joining the showroom it was agreed she could also lead the part-time teaching of the apprentices. Advertising for the apprenticeship started in early 1962. It was anticipated that intake could be 3–4 girls up to three times a year (January, April and September) as part of the 'Earn as you learn' scheme, although at first the school found it difficult to find willing participants, not because of the initial trainee pay but the pay once they had qualified.

It was hoped City Livery Companies might help towards the training costs which would be around £150 per student. The Broderers gave a donation of £500 to mark their 400th anniversary, to get things started. The Clothworkers' Company came on board with £150, as long as they could support a named student.

The apprenticeship was launched, with some trepidation. It was seen as very different from the Training School and young women enquiring

of the opportunities at the RSN were told in no uncertain terms that the Training School had closed. The programme began with the financial support of the Broderers, Gold and Silver Wyre Drawers, Clothworkers and Drapers as a two-year trial.[1] Initially only one person started, and Miss Margaret Richmond graduated from the two-year course in summer 1963.

However, after the initial trial it reverted in some ways to the type of teaching of the old Training School, but over time added the workroom techniques and some further development of the designs for each

(top left) **Early apprenticeship development of churchwork by Shelley Cox**
[Photograph: John Chase]

(top right) **Jacobean crewelwork by Helen Stevens**
[Photograph: John Chase]

(bottom left) **Early apprenticeship canvas stitches by BCA 1962**
[Photograph: John Chase]

(bottom right) **The apprenticeship was very much focused on practical applications, hence here a canvaswork bag.**
[Photograph: John Chase]

technique. It was also agreed that the minimum age for apprentices would be 16 and it was decided to offer five to six girls places in case any decided to leave, up to an absolute maximum of 10.

The 1963 annual report stated that 219 private lessons had been given in the showroom, reiterating why the showroom needed professional staffing, but it was hoped that in time the apprentices would themselves be able to give these private lessons.

The principal change in the classroom work of the apprenticeship was that the pieces worked became much smaller than those of the Training School and increasingly, over the 47 years of the course, apprentices had more opportunity to introduce their own design ideas. However, it was only after 2007 that they were encouraged to create a signature piece from scratch where the techniques were not stipulated and where the apprentice could choose every aspect of the final piece.[2]

Meanwhile money was still tight. There was another general downturn in the economy at the beginning of the 1960s and the flats converted from the top three floors of Prince's Gate were still on the market in 1964, adding to the financial woes. By 1965 the prices being asked were reduced again, taking them to little more than the amount the RSN owed the bank. At the same time the RSN-occupied rooms seemed to require more and more maintenance, and property matters dominated many Council minutes.

Miss Evans retired at Easter 1962 after 52 loyal years of service. She was 82. Undoubtedly loyal but latterly, work given to Miss Evans always overran the time estimated and as such her work was completed at a loss to the organisation. She had joined the long-service pension scheme in 1931 when it was launched and received a payment when she was 65 but it was agreed that she should receive a cheque for £50 and a framed testimonial signed by the President HRH Princess Alice, Countess of Athlone in tribute to her long years of service.

In May 1963 Miss Rhoda Rasey retired as Head of the workroom. She had been at the RSN since 1924 and as Head of the workroom since 1936. When informed of her pending retirement, Lady Bessborough stated that Miss Rasey had taken up her appointment, carrying out the complex and sometimes arduous duties of this post with a singleness of purpose which could not easily be surpassed. She was presented with a cheque for £500.

She was succeeded by Miss Margaret Bartlett who graduated from the Training School with the mark 'Very Good' in 1938. She entered the workroom in 1939 but left during the war, enrolling in the ATS. She had returned to the RSN in 1946. Although during her tenure there were no major royal projects, such as her predecessor had seen, there were to be some of the largest projects the RSN has ever undertaken. There were also some new innovations when in September 1963 the workroom undertook the first demonstration of simple stitches for children on BBC Television.

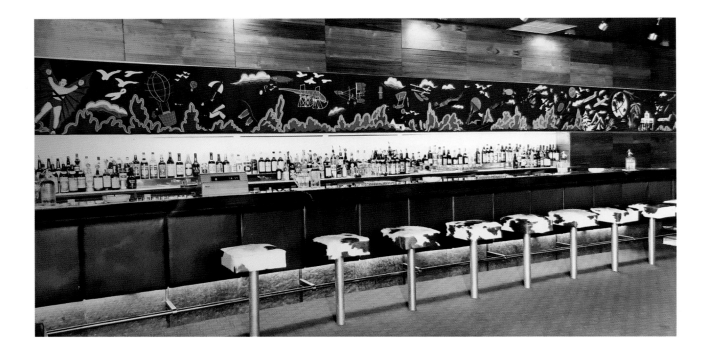

In the 1960s and '70s the RSN undertook many commissions for churches of all denominations in the UK and for churches in America and Canada. Mostly these were one-off frontals but occasionally the whole liturgical set. Recent research during the *Worship and Glory* exhibition in 2013 showed that many of these are still in use today.

The appliqué hanging in the bar of the Manchester airport hotel
[RSN Archive]

Manchester Airport Hotel Commission, 1964–65

The school acquired a particularly interesting commission for a large wall panel to be executed in a contemporary idiom, for the lounge bar of the airport hotel at the recently constructed Manchester airport. It was for Charles Forte's company[3] and the panel was to decorate behind what was referred to as the longest bar in England at the time. The theme was the history of aviation from the bird man to Concorde. This was all depicted in appliqué with a light touch of surface embroidery.

Miss Bartlett and three other members of the workroom staff spent several days at Manchester engaged in the task of mounting the panel. Mrs Hamilton-King attended the opening ceremony, led by the Mayor of Manchester, and reported back that she had received enthusiastic comments on the piece.

The Hastings Embroidery

The idea for the Hastings Embroidery came from Group Captain Ralph Ward who had devised the idea after seeing the Bayeux Tapestry, some time before he was appointed as the organiser of the 900th anniversary celebrations. The V&A recommended that he contact the RSN to realise his project. It was to be worked in a series of 27 panels each 9 feet by 3 feet (270 × 90cm) in appliqué and stitch portraying 81 events, nine per century, in the history of England. The contract was signed 29 June 1965.

The RSN had based the estimate on the Manchester project, in terms of level of detail, and they had stressed to the client that accuracy in historical detail would be less important than colourful and pictorial interest. In other words, that the RSN's work would be an interpretation. The original estimate was £6,500 and it was already known that a minimum of 12 panels should be ready to be shown at the Ideal Home Exhibition in March 1966 with a further two panels being worked on at the four-week exhibition. Council raised concern about whether the RSN had sufficient people to complete the work. Mrs Hamilton-King said she had four qualified workers, past staff who could be called upon and the nine new apprentices to meet the labour requirements.

There was also some concern about the staging of the panels at the Ideal Home Exhibition but in the end the *Daily Mail*, overall sponsor of the show, took over all the details and the support of the RSN team at the show. Twelve panels were on display with a further two being worked on.

However, by December Mrs Hamilton-King had to bring to the attention of the Management sub-committee that additional work had been requested by Group Captain Ward in the form of much more

The Queen Mother visiting the RSN to see the Hastings Embroidery, talking with Elizabeth Elvin (left) and Miss Bartlett

[RSN Archive. Photograph: Fox/Getty]

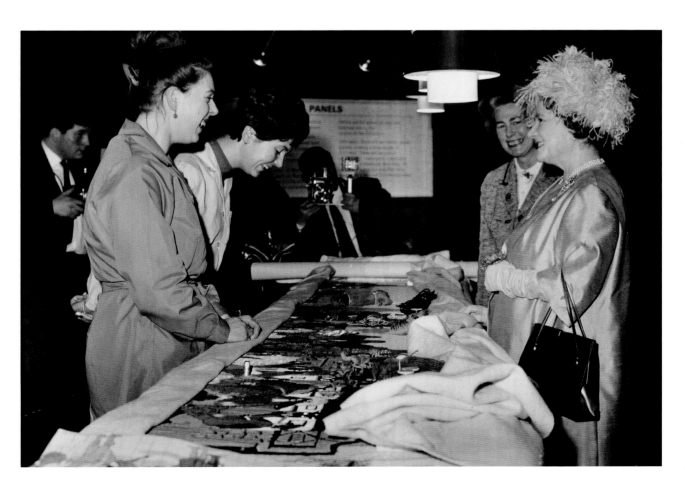

detailed embroidery. He had also added the requirement that each of the 81 labels for the scenes was to be embroidered. Mrs Hamilton-King estimated that the labels alone would cost a further £1,000. It was therefore decided that a letter should be sent to Hastings Borough Council and a delegation should go and meet them to discuss the matter, headed by committee members and the RSN's auditor.

Some papers reported that one of the roles of the panels was as consolation that the burghers of Bayeux would not allow the Bayeux Tapestry to come to Hastings, and the other issue was over the choice of events featured. The guide for the Britain–France reception at St James's Palace which featured projections of both the Hastings Embroidery and the Bayeux Tapestry noted that 'one of Britain's leading historians said that no matter to whom the list of events was submitted, no two historians would agree which were the most important events in British history … the list would always give rise to controversy'.[4]

The total cost for all the panels was now more than double the original estimate. The delegation reported back at the next meeting of the sub-committee to say that Hastings Borough Council had agreed to pay for the labels, to a maximum of £1,000 and would pay for any other additional costs, such being agreed by both sides, if they could do so over a five-year period, the money being raised through exhibiting the panels. This was considered a most generous and satisfactory outcome for the RSN and had been achieved by committee member Sir Gordon Russell[5] as chief negotiator, and by Hastings Borough Council's delight with the panels and their recognition that the embroidery was of outstanding merit and would be an heirloom for the future. The Queen Mother

One of the design panels for the Hastings Embroidery

[RSN Archive. Photograph: Susan Kay-Williams]

visited the RSN while the panels were being made and enjoyed chatting to the team about the work.

The Hastings Embroidery exhibition was opened in August by Princess Alice as part of the 1066 anniversary celebrations, although there were still some panels to be completed. As the centrepiece of the celebrations, the 243-foot-long (74 m) embroidery was widely praised and much visited. When it closed in Hastings, to be sent to the Royal Academy in London, 223,831 people had visited the embroidery and it was described by the local paper as 'one of the greatest attractions of the ninth-centenary celebrations'[6] almost in surprise. It had received international interest with visitors from France, the USA and across Europe, and local residents visited repeatedly. Hastings paid off the outstanding amount within a year. The panels were exhibited again in Hastings in 1975 and most recently in Rye, next door to Hastings, in 2019.

A Change of Principal

In February 1966, minuted under Any Other Business, Mrs Hamilton-King said that she had been approached by Lord Dulverton, in confidence, about a project to commemorate the D-Day landings (Operation Overlord) and that he had approached the RSN 'entirely because of the advance publicity given to the Hastings Panels'.

However, before anything further happened, Mrs Hamilton-King decided to retire, announcing she would step down in June. This time the RSN sought not a principal but a director, perhaps not least because it was not now a job managing a school so much as a mishmash of activities including being a landlord, building manager and overseeing the remaining departments. Mr David Lloyd commenced as Director on 4 July 1966.

Like her predecessors, Mrs Hamilton-King had given so much and had had so many things to contend with that it had almost worn her out. The level of commitment that was expected of the heads of the RSN is perhaps shown best in Mr Lloyd's letter of appointment. It ends: 'You will devote the whole of your time, skill and attention to the school's affairs and will not participate in any occupation which comes into competition with it in any way.'

Modern Embroidery

At Mr Lloyd's first committee meeting in July 1966, Chairman Lady Vaughan-Morgan talked about the forthcoming term of the evening school, which would be under the auspices of the Inner London Education Authority (ILEA) replacing the LCC.[7] She also talked about the possibility of adding an afternoon class (this is referred to as being aimed at young wives who did not work). She also stated that 'certain changes in the teaching syllabus were under consideration, with a view to "broadening" the present curriculum'. However, broadening was not going to be the same as modernising.

David Lloyd had been brought in for his business background rather than stitch knowledge, so he referred to the committee correspondence he had already had with a Miss Arnold about the RSN and modern embroidery. The committee decided that a reply be sent to Miss Arnold, explaining that, 'while it was the intention of the Royal School of Needlework to uphold the traditional styles and types of Embroidery, any new developments in this field would be kept under constant review'. To a similar enquiry from *The Sunday Times* the reply was that the Hastings panels and other work had kept the RSN very busy, but they would turn their minds to modern embroidery as soon as possible.

There would be changes to the apprenticeship curriculum, but for the RSN, technique is always paramount and sometimes that got in the way of seeing how the apprentices could incorporate the modern. Modern had to wait awhile.

While there had been several major projects, finances were still not in good shape, and other income sources had to be considered. In 1967 RSN Patron, Queen Elizabeth The Queen Mother visited to see the embroideries left at the school which had previously been owned by Queen Mary, and made suggestions as to their disposal. Subsequently some pieces were given back (one to the Women's Institute), while other pieces were sold, though unfortunately there are no details of these.

Early in 1968 the tapestries that lined the walls of the RSN, were sold to Vigo Art Galleries for £900. This disposal was summarised by Lady Vaughan-Morgan as 'disposing of pieces of work that served no useful purpose for the school'. One of the RSN's greatest treasures, the 12 Litany of Loreto pieces were once saved from being sold at auction by the quick thinking of Miss Bartlett and the Mini car of Elizabeth Elvin. Miss Bartlett, learning that Council was looking for ways to make money, feared for these pieces and quickly found them, wrapped them up and asked Elizabeth to bring her car round to the entrance where the two of them piled all 12 into the car, and Liz took them home until all danger of them being sent to auction had passed.[8]

The Overlord Embroidery
The Overlord Embroidery project was the brainchild of Lord Dulverton, to commemorate the D-Day landings. The cartoons were designed and drawn by Sandra Lawrence and the RSN was asked to make the panels. At the preliminary stage Mr Lloyd reported that he was in contact with Miss Sandra Lawrence, that she was working in close co-operation with the school, and that she appreciated the necessity of 'tailoring' the design to the special requirements of the embroiderer's craft. When asked about the completion date, Mr Lloyd replied that he thought that Lord Dulverton might have it in mind for the 25th anniversary in June 1969. However, by October 1968 only one sample panel had been made, paid for by Sir Walter Coutts, but this at least allowed the RSN to establish much more realistic costs than had been the case at the start of the

Mr David Lloyd, Principal of the RSN from 1967 to 1980, was a great help to Miss Bartlett when dealing with military men about the Overlord Embroidery.

[RSN Archive]

Hastings panels. In preparing the formal contract they knew to include caveats for increased prices over time or if there were significant changes. The original specification was 22 or 23 embroidery and appliqué panels of 8 feet by 3 feet (240cm × 90cm) giving an overall length of 180 feet (54 metres). The specification noted that the RSN would also endeavour to match colours but could give no guarantees (given the length of the project). With the sample panel and these caveats, Council felt it could go ahead with the project, it would take up to three-and-a-half years to complete the whole thing. Miss Bartlett kept a diary of the project and recorded some of the challenges.[9]

The idea was to use appropriate materials for the uniforms, while all the faces would be worked in silk shading embroidery and all the surface details stitched. By the signing of the contract in November, the commission had already been extended to 30 panels, but the RSN price was per panel. By December, Miss Lawrence (as she is referred to in the book until very near the end) was already bringing in 20 feet (6 metres) of designs.

From the beginning there were complexities. Sandra Lawrence produced the drawings, these had to be approved by Lord Dulverton's committee, then they came to the RSN who interpreted them in stitch, before being approved by Lord Dulverton's committee again. Meetings ensued with Lord Dulverton, and on one occasion with the Chiefs of Staff during 1968, all the time changing the brief.

Work commenced in early 1969 and Lord and Lady Dulverton and their committee visited the RSN in June to see the first two completed panels and, according to Miss Bartlett, were very pleased with the results.

Throughout the diary there are questions about the colours for different service personnel, what materials can be used, and multitudinous details, even down to the trim of an airman's moustache. There were repeated visits from Sandra Lawrence, Lord Dulverton and his committee and the War Office. Plus, the RSN's Patron had a personal interest as two panels would feature King George VI. Mr Lloyd informed Miss Bartlett that the Queen Mother would see the early completed panels during a special event at the Banqueting House in Whitehall on 1 June 1970. Staff from the RSN as well as the other major players were involved in the event. A note in the book states that hats were not required. The RSN party was Lady Reigate (Chairman), Mr Lloyd, Miss Bartlett, Miss Mason, Miss Winter, Miss Thomas, Miss Grimshaw, Miss Willows and Miss Hogg. Miss Bartlett notes about the 1 June visit: 'Great success 7 Panels on view plus 9 painted cartoons at Whitehall Banqueting Hall, HM Queen Mother and HRH Princess Alice present'.[10] A letter was later received from the Queen Mother congratulating everyone on the work. With space now at a premium at Prince's Gate the seven finished panels were taken to the vaults at Coutts Bank for safekeeping.

Wendy Hogg joined the RSN in 1969 on a month's trial at the age of 19, specifically to work on the Overlord. Passing her trial, she went on to work on this extensively. Authenticity was paramount; for example, no lettering on a map, just the contours. To obtain authentic materials, the RSN contacted the different countries and authorities, including writing to San Antonio, Texas for the correct material for Eisenhower's uniform. It was also important that the major players were depicted as they would have been at the time, down to their battle honours. The RSN still has an envelope containing the appropriate ribbons which Lord Montgomery wore at that time. The various colours and stripes were then embroidered onto Monty's uniform, but it was not without its issues; the diary records: 'Colonel Neave Hill will confirm Gold Stripe in Monty's tab and send sketch of Army Flash.'[11]

Monty was not the only one for whom there were problems; the book records: 'Miss Lawrence has not been able to obtain the sequence of medal ribbons for HM The King so we cannot complete panel.'[12]

Meanwhile, behind the scenes a General Brown was phoning regularly with more details and requirements. It is clear that calls were usually taken by Mr Lloyd, but occasionally when he was absent, they had to be taken by others. Mr Lloyd clearly acted as a buffer between Miss Bartlett and the orders of the military. By September 1970 Miss Bartlett noted the first seven panels had been completed and charged, and the next seven were in various stages from 'charged not mounted', awaiting a clarification of instruction, 'Complete not passed' or 'in hand'.

Achieving approval for each panel could take some time. For example, on panel 17 the Scottish piper was not approved and Miss Bartlett writes, '17 Bag pipes to be adjusted tartan too straight. Scottish regiment piper to come in to RSN with Bag pipes.'[13] Mr Lloyd then made new drawings of the piper in motion, but these had to be sent to Miss Lawrence for her approval.

When, in late 1971, Sandra Lawrence said that her contract only ran to the end of December Miss Bartlett said she could not have everything completed by then, compounded by the fact that Sandra Lawrence wanted to take all the drawings away for the War Office to photograph. The Chairman told Mr Lloyd to refuse, as all work would have to stop.

At the end of 1971 Miss Lawrence went to Thailand for two months. This caused major consternation and the date of completion was put back to June 1972. Meanwhile the Imperial War Museum (IWM) wanted to come in and film stitchers at their work. Four RSN workers were featured, with Miss Essam working a face on a separate frame. The film went on to win a silver award at the Berlin International Film Festival in 1975.

By 1972 it was all becoming a bit fractious with talk of alterations, not helped by General Brown referring to the wrong panels. For example, it was agreed that the sailors should have a change of hat colour as they had not had white hats on the day; this necessitated seven changes on four panels.

Making of the Overlord Embroidery.

Then the number of panels began to grow again from the contracted 30 – the committee extended it to 32, then 33 and finally to 34, although the final panel was slotted in as 29A to show the devastation of the city of Caen. This final panel was worked almost exclusively by Wendy Hogg. Throughout, there had been alterations, even after the drawings were supposedly approved by the committee. On the final panel, a squad of soldiers is seen walking down the road. Lord Dulverton said they would not have walked down the middle of the road but rather at the edge of it in case of aircraft and needing to jump into a ditch to take cover. Miss Bartlett solved this by making the road narrower so that the soldiers were nearer to the edges.

The first full showing of all 34 panels was at the Guildhall in London in summer 1975 but there was much debate about what was to happen

to them after that, as the government had turned down funding for the IWM extension. The panels went to Edinburgh in 1976 and then came back to London and were shown at the former Whitbread brewery in Barbican, London in 1977. There was talk of the panels going to the US and Canada. In the end it was the drawings that went to America.

There were many press calls in the lead-up to the Whitbread opening, interviews were given mostly by Miss Bartlett and Wendy Hogg, although by the time of the launch almost everyone had been interviewed about it, including Miss Essam. Finally, launch day arrived – 6 June 1978 – which the Queen Mother was to attend. Alas, she complained about the shadow on the King's face, not an issue of the stitch but rather one of lighting. However, there were still some requests for alterations to the piper.

(top) **Close-up of the piper on the Overlord Embroidery, panel 17**

(above) **Panel 17 featuring the piper, the panel which saw the most changes.**

[The D-Day Story, Portsmouth]

Wendy Hogg and colleague review their work on panel 28 of the Overlord Embroidery.

Its final homing at the D-Day museum in Portsmouth took place on 1 June 1984, the ceremony being performed by the Queen Mother, which Mrs Field, Miss Hogg and Miss Bartlett attended. In 2009 Wendy Hogg made her last visit to the museum to talk about the making to Queen Elizabeth II and The Duke of Edinburgh for the commemorations of D-Day 65 years earlier. The RSN party this time also comprised Brian Levy (Chairman), Dr Susan Kay-Williams (Chief Executive) and Elizabeth Elvin.

Lord Dulverton was very pleased with the response to the piece and passed on some feedback he received: for example, from Mrs Leslie King, 26 July 1975: 'Oh Oh – how moving and splendid the Embroidery is – strange almost illogical that it should have so much more impact than any painting could.'

In the middle of the making of the Overlord, the RSN reached its centenary in 1972. Celebrations were rather muted as they could not find a suitable venue for an exhibition. The head of the V&A turned down the RSN as it was considered the RSN work was too big for a small room and too few for a large room. So instead, they had a party at Merchant Taylors' Hall, and this was considered a great success but was not used as a fundraiser.

ILEA Course Expansion

In the 1970s the RSN worked with the ILEA to move on from just evening classes to a two-year certificate with a specific syllabus that was part stitch, part upholstery and incorporated items that were workroom based, including topics such as making up three-dimensional objects, quilting, box construction, ecclesiastical garments and machine embroidery. Eventually many of these topics would be included in the apprenticeship with the exception of the written component, which was an advanced study of an aspect of embroidery of the student's choosing to demonstrate the development of the student's own ideas.

The concept was that the student would have direct teaching in the first four terms, but over the final two terms the student would follow more self-directed study. This reflects a further and higher education approach to learning but was not fully integrated with the apprenticeship.

Friends of the RSN

Lady Mark Fitzalan-Howard (Chairman in the mid-1970s) introduced the idea of a Friends organisation in 1976. Since the demise of the Associates, there had not been a formal mechanism for supporters of the RSN to get behind it.

For an annual fee, Friends would be entitled to a 10 per cent discount on all purchases and private lessons. The scheme was launched on 1 October 1976 with an Annual category for adults and a reduced fee for under-16s (a discount was offered to those who took out direct debits, allowing the fees to be collected automatically the following year), and a Patron category for a one-off fee of £50. Friends would be invited to events and on the last Friday of each month there would be an expert embroideress in the shop to give advice and help to Friends.

By the end of the year there were 184 Friends, including 21 Patrons.[14] There were special activities for Friends, including free admission to the Jubilee exhibition, and the following year these included an Open Day and a weekend at West Dean College as well as lectures in spring and autumn.

At its height the RSN would have nearly 2,500 Friends in the 1980s; more recently the number has been around the 1,000 mark. Today, Friends are appreciated for being active advocates, with many of them in regular contact with the school.

Silver Jubilee Exhibition

The RSN had not held an exhibition for some time and, in conjunction with the Queen's Silver Jubilee, they approached the Royal College of Art about holding one there. *Threads of History* comprised royal pieces

Invitation to the centenary dinner at Merchant Taylors' Hall

[RSN Archive. Photograph: John Chase]

and more recent work by apprentices, and the workroom and was opened by the patron, Queen Elizabeth The Queen Mother. As souvenirs there were to be special cushions illustrating symbols of London, to be available at the exhibition, Barkers and Debenhams. Altogether the exhibition brought in over £12,000.

Following this, an American museum was interested in showing items from or made by the RSN and said they would pay all costs for two Council members to accompany the items to the Henry Morrison Flagler Museum in Florida and then to St Petersburg, Florida. Lady Mark and Mrs Pettifer made this trip which lasted for six weeks. The RSN still needed income and consideration was given to selling more of the items in the Collection, but it was realised that these were part of the travelling exhibition and therefore were part of the treasures of the RSN and should not be parted with lightly.

Through the 1970s and into the 1980s, there was a resurgence of interest in hand embroidery especially through kits. In 1970 the *Daily Telegraph* published a kit idea produced by the RSN where people could apply for the transfer: 8,000 copies were ultimately requested.[15] This was just one of many designs and promotions for kits made in conjunction with magazines and newspapers over these two decades, including *Good Housekeeping* and *Antique Collector*. In 1980, the RSN produced a wedding sampler that could be personalised for any couple, designed by Sue Skeen, a designer brought in by the RSN in 1978 for the paint room and for design. The wedding sampler achieved sales of £10,000. In the same year, the RSN created a kit worked from a William Morris design at Smeaton Manor, Northallerton, North Yorkshire for an exhibition of

(left) **Worked sample designed by the RSN for the *Daily Telegraph* and offered as a kit**
[Photograph: John Chase]

(right) **The standard created by the RSN for Yale Law School**
[© Yale Law School]

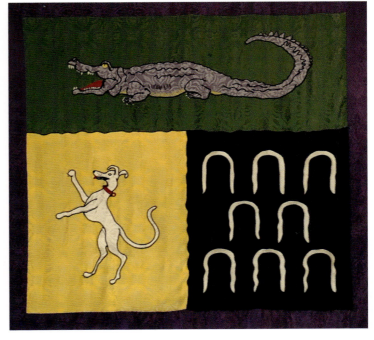

Morris's work at the Fitzwilliam Museum, Cambridge and promoted it in *The Lady*.

Also, in the 1970s Erica Wilson was in touch about the possibility of opening a shop in London in conjunction with the RSN. By this time Erica Wilson's television programme from the US was also available on the BBC, but in the end Council decided they could not do this. They did, however, start attending some of the key annual open-air events such as the Game Fair and Badminton. At their first visit to the Game Fair in 1979 the stand was visited by HRH The Prince of Wales who showed great interest in the exhibits and the work of the school.

As well as new projects the RSN also worked on conservation. This included the Blenheim Tapestries, in sequence from the late 1960s, although for the first one the estimate was given before cleaning and much more work was found after that process which was a cautionary lesson for future tapestries. There were also international commissions including altar cloths and vestments for several churches in the US and Canada and standards for Yale University.

From the 1960s through the 1970s the RSN also worked many sets of regimental colours (often in pairs), regimental flags and guidons. Miss Bartlett commented that these were not always profitable as the Ministry of Defence kept a tight lid on costs, but it was regular work as Miss Bartlett reported at least one set being made at each Council.

The Pineles Panel

Mr Edward Pineles was a private individual who lived in France. In 1977 he ordered a panel with a coat of arms and extensive goldwork surround. He was originally told by Miss Bartlett that it would be ready in 18 months. However, due to a combination of factors (some now lost to time) it was not finished until 1982. The piece, which has since been donated back to the RSN by the Pineles family, bears witness to the perceived slowness of the RSN team, by including a goldwork snail in the bottom corner. Nevertheless, Mr Pineles returned to the RSN for six heraldic cushions to be created in 1989, with a further three commissioned at the end of that year. Mr Pineles died at the end of 1997.

Miss Ruby Essam had retired in 1976 aged 79, when she was given a pension

The Pineles panel, featured in an exhibition at Christie's, was made by the RSN between 1977 and 1982. Although it took a long time, Mr Pineles was very pleased with it and subsequently commissioned six additional but smaller pieces.

[RSN Archive. Photograph: John Chase]

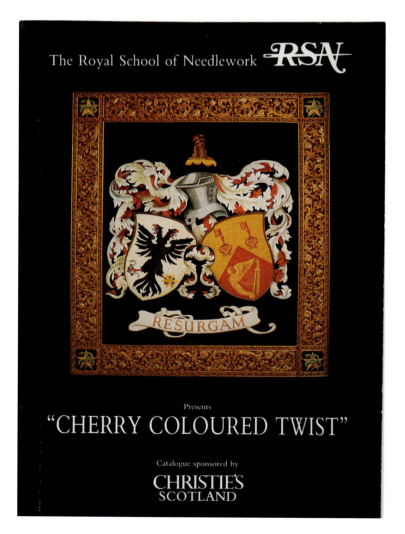

The Royal School of Needlework RSN

RESURGAM

Presents

"CHERRY COLOURED TWIST"

Catalogue sponsored by

CHRISTIE'S
SCOTLAND

of £36 per week. Adding her Training School time to her workroom service, she is the longest-serving person at the RSN: after arriving in 1913, and completing her diploma in 1916, she went straight into the workroom and stayed there for 60 years. When another worker retired aged 69, David Lloyd introduced a rule whereby after attaining their 59th birthday workers were required to apply annually to continue their employment with the school as a way of reducing the staff who could not meet the speed of work requirements and because by now there was the State Pension. Miss Essam's leaving party was an At Home sherry party and had been seen as a special opportunity for the Council to meet the staff in person.

Miss Essam is probably the longest-serving member of staff at the RSN. She arrived in 1913, graduated in 1916 and was employed in the workroom until 1976 – a total of 63 years.

[RSN Archive. Photograph: John Chase]

The President Lady Caroline Somerset
At Home
at The Royal School of Needlework
on 6th July 1976
On the occasion of the retirement of
Miss Ruby Essam

R.S.V.P.
Miss M. Byers
25, Princes Gate
London S.W. 7

6 p.m. - 8 p.m.
Reception

CHAPTER 6

The Most Challenging Decade

This piece was made for the SAS following the Iranian Embassy Siege, after they had planned their attack in the RSN premises.

[RSN Archive. Photograph: John Chase]

The End of an Era

In 1980 Miss Bartlett was awarded the British Empire Medal for services to embroidery and probably for the Overlord Embroidery above all.

Like the 1950s, the 1980s was a turbulent decade for the RSN. Some developments were an endeavour to stretch wings and try new ideas, such as the Small Birds[1] children's programme and the Youth Training Scheme[2] (YTS) on which the RSN started as enthusiastic participants, seeing it as a way to introduce young people to embroidery and then encourage them on to the apprenticeship and the workroom. Some developments were concerned with existing in a changing world. But in 1980 there was a completely unexpected interruption when the Iranian embassy two doors down was besieged. As the layout of the RSN and the Embassy matched, all staff and students were sent home while the special forces used the RSN rooms to plan their raid. Later, the RSN made an embroidery for the SAS.

From the beginning, the apprenticeship had a different focus from the Training School. The original idea had been to train young women to work in the workroom and this dictated aspects of the curriculum. It needed to incorporate the skills required by commercial stitchers, not just those for passing on to others. As well as particular stitches and techniques, this also included speed of stitching, attention to detail, listening to what was actually required and working to a timescale/brief. Anne Butcher began the apprenticeship in 1982 and is now Head of Studio and Teaching. She recalls that from day one, attention to

detail was drummed into the apprentices by tutor Sally Saunders and
that, while it might be possible to take threads out and redo work on a
personal project, that was not the case on a customer's work, it needed
to be right first time.

In 1981 Council started talking about the apprenticeship becoming
a three-year programme by introducing City and Guilds and design
elements. The first assessor, Anthea Godfrey[3] approved of the new
structure of apprentice training and the work she saw. However, there
were space issues at Prince's Gate with rooms frequently occupied by
two classes and apprentices or private lessons squeezed into the staff
room. In 1981 they had held the *Royal Connections* exhibition at
Prince's Gate, featuring the coronation robe of George IV, but this had
reduced space and necessitated the cancelling of classes for some time,
which impacted income.

Prince's Gate had become more and more expensive to run and
increasingly difficult to maintain. Minutes of all the committees were

more focused on the fabric of the building than on forward plans: floors needing relaying, ceilings required nets to retain the parts which were falling off them, and meanwhile income was decreasing. To try to tell a better story outside of the RSN, two of the trustees produced a booklet on the history of the RSN called *RSN Yesterday and Today* featuring a young apprentice on the front cover.

In 1980 Mr Lloyd had retired, but Council had not looked externally for a new Director. Mrs Field, Head of Education was initially paid extra to oversee the workroom and other areas and subsequently named Principal. Later, Council was uncertain of the calibre of the Principal and the Bursar Mr Piggott so in 1984 there was an extraordinary general meeting about whether an Administrator should be appointed as a role to overarch the two senior staff. It seemed undecided if this person was to be head of the school or just of the financial aspects. Eventually an Administrator was appointed to a role which oversaw financial estimates and HR, but they only stayed for a year.

At the same time, Miss Bartlett went part-time and Elizabeth Elvin, herself part-time, and Wendy Hogg were made joint heads of the workroom.

YTS was run as part of the RSN between 1983 and 1989. Over that time, the nature of the programme changed several times, as is often the case with government schemes. The programme was run by Wendy Hogg. The idea was to take fifteen 16–17-year-olds for one year and then select from them five who might go on to the two-year apprenticeship. In the first year 70 applied for the 15 places, all girls.

In July 1983 it was noted that the school had quite a large sum of money in hand against eventualities. However, just a year later there were significant debts: an overdraft of £68,000 in 1984 had risen to £155,000 by early 1987. Council had started to compile lists of the Collection again with a view to items going to Christie's[4] but matters had gone way beyond that. It was time for drastic action and the only asset was Prince's Gate. It had to be sold and the RSN move. From 1979 the minutes referred to the option to move to Hampton Court Palace (HCP), but this was only looked at in earnest from 1984 and it was only intended to be for the workroom. Even so, working with the civil servants[5] who then managed the Palace, it took three years for a room to be agreed and prepared. That was not the only problem, workroom staff also had to be convinced to move which necessitated pay rises and season tickets being provided before they would consent. One of the main reasons for the move was that, initially, it was offered as Grace-and-Favour which means without the need to pay rent.

Then, at the last minute, there was a hiccup when Hampton Court were horrified to learn that the RSN would have customers and visitors and that they had offered flexitime to workers who now had longer

journeys; eventually this was resolved and the workroom finally moved in mid-1987.[6] While inside the room might be of a suitable size, access was challenging and those who participated in the move remember the challenge of getting the long frame poles into the rooms – they had to go in via the windows. Mrs Elvin was asked if she would go full-time; in return she asked to be sole head of the workroom 'without Miss Bartlett's assistance or attendance' and to be compensated for the loss of the higher income of teaching. At this point, at the age of 69, Miss Bartlett chose to retire. Elizabeth Elvin moved to HCP initially for four days a week, eventually increasing to five. The RSN opened its workroom in Hampton Court in 1987 and the following year had its first royal visitor when the Queen Mother visited.

While not many of the workers agreed to go, Mrs Field (who also left when the move out of Prince's Gate occurred) had thought that additional staffing could be achieved by adding to the workers the YTS students who would be taught to make up cushions and repair samplers. She then thought to add the mature students who were willing to pay substantial fees for the one-year course. She thought they might work on restoration and repairs, including ecclesiastical pieces. As Mrs Field saw it the YTS students were paid for by the scheme and the mature ladies would pay for the privilege of being there, so it would be at little cost to the RSN.[7] While this might tick the box for potential cost saving it did not necessarily meet the requirements for quality, consistency and standards, nor the teaching that the one-year-course students might seek. It did not happen.

It was not as if there was no money coming in; Council members were trying hard to generate additional funds. Following the long-standing link with Cunard through the *Queen Mary* and *Queen*

Elizabeth ships, the RSN was invited aboard the *QE2* to hold a small exhibition and to demonstrate, as well as to sell kits and other items. Chairman Lady Mark Fitzalan-Howard and Council Member Mrs Elizabeth Pettifer took on the challenge. On a voyage to Norway Lady Mark and Mrs Pettifer demonstrated and sold kits, and altogether raised £820 and received a positive letter from a Cunard executive who was on the trip. On a voyage in 1982, Mrs Joe Loss (the band leader's wife) asked for an embroidered lion for her husband, and the Chairman worked this for her. Erica Wilson was also in touch again saying that kits were selling well in her shop in New York thanks to the cruise. On the next cruise, Mrs Pettifer and Mrs Luke raised £4,500, $200 and recruited three new Friends. The Bobbin Ball, a formal dance for young people in 1984 raised £6,000. A special exhibition in Tokyo in 1985 realised £10,000 and brought in the first Japanese students.

Council also tried to reach commercial deals to replace the shop at the RSN. The V&A gave permission for the RSN to create several kits based on the Oxburgh Hangings which were to be sold through John Lewis, and the RSN negotiated a sales area at Liberty's in 1987, though they were slightly overwhelmed when the initial estimate for shop fittings was more than £10,000. The Liberty outlet was reasonably successful at first but then profits fell, and it was closed before the end of the decade.

The biggest problem though, was where to locate the rest of the RSN when Prince's Gate was sold. Council members visited many sites but found nothing suitable. Three different estate agents were approached for assistance. In the end they settled on King Street in Covent Garden – a six-floor building, though much smaller than Prince's Gate. It was meant to accommodate the shop, mail order department, paint room, upholstery, classrooms and administration.

With Mrs Field's departure a new Principal was needed but instead, with the organisation now in separate places, they sought a new Director of Education and appointed Jenny Fitzgerald-Bond from the ILEA. Shortly after the move to King Street the shop was closed, it was losing too much money, and a new marketing person, Miss Shone was brought in to lead the mail order and paint room activities.

By 1988 the RSN was in six separate parts:[8] Jenny Fitzgerald-Bond led the classes and courses which were in two locations, while also overseeing the YTS in another location; Wendy Hogg ran the YTS; Miss Shone ran marketing and trading; Elizabeth Elvin ran the workroom. The Friends organisation was run by volunteers and was now located in Kensington High Street. The Collection that remained, after yet more had been sent to Christie's, was temporarily at the Savoy until the RSN was given a six-month notice to clear it.

The Friends was the only part which was making money. There were more than 2,200 Friends, including international supporters, and as it was run by volunteers there was little cost save for rent and the production of the newsletter.

Both sides alike worked by Anne Butcher, apprentice 1982–84

While the sale of Prince's Gate was going through the RSN needed a bridging loan; this and the overdraft were costing £8,000 per month in interest. The shop was closed but losses continued in the mail order department, so this was outsourced on a five-year contract. The YTS had been a drain on the school since the beginning and the hoped-for students progressing into the workroom never materialised (probably due to the low pay), so it was ended in 1989 and Wendy Hogg returned to the workroom.

Jenny Fitzgerald-Bond came in with strong ideas for developing the classes but then had to confront reality. The space that was available at King Street was not big enough to make the classes viable. They had taught on a 1:18 basis, especially for the ILEA classes, so there had to be space in the classroom to accommodate that number of students. Meanwhile Miss Shone had also looked at what she had to work with and the non-viability of it all, plus the fact that the organisation was haemorrhaging money.

Additionally, there was a clash over the purpose of the apprenticeship: was it to train workers for the workroom or teachers, which were now desperately needed?[9] The focus of the apprenticeship curriculum was on commercial skills such as both sides alike and whitework. Meanwhile teachers were being brought in who had not received a full RSN training, such as Jean Panter[10] who, having been taught by both Elizabeth Elvin and Wendy Hogg, went on to teach for the school in the 1980s.

Council, at this time, had been working hard; they held endless meetings, they visited possible locations, undertook meetings with staff and with managers, but still the upheaval led to major uncertainty and King Street was simply too small for the activities that the RSN was undertaking. Meanwhile, although following the sale of Prince's Gate, they had managed to dedicate £100,000 to investments, less than two years later, by 1989, the organisation was almost bankrupt again. The new overdraft was increasing at more than £20,000 a month. Jenny Fitzgerald-Bond estimated figures for the 1989–90 classes but her summary was stark. The projected fee income was unrealistic. The space was too small, and the uncertainty meant that classes in 1988–89 were only at 52 per cent capacity because of late planning, which meant students could not get grants. Even at full capacity the reduced space across two venues was not enough. Mrs Fitzgerald-Bond and Miss Shone concluded that the RSN was almost bankrupt, had no direction and they could not produce the sums required. They both tendered their resignations at the Council meeting on 26 April 1989.

All sources of income were pursued, even selling the painting that Sir Albert Stern had left them, which had hung on the wall at Prince's Gate – it raised £7,000. The Walter Crane designs and drawings were taken to auction and only removed from the sale at the last minute.

On top of everything else, both the workroom and the paint room were losing money, but this was put down to teaching the apprentices, as the workers could not be stitching commercially while teaching. By November 1989 the overdraft stood at £130,000. The only option remaining, less than two years after buying it, was to sell King Street. Perhaps not surprisingly there were also significant resignations from Council and the Finance Committee at this time, including by the chairman.

On Jenny Fitzgerald-Bond's departure it was Mr Piggott (the man behind the scenes who had got on with all the moves and changes) who was asked to take on the overarching role after he pointed out to Council that each part of the RSN was being run separately. He was not, however, given the title of principal or director and what he oversaw was a shrinking vista. The loss of King Street meant the end of courses, except for the apprenticeship. The paint room was downsized and moved to Hampton Court, who had agreed to additional rooms, as did the administration.

By 1989 the RSN was a shadow of its former self. Not since the beginning of the 1960s had there been such a retrenchment. Externally, Council tried to present all this in a positive light, issuing a press release in 1989 entitled 'To meet demand for professional embroiderers Royal School of Needlework to Double Number of Apprentices. Covent Garden premises to be sold to endow pupils'.

The release began in a very upbeat way talking about increasing the number of apprentices, but the corollary was the loss of all classes, because the workroom must continue. The press release gave the idea that the income from the property sale would endow the training places, alas this was not so. The money went to pay the debts.

Work and Events in the 1980s

As has been seen before, the RSN can be a tale of two parallel lines: internal and external. The Chairman's annual reports in 1988 and 1989 make no mention of the impending catastrophe. Instead, they talk of work accomplished, clients pleased and to add to the positive, the people presenting the certificates to graduates these years were celebrities and significant figures: 1985 Elizabeth Emanuel (co-creator of Princess Diana's wedding dress) and the Queen Mother visited the apprenticeship exhibition; 1987 The Lord Mayor of London; 1988 actress Nanette Newman; and in 1989 actress Una Stubbs, both actresses were keen stitchers.

In the 1980s, as well as creating designs in the paint room, Sue Skeen was undertaking a PR role for the RSN, and several articles followed in popular magazines of the time such as *Pins and Needles* in 1984 which interviewed apprentices and Miss Bartlett

(below) **The RSN contributed lace given by Queen Mary to the wedding dress of Lady Diana Spencer.**
[Photograph: Anwar Hussein/Alamy]

(opposite) **The cover of the** *Radio Times* **in the week of the wedding of the Prince of Wales to Lady Diana Spencer, worked by the RSN**
[RSN Archive]

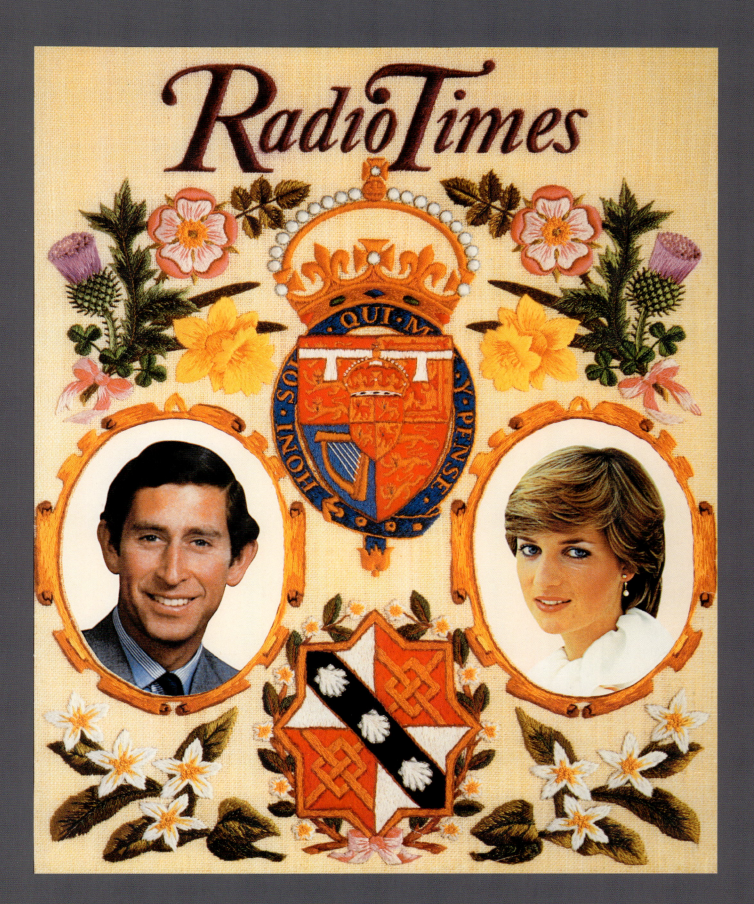

as head of the workroom to try and promote the apprenticeship course. In 1987 Anne Butcher was interviewed as a Living National Treasure by *Country Life* magazine.

Samplers were still popular, with one William Morris-design chair seat cover for the *Daily Telegraph* selling more than 3,300 packs, raising £20,000. The RSN also created designs for Ehrman's including a Longleat rose sampler. A new retail catalogue was produced in 1986 with 140 designs, at a cost £9,000 to print.[11] The RSN could not really afford this, but a positive response was seen. It included the Mouse and Rose design which sold more than £6,000 worth of kits.

Special projects included an appliqué of Worcester CCC's grounds for legendary cricket commentator John Arlott in 1980, and in the same year, after HRH The Prince of Wales saw the RSN at the Game Fair, when a banner was needed for the Prince of Wales's Royal Regiment Cadet Force, he insisted that it should be made by the RSN.

For the 1981 royal wedding the Emanuels asked the RSN for a piece of lace for Lady Diana Spencer's wedding dress. In the RSN Collection was found a piece of lace that had been given by Queen Mary. It is told that once selected a member of the RSN workroom took home the pieces to clean, hung them on her washing line and then made any necessary fine repairs before it was given to the Emanuels.[12]

The RSN created two royal wedding kits: one for the *Daily Telegraph*, a Royal Wedding Sampler, sold 7,000 packs; and 4,000 packs were sold of the *Sunday Telegraph* Wedding Kneeler. The RSN also designed and made a tablecloth for *Woman's Own* to present to Their Royal Highnesses and the RSN designed the wedding issue of the *Radio Times* with an arrangement to sell transfers through the magazine – 2,600 were sold. For its own gifts the RSN embroidered a pair of slippers for the Prince of Wales and a cushion for Lady Diana Spencer.

Other significant commissions in the 1980s included the logo for the Pope's visit in 1982, and work on the Pugin bed from the Speaker's House at Westminster. The V&A restored the bed and asked the RSN to make the hangings. For a commercial company in Sutton, south London, the RSN made a large appliqué and embroidered hanging of a rural scene.

At the end of the decade two big projects were highlighted by the Chairman in her annual report: the Townswomen's Guild panel, which was unveiled by Prime Minister Margaret Thatcher[13] and the Children's Society panel, unveiled by Queen Elizabeth The Queen Mother as Patron of both organisations.[14] To mark the Children's Society's centenary, the RSN also created hundreds of kneeler kits for the Church of England.

CHAPTER 7

At Hampton Court

Elizabeth Elvin had been one of the few staff who wanted to move to Hampton Court Palace (while still leading the fight for more pay and season tickets) and began as part-time Head of Workroom. In 1990, at the first Council meeting held at Hampton Court Palace, given that virtually all that remained of the RSN was the workroom, paint room and the apprenticeship, Council asked Mrs Elvin to work full-time, and made her Principal.

The Apprenticeship at Hampton Court Palace

Immediately following the move, the apprenticeship reverted to being a two-year programme before returning to being a three-year programme from the early 1990s (the first two years being spent in the classroom and the third being based in the workroom).

There were several reasons for these changes, finance always being the major one. The RSN never had any government funding towards the programme so had to raise all the funds itself, including for a small stipend for the apprentices. Throughout, the major supporters were livery companies. Secondly, as the work being requested of the studio changed, it was necessary to have a better trained workforce.

There were many curriculum developments from the old Training School programme, and these happened over time. For example, in the 1980s apprentices were required to write essays, but this requirement had been removed by the 1990s, and in the end, the most that apprentices were asked to write was their technical file, which would become their life-long *aide-mémoire*. Some things reverted to

the Training School's pre-1961 briefs, at least initially, while other long-standing techniques were updated or given a twist. Jacobean crewelwork began where the Training School had finished but took the monochrome aspect and expanded it. By the 1980s the brief was based on the tree of life and apprentices were encouraged to create their own design, and one that was twice as big as those worked by the end of the apprenticeship programme.

Silk shading was changed to appear at three levels, likewise goldwork. Canvas stitches were to show the range of texture that could be achieved on canvas, and it became pictorial, so using the stitches and textures effectively rather than just as a sampler as had been the case in the Training School diploma. The early apprentices were still required to work a piece of petit point to show that even by using just one stitch, they could work a design competently and with speed. Canvas shading became

more important as it was necessary to learn the best ways of shading
when constrained by the rigidity of the squared canvas ground fabric.

Perhaps the two biggest changes were to blackwork and the lessening
of religious iconography for the final pieces, though this was not a
straight-line progression. From its introduction to this country in around
the 15th century, blackwork had been an infill technique used within a
shaped outline stitch, with the visual aim of representing lace patterns.
The shape could be anything from a flower to an animal. During the
apprenticeship the technique was transformed, continuing to use the
patterns but interpreting them pictorially in terms of shade and shadow.
The RSN was the first to introduce this approach to blackwork and it
has transformed how blackwork is used today. The squared patterns lend
themselves to buildings or other geometric shapes, but exploring the use
of shading has led to blackwork being used particularly for portraits.

The finale of the Training School diploma course had been the churchwork piece, beginning with Pomegranate, Crown and Fleur-de-lys (which taught basic goldwork), then moving on to the more advanced and creative goldwork in the cross with, then, a number of other techniques being featured in the range of motifs, badges and other elements surrounding the cross. Before the end of the diploma this brief had been made looser, separating off Pomegranate, Crown and Fleur-de-lys (although they were still taught) and instead working this piece as a cross in metal thread accompanied by two saints, one in appliqué and one in tapestry silk shading. Over time, the brief changed again. It became known as Figure, Symbol and Animal. Initially these had a religious emphasis but eventually it was realised that the worked pieces did not need to be religious for the apprentices to demonstrate the techniques. As such, it opened the door to more creative thinking and later pieces included one featuring *Alice in Wonderland*, the Queen of Hearts and the White Rabbit, another which featured a businessman, the pound sign and a shark, and a third of Icarus flying towards the sun with his wings taking animal form.[1]

Silk shading was given a boost when Derek Watson, the son of an active stitcher who had made work for the Queen Mother, inaugurated a competition in her name, Hilda Watson. The first-year apprentice who achieved the highest marks in silk shading, would, in the third year, have the honour of making a piece for the Watson family. This was always an animal and, as Derek Watson was a farming journalist, usually a farm animal.

(top left) Perhaps the biggest change of the apprenticeship was with blackwork, moving on from infilling shapes to creating pictures. It could be used for some dramatic effects. 'Hamlet' by Alexandra Lester.

(top right) Lucy Rogers created this embroidered pound sign as her Symbol.

(below left) As well as basic and coronation goldwork, apprentices were also introduced to creative goldwork as seen in this fish created by Bella Lane.

(below right) Students learned about the use of negative space. 'Tiger' by Sarah Homfray.

(left) Apprenticeship project in 2005 to commemorate the Battle of Trafalgar

[RSN Collection. Photographs: John Chase]

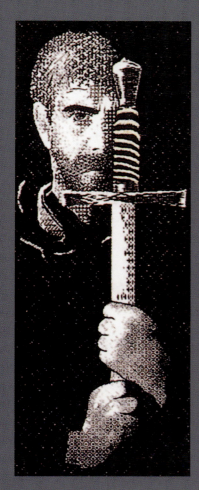

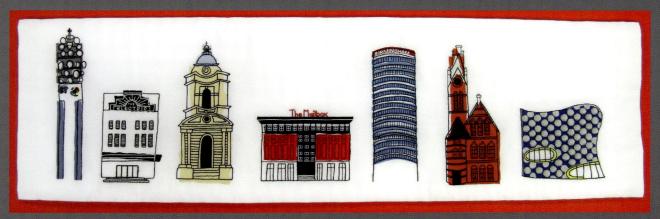

(opposite) **The apprentices undertook joint projects such as this piece, based on the chimneys and symbols of Hampton Court Palace for the 125th anniversary exhibition in 1997.**

[RSN Collection. Photograph: John Chase]

(top) **Appliqué became more open to the apprentices' own designs. Here Rachel Doyle features the iconic buildings of Birmingham old and new.**

(above left) **A major change of the apprenticeship programme was to the churchwork piece. This was now secularised and became known as Figure, Symbol and Animal, where the Symbol should include metal thread work with a naturally shaded animal and a tapestry shaded figure. Rachel Doyle here celebrates *Alice in Wonderland*.**

(above right) **Tassel was introduced from the upholstery side of the workroom, although apprentices' tassels were one-offs and could be embellished to a theme. Made by Jacqui McDonald.**

[Photograph: John Chase]

Two further topics were introduced, responding to a rise in interest in the embroidered boxes of the 17th century, that is box-making and stumpwork or raised embroidery. Church vestments was another subject straight out of the workroom. Apprentices made scale versions of a burse, stole, alms bag, banner and a cope to understand the principles of how they are made. Creative box was added as an extension to basic box, and, because it is never quite known when it might be needed, coronation goldwork.

Also introduced in the late 1990s was the joint project, where the first two year-groups of the apprenticeship would work together on a piece. The largest of these celebrates being at Hampton Court and features a lion, two griffin supporters, the rose window and a selection of chimneys, being some of the key symbols of the Palace building. There was the recreation of an 18th-century dress and two gauntlets made to commemorate the 1805 battle of Trafalgar. These projects fostered teamwork, but more than that they reinforced the aim of the RSN which was that a group of people should work on a piece and it should appear as if it were the work of a single person. During the latter stages of the apprenticeship, this was learned from making a series of kneelers for the Clothworkers' church, St Olave's, in the City, a project which was continued into the Future Tutors programme. While this used the simplest of stitches, it had the greatest potential for revealing any stitching that did not match.

By the early 2000s the fundraising was getting harder and was not covering the cost of the course, albeit that several other livery companies had come on board such as Dyers, Girdlers, Haberdashers and

(left) **Coronation goldwork was continued in the apprenticeship to keep the skills alive. This example by Shelley Cox.**

(right) **Highland cattle embroidered by Sarah Homfray was one of the Hilda Watson award winners.**

[Photographs: John Chase]

(above left) The RSN was asked by Hampton Court Palace to recreate the King's Throne Canopy of William IV, following the fire at the Palace. The request was a little unusual as the RSN was asked to make it to mirror the condition of its predecessor, so while being newly made, it needed to appear as if 300 years old, complete with tarnished metal thread and conservation netting.
[RSN Archive]

(above right) Banner for the Worshipful Company of Gold and Silver Wyre Drawers, one of several livery companies with which the RSN still has connections
[RSN Archive].

(left) Sample panel for Eurotunnel designed by David Gentleman and embroidered by the RSN
[RSN Collection]

Needlemakers. There was less work for the studio by the early 2000s and
it could not promise to take on any of the apprenticeship graduates, and
although many were and still are teachers for the RSN, the course was
not aimed at teaching and did not include a teaching qualification of any
kind. It was this, and the ongoing financial issues which really brought
the apprenticeship to an end. Many apprenticeship graduates have
gone on to teach for the RSN, but they had to seek their own teaching
qualifications.

The work of the studio was still very varied. Sir Alastair Morton,
head of the Eurotunnel project wanted a series of appliquéd panels and
had David Gentlemen design a first one which the RSN duly made up.
However, the funding could not be found for the series to be continued
and the sample panel is still at the RSN.[2] A number of commercial
companies sought out the RSN to produce embroidered pieces for
advertisements, ranging from KP nuts to Evian water. Military and
livery banners were still being produced. For Historic Royal Palaces
the RSN was commissioned to recreate the Throne Room back cloth,
following the fire at Hampton Court, with a special brief to make it
look old, and altar frontals and vestments were still in demand, but now
often with a new look to them. There were also anniversary pieces such
as for the 40th anniversary of the Duke of Edinburgh's Awards which

Panels to celebrate the 40th anniversary of the Duke of Edinburgh's Award. The panels were designed by Nicola Jarvis and prepared by the RSN workroom for DofE participants to stitch. On completion, the panels were returned to the RSN for making up and mounting, and were launched at the 40th anniversary event.

[RSN Images. Photograph: John Chase]

apprenticeship graduate Nicola Jarvis designed; the team colour-matched the panels before they were sent out to the regions to be worked before being returned to the RSN for checking and mounting.

The rebuilding of the external teaching by the RSN happened slowly during the 1990s, starting with a summer school and the one-year certificated course for small numbers of students. However, in 1997 the RSN had to start paying rent and new sources of income were required, so a programme of weekend short courses was started along with the re-opening of a shop. In 1997 the RSN first discussed having a presence on the internet and subsequently launched a website with seven pages.

125 Years of Excellence, 1997
Making up for the very low-key centenary year, for the 125th anniversary the principal and Council wanted to hold a big exhibition

reminiscent of those in the 1950s. Entitled *125 Years of Excellence* it was held at Hampton Court and endeavoured to feature some of the major commissions the RSN had completed, and which were still in existence, beginning with the Royal Albert Hall Hammer Cloth to represent the RSN in the 19th century. There were coronation pieces, military pieces (including a coat for a regimental goat, as mascot), pieces from the Overlord Embroidery, and as an example of new work, a suit by Paul Smith embroidered with insects, a hat by Philip Somerville which was later raffled off, and Anne Butcher's hand-embroidered wedding dress from 1993 when she was first Head of Workroom.

Royal Opera House, 1997–98

The RSN was very pleased to be asked to work on the curtains and pelmet of the Royal Opera House in Covent Garden after its refit. These were large pieces and, for the curtains, needed special consideration as they would be opened and closed frequently.[3] This in many ways took the RSN back to much earlier days when it created curtains for newly built theatres at the end of the 19th century.

Even for regular visitors to the Royal Opera House it can be difficult to estimate the size of the crest on the pelmet so the picture of a member of RSN staff sitting in the middle of it really helps put the piece into perspective and shows why appliqué was chosen as the principal technique, as others, such as silk shading, would have taken much longer and been far more expensive. In this instance, appliqué was not only

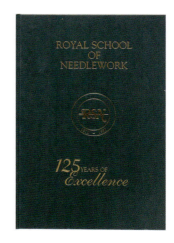

(above) **Cover of the catalogue for the 125th anniversary exhibition held at Hampton Court Palace**

(below) **The auditorium of the Royal Opera House with the crest and the curtains embroidered by the RSN**
[Image courtesy of the ROH © 2016 ROH. Photograph: Sim Canetty-Clarke]

Making the crest for the
Royal Opera House

[*The Times*]

appropriate for speed, but it was also appropriate for the room, giving
a three-dimensional quality which enables it to be seen clearly by the
audience within the context of such a large space.

Between 1998 and 2003 the RSN prepared several items for Wells
Cathedral which had been designed by Jane Lemon. The first was an
altar frontal for Christmas and this was followed by a set of Millennium
vestments for the Dean and Chapter as well as additional altar frontals.
In Jane's typical style, the items had sweeping designs that anchored
them to the cathedral.

The Millennium Sampler

With the millennium in sight the joint project for 1999 was to create a
new sampler. The design was of a computer screen and across it would
be an icon for each letter of the alphabet. Some of these icons have
retained their potency and reference such as the Olympic rings and
the Nike Swoosh, others turned out to be only of the moment such as
Millennium Man, and others, once mighty, have faded away, Kodak for

example, but it is a fascinating snapshot of a moment in time for all the icons and even the look of the computer screen which, only 20 years later seems so old-fashioned.

In the making, there was one element which took sampler making back to the 18th century and that was the issue of what to do when you ran out of space. A count of the letters represented on the main screen totals 24. The final two, 'y' and 'z' appear as part of the 'on' button lower down the screen.

As memories will fade, the symbols represent:
A – @ symbol, B – barcode, C – Cable & Wireless, D – dollar sign, E – European Union, F – female, G – genome sequencing (image is the double helix of DNA), H – English Heritage, I – information centres (tourism and others), J – scales of justice, K – Kodak, L – National Lottery, M – Millennium Man, N – Nike Swoosh, O – Olympic rings, P – Penguin (publisher), Q – Mary Quant, R – ribbons for charitable causes, S – Save the Children, T – treble clef, U – London Underground, V – Vegetarian Society, W – Windows, X – x-ray, Y – yin and yang, Z – zeta waves.

The RSN Patron

By the time of her death in 2002, Queen Elizabeth The Queen Mother had been associated with the RSN for 79 years, since 1923. Throughout this time, she remained a stalwart supporter even in later life, putting her name to a fund to support the apprentices. In return, the RSN was pleased to make many gifts for her, either directly from the school or on behalf of others.

In the 1990s activities included working a cushion for her 90th birthday and members of staff walking in the Queen Mother's 90th Birthday procession wearing hats with needlework accoutrements. For her 100th birthday the RSN made a cushion featuring her beloved Castle of Mey.

The RSN's Millennium Sampler designed and worked by apprentices depicts a computer screen.

[RSN Collection]

On her death, letters of condolence were sent, but also a request for Queen Elizabeth II to become our Patron. The RSN was fortunate that this was one of the small number of patronages she took on from her mother.

In the same year, the RSN was asked to make Queen Elizabeth II's Golden Jubilee balcony hanging. This was a physically huge project and necessitated access to one of the throne rooms at Hampton Court Palace to bring the whole piece together. The RSN produced all the central elements: the trails of flowers, the crowns, the 'E' monograms, the 'C' logos for the Commonwealth, but the individual national roundels from the Commonwealth countries were to come from the countries themselves. Some did but others did not, and local school children were

In 2002 the RSN was asked to make a hanging that would drop from the Buckingham Palace balcony for Queen Elizabeth II's Golden Jubilee. The piece was so large that extra space was required in order to complete the work. Seen here is the finished Queen's balcony hanging.

[RSN Archive. Photograph: Matthew Fearn PA Images]

asked to help. Originally the roundels were to be attached in the order in which the countries became members of the Commonwealth but in the end their order was determined by their date of arrival and, more importantly, how they would best work on the back cloth, allowing it to hang to best effect.

The country of origin for some of the roundels is very clear, either because they feature a flag or part thereof, such as for Pakistan, or a quintessential icon such as the maple leaf of Canada but the one which always confuses people is that from Australia which is an orange landmass, set in a mid-blue sea surrounded by the light blue of the

Elizabeth Elvin, Principal from 1990 to 2007, here seen stitching in a publicity shot for classes she was to lead in the US

[RSN Archive]

stars of the Southern Cross. It is at the top on the left-hand side but no Australian visitors to the RSN ever recognise it.

It was hoped that the hanging would be shown elsewhere once the jubilee celebrations were over, but its immense size made that impractical, and was compounded by many of the roundels having items stuck on, making them a conservator's nightmare.

Another modernisation was to rename the workroom as the studio, as something more contemporary and proactive. To show that it was moving into the 21st century, it launched a CD-ROM to enable people to design their own canvaswork kits. Then, in 2003 came a new type of exhibition.

Leighton House was the venue for a one-week exhibition to showcase what contemporary embroidery could be. Work was created by studio members, by apprentices and loaned by apprenticeship graduates; many pieces were for sale. This attracted a wide range of interest and generated sales, further commissions, enquiries and new Friends.

This exhibition gave people an idea of what contemporary embroidery could be in context, on chairs, for unusual hangings, as fine art pictures or as contemporary handbags. This was a different approach for an RSN exhibition and references the beginning of the RSN as the makers were paid their salary at the RSN while making something to sell for the RSN, even if some of the items did not sell for some time.

As the Principal wrote in the catalogue introduction: 'This is an exhibition which celebrates the diversity of embroidery. My hope is that it will enthuse and inspire many to new levels of appreciation of the creative, artistic, and technical skills of the embroiderer.'[4]

To reinforce what the RSN studio could offer, several pages contained messages of what the studio could do for all kinds of interiors. Following the positive response, some Council members wanted there to be more such exhibitions, but they were costly, from the hire of the space to allocating studio time to working the items.

In the early years of the new millennium the focus was on trying to hold exhibitions and to open new areas to RSN embroidery. With this in mind, Elizabeth Elvin was invited to go to the United States, and, specifically, the RSN was engaged to work on curtains in the Arts and Crafts style for a privately owned hotel in Iowa. After an initial visit in 2001 this led to short classes being taught directly in America between 2003 and 2005.

Back at base, financial issues were raising their head again. The production of management accounts was not up to date and there was a growing deficit. In 2003 the loss was £158,000. By 2007 this was £300,000 and completely unsustainable. The principal's reports were all about fundraising, but the deficit was an insurmountable gap to fill through fundraising. Once again there was too big a difference between income and expenditure.

Canvas shading on the large
scale, working from a design
by the artist Basil Al-Kazzi
this piece is 1.2 metres
square and took over a year
to make with all the colour
combinations and blending.
[RSN Archive]

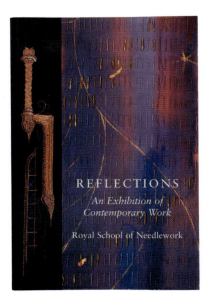

(top left) **Banner for the Hussars**
[RSN Archive]

(top right) **Embroidered triptych 'Stillness of Dawn' by Lisa Hughes, from the** *Reflections* **exhibition**
[RSN Archive]

(above left) *Reflections* **was an exhibition of contemporary embroidery made by apprentices and staff in the workroom. Intended as a selling exhibition, it also showed what embroidery could be.**
[RSN Archive. Photograph: John Chase]

(above right) **As part of the 2002 World Cup in Japan Adidas wanted to offer a pair of David Beckham's boots as a prize and asked the RSN to stitch the name Beckham in Japanese on the side. This was particularly challenging as shoes are normally embroidered before they are made up, not afterwards.**
[RSN Archive]

CHAPTER 8

Tradition, Quality and Innovation

In February 2007 Elizabeth Elvin stepped down as Principal of the RSN, remaining initially as a consultant. She is still an assessor for the certificate and diploma courses and celebrated 60 years of association with the RSN in September 2021, when she was interviewed by the current Chief Executive about her experiences and the changes she had seen at the RSN.

Back in 2007 the Bursar also left. An interim finance officer was appointed while Council searched externally for a new Head. Council took the opportunity to review the job description and the title. They decided that they needed someone who had experience as a charity chief executive and of turning an organisation around, as well as having an interest in hand embroidery without needing to be an expert embroiderer themselves.[1] Assisting Council in their decision making was Mr Brian Levy who had a background in change management and who had been brought in by a member of Council to give advice and guidance.

While the recruitment process was proceeding, one of the new members of Council agreed to come off Council to act as interim manager. He reported at his first meeting that the RSN was a complex organisation, but that staff responded positively to change, that the departmental heads were 'capable people who respond to responsibility which they have not been given before'.

Dr Susan Kay-Williams was appointed. She was then Chief Executive of Garden Organic[2] the national charity for organic gardening and organic research. On appointment, before Dr Kay-Williams had taken up the role, the Chairman, Countess Charles de Salis stood down and

Final Major Project by Elliott Reynolds

[Photograph: Tas]

Dame Zandra Rhodes poses
with the final apprentices
in 2009 following their
graduation ceremony.

[RSN Archive]

Mr Brian Levy was voted in. The new Chairman and Chief Executive
partnership began on 20 August 2007.

With expenditure far exceeding income until 2007, the first
requirement was to set a viable strategic plan and work towards an
annually balanced budget. It is fortunate that this work had started
a year before the banking crisis erupted. As it was, the new principle,
which remains active, is to earn and raise more income than is expended
on an annual basis. This was achieved every year from 2009 until the
pandemic. To achieve this, some tough steps had to be taken initially;
once again, some people had to go; some of the activities, such as lavish
external exhibitions, had to cease. Instead, there was greater focus on the
teaching and running of a variety of courses that would not only sustain
the RSN in the future but also underline its position as the international
centre of excellence for the art of hand embroidery.

The decision to end the apprenticeship had already been taken by
Council early in 2007. The scheme was expensive and, due to declining
workloads, it was not able to fulfil its aim, which was to offer graduates
a place in the studio. What the organisation needed was more teachers
but, while the apprentices did undertake teaching for the RSN they did
not have a teaching qualification.

In the first instance, the RSN wanted to explore new options and
the one it focused on was a two-year foundation degree. Foundation
degrees were new, a pet project of the Labour government. The idea was
for these to be a more practically focused degree. Council considered it
imperative that practical stitching remained a core part of the course, not
just learning about the academic history of stitching.

To establish the degree programme, the RSN needed to find a
validating partner. A number were considered but the eventual decision

was to partner with the University for the Creative Arts (UCA).[3] It was believed that they would support this fledgling organisation in meeting the various and demanding needs of higher education. To prepare the syllabus the RSN appointed James Hunting as someone with previous higher education experience who was both a lecturer and a stitch practitioner. James drew up the first course and the RSN underwent both institutional and course validation in early 2009, enabling it to enrol its first 11 students in September 2009, but not without an unexpected blow. As a result of the financial crash of 2008, government was changing the way they funded higher education. Just 20 days before the first students were due to start, the RSN was informed by the Higher Education Funding Council for England (HEFCE) that foundation degree funding was now only available for science courses not arts courses. It was a devastating blow. The RSN had already invested such a lot in the new programme, having raised more than £250,000 to rent and fit out additional rooms at Hampton Court Palace. Thanks to two legacies received that year, from Life Friend Victoria Adams and former RSN teacher Jean Panter, Council was able to proceed.

Fundamental to the degree course from Council's point of view was that students were taught an introduction to stitching by RSN tutors, but then, to elevate their study to degree level, they were challenged to take that stitching in different directions by exploring art and design and reinforcing it through contextual studies. The first stitch tutor on the degree course was RSN graduate Nicola Jarvis.

Some of the RSN tutors were sceptical about this new direction. The degree takes a very different approach from the apprenticeship. For example, on all other courses students are taught to finish their work and mount it, so there was consternation that the degree students left work unfinished and on the frame. But the degree course is not aimed at developing RSN teachers but rather to develop graduates who could take their embroidery creativity forward into a variety of careers such as fashion and film.

Some of the students wanted to complete a third year to gain a full BA (Hons) award and so in 2011 the RSN gained validation for what was known as the BA top-up, enabling those who wished to do so, to continue seamlessly, graduating with a BA in 2012. The students' final show was held at UCA Farnham Campus, and it is fair to say that the senior staff at UCA were pleasantly surprised by what had been achieved and the variety in the work. Everyone who visited the show got to see the RSN work because it was displayed in the foyer.

Under the current course leader, Angie Wyman this fledgling course was enhanced and finally evolved into a fully formed BA degree in 2014, still with practical hand stitching at its core, taught by graduates of either the apprenticeship or its successor, the Future Tutor Programme.

A key part of the programme is the opportunity to work on live projects whether on site or at the workshops of the likes of Alexander McQueen, Ralph & Russo, Jasper Conran, Mary Katrantzou, Hussein Chalayan, and others. At times it has felt as though certain companies had the RSN students on speed dial, but there was one very good reason for that, which is their technical knowledge. As students and graduates have said, when called in to a couture house, they had the advantage over fashion design students who may not have carried out any actual stitching, often being called on to show the other students what is needed and how to make a start. It is these professional skills which will hold them in good stead for the future.

In the degree studios students have worked on projects for Patrick Grant's E. Tautz company for the runway, Nicholas Oakwell for the GREAT Britain exhibition in Shanghai, Kirstie Macleod, *Game of Thrones*, Sheme shoes, and Susan Aldworth for an art installation, while individual students have worked on collaborations with the Jane Austen's House museum and Liberty, and competitions such as the Bradford Textile Society and the Glovers' Company.

Degree students have gone on to achieve success in the competitions they enter while on the course and following graduation, and have made varied career choices including working in film costume, making

(left) **Patrick Grant first approached the RSN in 2013 to explore the archives, and from that came a partnership which saw RSN degree students working with his team at E. Tautz to work the motifs for this jacket which went down the runway in January 2014.**
[© E. Tautz]

(right) **Nicholas Oakwell came to the RSN to help him realise a dress for the GREAT Britain exhibition in Shanghai in 2016.**
[© The GREAT Britain Campaign UK government. Photograph: Greg Williams]

(above) **First-year students worked pillowcases as part of a project for Susan Aldworth's '1001 Nights' installation in the exhibition *The Dark Self* at York St Mary's, 2017.**
[Susan Aldworth. Image courtesy of the artist. Photograph: Paul Hughes]

(left) **Both the RSN and the degree students worked on this project for *Game of Thrones*. The studio worked the corner roundels for the Lanisters and the degree students created the fabric for the White Walker's outfit as well as building the torso. The overall dimensions are 6 metres by 4 metres.**
[Photograph: UAL/ Embroiderers' Guild]

embroidered jewellery, undertaking private commissions, teaching, working with women's community groups in India, the Middle East and Africa. To date, RSN graduates have worked on films including *Doctor Strange*, *Murder on the Orient Express*, *Emma* and *Mulan*.

The RSN Certificate in Technical Hand Embroidery

In 2004 it was minuted that Courses Co-ordinator, later Head of Education, Gill Holdsworth had transformed what had been known as the One-Year Certificated Programme. On the original course students studied four techniques over a year but only a small number could be accommodated. Gill had the idea to radically change the delivery of the programme and instead of asking students to commit to a whole year, she rechristened it the Certificate Programme in Technical Hand Embroidery and broke it up into four techniques so that people could sign up for one technique at a time. She introduced much more flexibility in attendance, enabling people to come weekly, fortnightly, or more randomly.

Initially, the certificate was only offered Monday to Friday but following the success of the revised programme it was expanded to seven days a week at Hampton Court and is the basis of the teaching in Durham, Bristol, Rugby, Glasgow, America and Japan and the intensive courses in the summer.

So enthused were people after the certificate that they then wanted more and in 2009 the RSN introduced the diploma to offer students a choice between this and the degree.[4] The diploma requires a minimum of six modules: four new techniques and two at a higher level. Once completed students can take additional modules or the three advanced modules: advanced whitework, creative box or both sides alike.

This added flexibility has enhanced the course significantly, encouraging much wider participation. By early 2020 there were around 350 people registered from all over the world for this most demanding of technical hand embroidery courses.

(left) **Degree students were invited to design for a Chinese shoe company, Sheme. The three designs selected were by Sabina Lima, Eliza Tutere and Erin Ledsom.**

(right) **Degree students were invited to create site-specific installations at Jane Austen's House in Hampshire. Here Charis Bailey has embroidered a line from *Mansfield Park* onto the edge of a piece of lace appearing out of an 18th-century inkwell.**

[Photograph: Susan Kay-Williams]

(above left) **Final Major Project by Livia Papiernik-Berkhauer**
[Photograph: Tas]

(above right) **Final Major Project by Jasmine Dawson**
[Photograph: Tas]

(right) **'The Preciousness of Life' by Lucy Martin**
[Photograph: Tas]

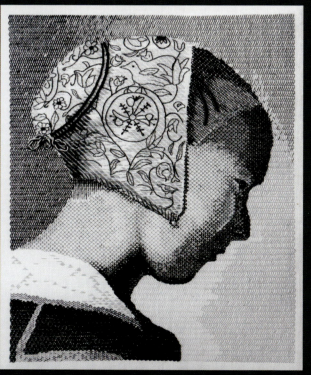

(top left) **Jacobean crewelwork by Liz Hands**

(top right) **Jacobean crewelwork by Diana Cargill**

(above left) **Blackwork by Gillian Wilde**

(above right) **Blackwork does not need to be in black, Carole Holmes's interpretation of the**

(top left) **Silk-shaded lily by Susan Cameron**

(top right) **Silk-shaded poppy by Eileen Dalziel**

(left) **Chinese lanterns in canvas stitches by Belinda Calaguas**

(above) **Canvas stitches by Elizabeth Barnett referencing Wordsworth's golden daffodils, with Windermere in the background**

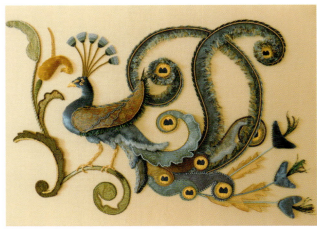

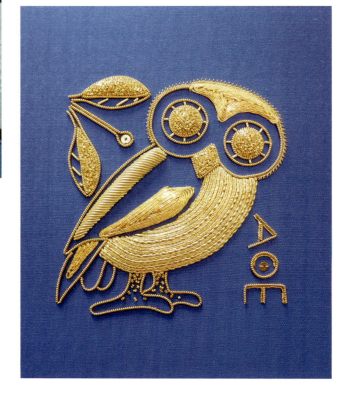

(top left) **Certificate goldwork** by Ayako Tanihata

(above) **Diploma appliqué cockerel** by Teresa McAuliffe from an original stained glass by Helen Robinson

(top right) **Peacock appliqué** by Kirsten Doogue

(centre right) **Diploma natural silk shading badger** by Kay Allan

(right) **Certificate goldwork** by Amanda Carter

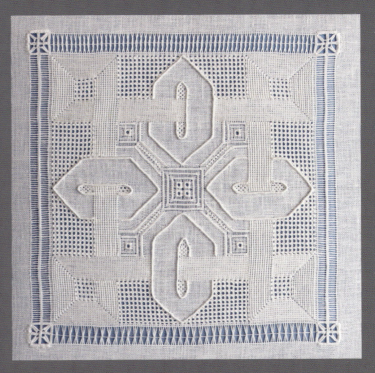

(top left) American student Sandra Arthur celebrated her kinswoman Betsy Ross, creator of the American flag, in stumpwork.

(left) Spanish student Nuria Picos Rodriguez used a matador's suit of lights as her inspiration for advanced goldwork.

(top right) The brief for stumpwork is one figure but here Ghislaine Peart excelled with three and a very effective appliqué background.

(above) Whitework is considered by many a most challenging technique. Angela Weedon here explored pulled and drawn thread work.

(opposite) Susan Chater, tapestry silk shading

(top left) **Mary Magdalene tapestry silk shading and metal thread work by Emma Frith**

(top right) **In this one work, diploma student Anja von Kalinowski combined five techniques: appliqué, blackwork, creative metal thread, natural silk shading and tapestry silk shading.**

(bottom left) **Advanced whitework by Lianne Hart**

(bottom right) **In Japan the pineapple is a symbol of welcome. For her diploma box project, student Kaoru Sato created this pineapple with removable lid and pineapple ring inside.**

Future Tutors

After a couple of years of the degree it was clear that those students were, by and large, not interested in going on to study hand embroidery technique to the level that was required to teach for the RSN. However, there was a growing need for new teachers. Only a fraction of the apprenticeship graduates had gone on to teach for the RSN in the long term. Interestingly, from the last cohort, four out of the six are regular teachers, the largest number from any year, but as many juggle work around childcare responsibilities they may move in and out of the pool of people whom we have available at any one time. If the RSN was to grow, then there needed to be more teachers available. To that end the Future Tutor programme was launched in 2012.

The Future Tutor programme is a three-year course which includes time in the RSN studio. Initially, this was planned as being for a period in each year, but practically, it was realised that the skill set that the students had in years one and two meant progress in the studio was too slow, so this was changed to be entirely in the third year. Finally, the course includes an adult teaching qualification to equip them for teaching, lesson planning and the role of learning outcomes to meet the needs of the students and the institutions where they will teach in the future. While many of the modules are similar to those on the certificate and diploma, students are held to a higher standard and have to incorporate all key elements of each technique within their work not just a few of them. In addition to the standard techniques, they have also been challenged to produce a signature project, one that combines techniques, or uses just one, but explores an area of stitching that crosses boundaries.

The Future Tutors pay towards their tuition because, as the RSN's own course, it is ineligible for any government funding, so the RSN has consistently raised funds to cover at least half of the course costs and for student bursaries. Because of the costs, most applicants are in their 30s or older. However, it has proved effective in producing new teachers and, in turn enabled the RSN to offer more classes at more locations. Specifically, this enabled the running of the first US summer school in Lexington, Kentucky in 2018 when 11 teachers went to the US for two weeks to teach more than 200 students, while simultaneously the RSN was offering Summer Intensive courses at Hampton Court and short courses in Ireland. This would not have been possible without this extra teaching capacity.

Short Courses

Short courses are the starting point for engaging with the RSN. They are open to anyone and take learners from beginners through to advanced courses. Back in 2007 there were just 50 courses a year being offered by the RSN and those were advertised up to a year in advance. One issue that limited the number of courses was physical space. This was a familiar problem, dating back through King Street and Prince's Gate. At

(opposite) **Future Tutor Jess Ingram's tapestry silk shading based on Lady Sybil from** *Downton Abbey*

(top left) **'Budgie' by Kate Barlow is worked in natural silk shading. This piece was selected for the Royal Academy Summer Exhibition in 2015.**

(top right) **For her Advanced Goldwork, Angela Bishop was inspired to recreate in goldwork the jewels from a portrait of Anne of Denmark at Hampton Court Palace.**

(above left) **Future Tutors are challenged to use blackwork for portraits to learn the use of shading and shadow. This piece is by Amy Burt.**

(above right) **Creative box by Amy Burt**

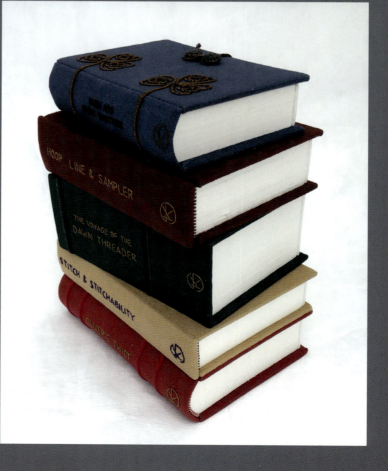

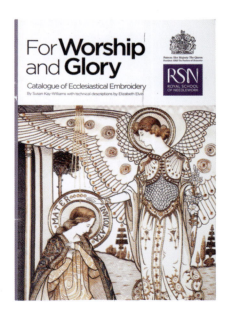

(top) **Creative box by Kate Pankhurst features Speke Hall in digital print and embroidery**

(bottom left) **For her Signature Project Kate Barlow created this 'sweetie dress' with three-dimensional raised-work sweets on a candy stripe dress.**

(bottom right) **Creative box by Kathryn Sanders comprises a stack of books with playful titles such as Voyage of the Dawn Threader and Stitch and Stitchability. The stack opens with lids and even secret drawers.**

(below) **The major exhibition at the RSN in 2013 was** *For Worship and Glory* **featuring ecclesiastical pieces in the Collection worked by and donated to the RSN. This later toured to Ely, Chester and Exeter cathedrals.**

Hampton Court, although the RSN had taken on more space in 2009, 2011 and 2015 it was all fully occupied by the degree.

By 2019 the short course programme was a balancing act between the number of rooms that might be available and what might be required in a year's time, although we now produced brochures twice a year where the second could include additional classes, it was always challenging to find the space balancing summer intensive certificate and diploma courses with the space to hold a short course.

The Collection and Archives

In 2007 there were both a part-time Archivist and a part-time Curator; they were responsible for two exhibitions, the first at Cumberland Lodge in Windsor Great Park in 2007 (the first of three exhibitions there), and in 2009 at the Royal Opera House.

Cumberland Lodge was a special location for the RSN because it had been Princess Helena's home. Although now used as a residential conference centre, pictures of Prince and Princess Christian and their children are still on show at the house. The first exhibition featured treasures from the RSN and was visited by the RSN's patron, Queen Elizabeth II.

The exhibition at the Royal Opera House featured objects from both organisations and was officially opened by HRH The Duchess of Gloucester, the RSN President. Unfortunately, the posts of Archivist and of Curator could not be maintained, and these roles have been taken on by the Chief Executive.

Opening the Studio Doors

Back in 2009 when visitors came, they came to see the studio at work. At certain times in 2009 there were only two things being worked on – the very large pieces for Dover Castle – and later when the Chief Executive went to give a lecture to a group, they commented that in the talk they had seen so much more, so a decision was taken to refocus visits. It was decided to focus instead on an exhibition on the walls and seeing the studio was an added extra. The aim was to reduce disappointment in only seeing a small number of items but also, as part of the public benefit of the RSN to start to reveal parts of the Collection and Archive.

It was also decided to recruit a team of volunteers who would lead the tours. The first exhibition was in 2010. Since then, up to 2020, there have been two exhibitions a year to which groups and individuals could come on pre-booked visits, and latterly there has been at least one open day a year when the studio and exhibition were open to anyone, often as part of Open House London.

The volunteers were given training in the history of the RSN and about the specifics of each exhibition. As a teaching organisation this did not just include information about the pieces on display but also contextualised each exhibition within a time frame or a culture or a milieu. It was also possible to highlight a variety of techniques through different exhibitions. The exhibitions alternated between those which were taken predominantly from the RSN Collection and those which featured the work of RSN students (Future Tutors, degree and certificate and diploma).

For the 140th anniversary the RSN reprised the title *Royal Connections* with some of the smaller items that had not been part of larger exhibitions, with the benefit of allowing visitors to get closer to the objects. This exhibition was opened by HRH The Duchess of Gloucester.

Others included *For Worship and Glory* – ecclesiastical embroidery from the RSN Collection. This was a huge success with people being

(above left) **Queen Elizabeth II's horse Carlton House, worked in blackwork embroidery by the RSN studio for her Diamond Jubilee**

(left) **An embroidered corsage of the flowers of the four nations made by the RSN studio for Queen Elizabeth II's 90th birthday**

(opposite) **Blackwork portrait of the Duchess of Cornwall (now HM Queen Camilla) worked by the RSN studio: Rachel Doyle, Kate Barlow, Alena Chenevix Trench**

[Photograph: Andy Newbold]

(left) HRH The Duchess of Cornwall (now HM Queen Camilla) meets the three studio staff who created her portrait, from left Alena Chenevix Trench, Kate Barlow and Rachel Doyle.
[Photograph: Andy Newbold]

(below left) In 2017 when HRH The Duchess of Cornwall (now HM Queen Camilla) came on her first visit as Patron, she was accompanied by our President, HRH The Duchess of Gloucester. Here in the studio chatting with Dr Susan Kay-Williams, the Chief Executive and Anne Butcher, Head of Studio
[Photograph: Andy Newbold]

(below) Scan the QR code to watch a video of Rachel Doyle creating the face of Her Majesty in blackwork embroidery.

able to see all 12 Litany of Loreto embroideries for the first time in many years. This exhibition also went to Ely Cathedral in 2015 where 8,000 people visited in the unseasonal month of February. Parts of that exhibition subsequently went to Chester in 2017 and Exeter in 2019. Others have taken particular themes, such as flowers, animals and people in embroidery.

In 2017 the RSN marked 30 years of being based at Hampton Court Palace. Two events were planned: an exhibition of recent work across all courses and the studio, entitled *Embroidered at the Palace* which attracted more than 5,000 visitors. The second was a tea party for Friends and Supporters held in the Garden Room at Hampton Court Palace. In a sold-out event, there were both new supporters and those whose connections went back to the 1940s and '50s.

Patronage

Queen Elizabeth II became Patron after her mother and came not only to the 2007 Cumberland Lodge exhibition but also the one held in 2011. This featured goldwork and the Chief Executive escorted the Queen and the Duke of Edinburgh around this exhibition where they had a discussion over the Lord Chancellor's Purse which is used for the State Opening of Parliament.

HRH The Duchess of Gloucester has been our President for many years. Like most of her predecessors as President she has been a very active supporter of the RSN, making many visits to Hampton Court and is a stitcher herself.

(above right) **Degree students were asked to create a selfie on a handkerchief. From the response to this project the RSN developed a schools' programme to Stitch a Selfie, initially funded by the Worshipful Company of Girdlers. Beth Duffy with her selfie.**

(right) **Degree Final Major Project from Elena Thornton. 2017 Winner Hand & Lock prize**

In 2017 Queen Elizabeth II asked the Duchess of Cornwall (now HM Queen Camilla) to take over as Patron and the RSN was very pleased to welcome her, initially on a joint visit with the Duchess of Gloucester and then subsequently on a solo engagement when she opened the *Faces and Figures in Embroidery* exhibition by confronting the stitched portrait of herself made by three members of the RSN studio.[5]

The Selfie Project

The degree programme also informed other parts of the RSN. The 'selfie' project was launched for schools on the back of work being done by the degree and a remembered project from the end of the apprenticeship about creating a portrait in stitch. The degree had played with format and with the 'fabric' by stitching on a handkerchief and a sieve which gave the idea for launching a programme for schools. Stitch a Selfie was originally launched in 2018 with financial support from the Worshipful Company of Girdlers. The idea was to offer a crate of materials to schools and encourage them to participate in making a self-portrait inspired by those shown in an accompanying booklet. It was specifically aimed at being gender neutral. Teachers were offered some stitch training to help them get started if they were not familiar with stitching. Just prior to the first lockdown the RSN was preparing to relaunch this project, offering schools the opportunity not just to stitch selfies but also mantras or positive phrases that make the stitcher feel good about themselves. Following the pandemic, we have seen teachers use this project to support the mental health and wellbeing of their students and this means the RSN will be further promoting this and other initiatives to help pupils through 2021–22.

Post pandemic the RSN has found better ways to deliver the project online which will potentially mean that it can be open to more schools whether as part of the Textile Studies activities or as part of PSHE.

The RSN has long encouraged student to participate in competitions for embroidery and textile arts of which the largest for hand embroidery is the Hand & Lock Prize which was first launched in 2000 for students and now has both a student and an open class in two categories: fashion and textile art. The prize has really come of age in the last five years and attracts a worldwide entry. The RSN students from both the degree and the Future Tutors take part and several have been prize winners, including four winners of the student prize for textile art:

Elena Thornton in 2017 (degree) for her neck and face pieces and Gold and Silver Wyre Drawers Award

Alex Standring in 2018 (degree) for her Fear and Faith headdresses and Gold and Silver Wyre Drawers Award

Martha Blackburn in 2020 (Future Tutors) for her hand stitched portraits and Broderers Award

Kate Pankhurst in 2021 (Future Tutors) for her Lockdown O'Clock and the Gold and Silver Wyre Drawers Award

Other prize winners include Jung Byun Future Tutor (2019) Broderers award for her peacock mirror, Charis Bailey (2017) graduate of the degree as runner up in the Open category fashion section, Lizzie Lowe Broderers Award (2018) Lucy Tiley and Hisae Abe (2020) third prize for textile art and fashion respectively, Millie Whitehead and Rebecca Offredi (2021) third prize for fashion and textile art respectively, Sabina Lima (2021) third prize, open category textile art – all degree students.

The Embroidery Studio

Over the last decade the commissions in the studio have been as wide-ranging as ever from commemorating the reign of Henry II for English Heritage to millennium vestments for Buckfast Abbey, from the insignia for Prince Philip, used by ITV for their obituary programmes to working on the wedding dress of Catherine Middleton and bringing together Cornelia Parker's Magna Carta embroidery to creating and restoring embroidery for *Salvage Hunters: the restorers*. What they almost all have in common is being made by a team of people.

(right) **Working on the Guest Hall Back Cloth for Dover Castle for English Heritage 2009**

(below right) **Collective working on the wedding dress of Catherine Middleton for Sarah Burton of Alexander McQueen**

The RSN studio created seven pieces for Dover Castle in 2009 which, in tune with the historical time they represented, were worked in Bayeux stitch. One of the team was Wendy Hogg. From her start on the Overlord Embroidery and then leading the YTS programme Wendy taught mounting, canvas stretching and other techniques of finishing to apprentices. She died in 2011, and the last big pieces that she worked on were the hangings for English Heritage for Dover Castle when she celebrated 40 years at the RSN.

Just as with every large project before, the RSN can rise to the challenge of both secrecy and amazing work when required. When we were asked to undertake the wedding dress of Catherine Middleton,

(left) Catherine Middleton and her father as they prepared to walk up the aisle. This was the moment when all those at the RSN who had been working on the dress were finally able to tell their families and friends what they had been working on.
[Photograph: Anwar Hussein/Alamy]

(above) The lace appliqué on the bodice, skirt and train of the dress, and around the edge of the veil was hand worked by the RSN, by a team of people working on the project in secret. The embroiderers used the Carrickmacross technique, which originated in Ireland in the 1820s. Hand-cut lace flowers, including roses, thistles, daffodils and shamrocks, were individually applied onto ivory silk tulle to a pattern developed specifically for each part of the gown by Sarah Burton of Alexander McQueen.
[LEWIS WHYLD/AFP via Getty Images]

we did not know for which designer it was, as the initial introductions were made through a third party, but everyone working on it knew what it was and who the ultimate client was and signed an oath to agree that they were sworn to secrecy. In total a team of over 60 people contributed, many giving up family time and other engagements to assist. But this combined working made the whole team feel so proud when Catherine Middleton stepped out of the car, and they were able to tell their families that they had worked on the wedding dress designed by Sarah Burton of Alexander McQueen.

In a long line of royal commissions this had all the RSN hallmarks: collective working that looked like the work of one person, never a seat should go cold, to get the job done on time and a wonderful result at the end. The RSN team was very proud to work on this and celebrated after the event by sharing the two tins of cake which were sent.

As can be seen from this list of work, the studio is still at the centre of the RSN with an incredibly varied range of work. Jobs may be one-off birthday or anniversary gifts, mending a seat cover that some small animal has chewed, transferring a much-loved embroidery from a moulting velvet background, or giving textiles an important new lease of life.

(opposite, top) In 2010 the Lord Chancellor's Purse returned to the RSN for some TLC. This included light cleaning of the raised cherubs and restoring the tassels.

(opposite, bottom left) The set of Millennium Vestments for Buckfast Abbey waiting to be packaged and sent to the Abbey. Originally wanted for Easter 2018, it was a challenge when the RSN were then asked to supply it in time for midnight mass the preceding Christmas.

(opposite, bottom right) St Amphibalus's Shrine cover being assembled at the RSN after all the embroidered panels have been completed prior to its being installed in St Albans Cathedral. This was worked by a small team through lockdowns and social distancing.

(above) The RSN was asked to create a crest for Savoir Beds' top-of-the-range four poster bed.

(left) HRH Prince Philip's insignia was commissioned by ITV and used extensively in programmes after his death.

(top) The insignia of the Fleet Air Arm. This whole embroidery is just slightly larger than a one pence piece.

(above) Brooch designed and worked by the RSN studio, inspired by designs in the great mosques of Abu Dhabi and Dubai.

(right) The RSN was approached by the Red Carpet Green Dress project founded by Suzy Amis Cameron. We were asked to embroider a dress which Vivienne Westwood's studio was realising for Naomie Harris to wear at the Oscars in 2013.

[Photograph: Abaca Press/Alamy]

(left) The studio never knows what it will be asked to do next. In this case it was a CD cover for an American R&B singer and it turns out black on black stitching is more challenging than white on white.

Response to the Pandemic

Like everyone else, the RSN was unprepared for the pandemic. The Chief Executive had just returned from visiting students in Japan. The RSN had launched the second US Summer School and was gearing up for another group event, while RSN satellites were developing strong summer classes. And then came lockdown in March 2020. In two days the RSN sent everyone home, the Future Tutor and degree students armed with as many materials as they could carry. Teaching went online for our two main courses. Certificate and diploma courses as well as short courses, were stopped. To be suddenly faced with returning hundreds of thousands of pounds was challenging. The RSN furloughed people immediately and halted all expenditure. Then the only option was an emergency appeal because it was believed that if the team could just buy themselves a bit of time, there would be a way forward. And so it proved.

RSN Supporters really rose to the challenge, they made cash donations (more than £70,000), they waived the return of fees, they bought from the online shop (200 orders over the Easter weekend alone), they supported the RSN Stitch Bank, and they became RSN Friends, all of which gave the small active team of staff a huge boost of confidence and drove a real commitment to turn the organisation around.

The RSN started offering one-to-one digital tuition to established certificate and diploma students online in April. As the Future Tutors and degree students grappled with the technical challenges, all the staff team learned, and everyone continued learning as the one-to-one classes began, but the feedback from the students and tutors was that there were ways to make it work. With the help of the school's IT manager

Rainbow: the first online short class designed and led by Sarah de Rousset-Hall, May 2020

Rainbow: the first online short class designed and led by Sarah de Rousset-Hall, May 2020

and the willingness of tutors to experiment, ways were found to make everything work.

The first online short course, based on a rainbow, was run in May 2020 and the response to it showed that there was not only a keenness for all things practical during lockdown but that the RSN could really meet a need. The team and tutors discovered many new ways in which they could offer courses – shorter windows of engagement spread across more days, at different times of the day, especially evenings, across time zones and offering more courses simultaneously than would ever be possible at Hampton Court. Perhaps the best example of this was a programme that was devised to take advantage of two RSN hallmarks: technical excellence and the number of tutors – Technical Tuesdays. The idea was to take one technique and teach 30 stitches from that technique, one a week across three terms of 10 weeks. Each session would last two hours and in that time learners would be taught a stitch in detail, see how it might be applied, and also see illustrative examples on pieces from the Collection. It was thought that this might be popular, so we offered 15 places. The team had not anticipated just how popular it might be and were almost overwhelmed when there were more than 40 people on the waiting list. However, thanks to the teaching resource in which the RSN has focused so much energy, additional tutors could be brought in, and the lead tutor ran a second class earlier in the day. In total, Technical Tuesday began with four full classes and lots of positive comments and participation, even from people who had previously taken certificate and diploma classes. Four classes, three running simultaneously, engaging people in many countries and 60 happy students.

From January 2021 the RSN was also, for the first time, able to offer the certificate online for new applicants by splitting the introduction into sections, so that participants really did feel that they were in the RSN. The new way of working gave enormous flexibility, the opportunity to repeat short classes a week later or a month later, rather than a year later and it also meant that the RSN could reach more interested participants through offering classes at different times of day thus enabling people from around the world to participate. In addition, the RSN has offered talks twice a month to anyone who wanted to join and there have been up to 600 people listening, giving the RSN a whole new international audience. The culmination of the first year online was the first International Online Summer School in July 2021 with over 270 participants from more than 16 countries. What would Lady Welby and Princess Helena think of that?

Since 2007 the RSN has developed and worked through a series of strategic plans to take the organisation forward, but with the pandemic everything had to be reconsidered. A new strategic plan that will embrace both physical and online delivery and put the role of stitching for mental health and wellbeing centre stage, has been developed to take the RSN through the anniversary year and well beyond. The RSN is looking to the future. When asked what I am most proud of during the pandemic the answer is the drive and determination of the active team. Collectively we were determined to pivot the organisation and ensure it was still here for the anniversary. More than that, though, was the fact that throughout 2020 the organisation did not have to dip into its investments, that they remain a solid foundation, built up over the last 15 years on which the RSN can build for its future: that is something of a first.

The RSN Stitch Bank and Digitisation

Also of great importance to the RSN is developing projects which really help it to build on its reputation as the centre of excellence for hand embroidery. Two projects have been planned for some time. The first was launched as the start to the anniversary year and the RSN hopes the second may begin during it. The RSN Stitch Bank is to be a stitch repository ultimately for every stitch in the world. Stitches fall out of favour and become lost and unused, so this project aims to find as many stitches as possible and add them to this database for use by tutors, students, scholars, curators, historians and, of course, stitchers. An early indication of the success of the RSN Stitch Bank is that it has been viewed by 50,000 unique users in the first two months.

The RSN Stitch Bank aims to become the biggest repository of stitch in the world

This is how you can contribute

(top) The major new initiative from the RSN is the RSN Stitch Bank, with the aim to conserve and preserve every stitch in the world. Launched in September 2021 it has already been praised as a game changer.

(above) Scan the QR code and this will take you straight to the RSN Stitch Bank

The most recent version of the crest, worked in time-honoured fashion by a group of tutors and apprentices collectively but in the end looking like the work of one person.

The most recent version of the crest, worked in time-honoured fashion by a group of tutors and apprentices collectively but in the end looking like the work of one person.

A longed-for project is the digitisation of the RSN Textile Collection and the RSN Archive. This will help tutors, students, academics and enquirers to find out more about the RSN and some of the people who have passed through our classes and workrooms. These are already two projects looking to underline the RSN's role into the future.

The story of the RSN has been one of turbulent times, but also one of the commitment and drive of individuals to help it succeed. While in the 21st century the organisation is open to men as well as women, with male teachers and is encouraging both boys and girls to stitch on the Selfie project, it remains committed to high-quality technical stitchwork, but is also aware of the importance of design and new ideas, hence our values of Quality, Tradition and Innovation.

At graduation parties I am fond of saying that everyone who comes to or takes courses with the RSN is tied by an invisible thread and that every now and again it becomes elastic and pulls people back to the RSN. This is just one aspect of the hold the organisation has over its staff and students; it creates an almost unbreakable bond of people committed to ensuring the art of hand embroidery will not die.

CHAPTER 9

Celebration and Coronation

The RSN team were keen to make the most of the anniversary. As has been noted through the ups and downs recorded in this book, it was not a given that the organisation would ever reach such an impressive milestone. However, even the pandemic could not stop the current team of staff and tutors from working to ensure we were around to commemorate the achievement, and our next 150 years got off to an exciting start.

To make the most of the year, our principal outreach was through holding exhibitions to enable more people to learn about the RSN, its work and its Textile Collection and Archive. By the end of the year, the RSN had been part of five exhibitions, four in the UK and one in the United States.

We had been scheduled to hold a second exhibition at Ely Cathedral in 2021,[1] but with the ongoing Covid-19 issues it was postponed. Following on from the original very successful exhibition we had taken there in 2015, at the request of Ely, we combined a second part of *For Worship and Glory*, featuring ecclesiastical objects from the RSN Collection, with recent work by RSN degree students. The request for recent work was because of the strong textile programme at King's Ely school. To make this exhibition truly special, we loaned all 12 of the Litany of Loreto embroideries, making it the first time they had all been seen together since 2013. Thanks to the team at Ely these beautiful pieces were hung in the Lady Chapel at eye level making it possible for visitors to have a very close look for as long as they wished. Nearly 5,000 people attended the show between January and March.

The main anniversary exhibition[2] was always planned to be at the Fashion and Textile Museum (FTM) in Bermondsey, near London Bridge. The museum was established by Dame Zandra Rhodes and is now part of Newham College. A large exhibition takes a great deal of planning, notwithstanding some of the pieces were going to come from the RSN Collection. It was, however, challenging to try to plan the exhibition when many of the venues from which we hoped to borrow pieces were closed due to the pandemic. This caused some concern about whether items could be identified and released in time, the last items were only agreed a month before the exhibition opened and seemed to be the furthest away, including one from the Highlands of Scotland. The focus of the exhibition was to tell the story of the RSN both as an organisation producing commissions and as the principal teaching establishment for technical hand embroidery. Along the way, though, the idea was to surprise people with the range of work the RSN had produced and the variety of people with whom we had worked. Having researched this book and having the

broadest knowledge of the history of the RSN and the Textile Collection, it was agreed with the FTM that I would curate the contents of the exhibition and they would curate the design of the exhibition.

The scariest part was not being allowed in to the building while the exhibition was under construction, only seeing it the day before it opened, but the FTM team had done a great job and with just a couple of tweaks it was what I had hoped it would be – something which would surprise visitors about the breadth and range of the RSN's work, from coronations to lingerie, from stitching as therapy to the degree work, from large hangings and screens to fashion and textile art.

In the first room, exhibiting pieces from the RSN Archive, we celebrated the first 30 years of the RSN and its strong links with art embroidery, and the Arts and Crafts and Aesthetic movements, featuring designs by William Morris, Walter Crane and Alexander Fisher. We also included an example of Burden stitch, so named by the RSN because it was highly favoured by Bessie Burden, who taught at the RSN in the 1870s.

(top left) **Ecclesiastical embroidery is an area in which the RSN has continued to specialise since the 1880s**
[RSN Collection. Photograph: Andy Newbold]

(top right) **Hand-stitched lingerie was made between 1916 and 1942 for an upmarket clientele**
[RSN Collection. Photograph: Andy Newbold]

(bottom) **Contemporary camisoles designed by second-year degree students in response to lingerie made by the RSN early in the 20th century**
[RSN Collection. Photograph: Andy Newbold]

For the historical parts we were delighted to be able to feature items which we had not seen before, such as the mantle worn by Edward VII at his coronation in 1902, the hand-embroidered wings for Army Air Observation Post insignia from 1942, and a dressing gown made by the RSN in the 1930s which had been given to the Collection only about five years previously.

To highlight the contemporary side of the RSN, we asked the second-year degree students to create their own responses to examples of lingerie made by the RSN in the 1920s and '30s. Each student was given the same camisole template and asked to create their own design for a 21st-century camisole. It was recognised that today a camisole can be an over-garment as well as an undergarment and the students explored every aspect of those possibilities with very individual responses.

We worked hard to seek objects from former customers and graduates, and the FTM said that ours was the exhibition that had benefitted from the most individual loans from different people. Lenders included Her Late Majesty Queen Elizabeth II and the Royal Collection, Patrick Grant, Sir Paul McCartney, Kirstie Macleod, Wells Cathedral, Ripon Cathedral, St George's Chapel at Windsor Castle, the Army Flying Museum, the Black Watch Museum, the D-Day Story museum, William Morris Gallery, Wemyss School of Needlework, and many of our tutors and graduates. The RSN was very grateful to all of them for supporting this event which really helped to tell the widest story of the RSN's history as well as its forward-looking future.

At the opening night we welcomed many guests including RSN supporter Dame Zandra Rhodes, Nicholas Oakwell and Kirstie Macleod, as well as many of our contributors, and we continued to welcome special visitors all the way through, amongst whom were Her Majesty Queen Azizah of Malaysia, our President, HRH The Duchess of Gloucester, many of our supporting livery companies and all our International Summer School students who were taking classes at Hampton Court. More than 12,000 guests visited the exhibition, and the best thing was when we heard people say as they were leaving that they were rushing home to tell someone else about the exhibition to encourage them to visit.

During this exhibition and as part of the RSN's further outreach, we hosted workshops and held special events for schools and families, funded by the Worshipful Company of Broderers, with the aim of introducing more people to embroidery. These events were incredibly popular and on family days frequently led to three generations of a family all stitching together. We were then delighted to receive feedback from parents and schools who wanted to continue stitching, and to hear that a number of school embroidery clubs had been established.

In 2022 we also launched our first Sip & Stitch event as a way of bringing people together through stitch and raising funds for the RSN Stitch Bank. We launched the event on World Embroidery Day – 30 July –

Recent graduates' work was featured at the FTM exhibition, as well as historical pieces
[RSN Collection. Photograph: Andy Newbold]

and were delighted to gain participants from as far afield as New Zealand and South Africa in our first year. From 2023, the RSN's Sip & Stitch has become an annual event, taking place to coincide with the RSN's anniversary in November, to avoid clashing with supporters' summer holidays.

Our international exhibition was our smallest of 2022, with only two Litany of Loreto works being shipped to the University of Dayton, Ohio. They were specifically requested by the university because the theme of the exhibition was the work of the Italian graphic designer Ezio Anichini who had drawn the original Litany of Loreto designs between 1914 and 1920. It was the American professor John Schaeffer, who had researched Anichini, who alerted the RSN to him being the designer of these works, so we were happy to send two of them to the exhibition and accompany this with an online talk about the whole embroidered series which attracted more than 600 subscribers from an international audience.

The Sunbury Embroidery Gallery is only a couple of miles from Hampton Court Palace so it might seem odd to hold an exhibition so close to home, but we recognise that the gallery enjoys a very different

(right) **The Sunbury exhibition featured work by Future Tutor and Degree students who graduated in 2022, including these pieces by Daisy Streatfeild**
[RSN Collection. Photograph: Susan Kay-Williams]

(below) **Working with Jay Blades, these Parker Knoll chairs are given new life**
[RSN Collection. Photograph: RSN Studio]

audience of local people compared with the international visitors who come to Hampton Court Palace. The exhibition focused on recent work by Degree and Future Tutor students which is not openly available to view for longer than a week at Hampton Court Palace. At the gallery, it was on show for two months, giving a large number of people the opportunity to see the work.

The RSN Studio has of recent years taken the opportunity to promote itself in the interiors market by exhibiting at Decorex, the annual trade fair for interior design. At the stand in 2022 the RSN Studio featured a piece that the organisation made in the 1980s, and yet, the landscape has a contemporary feel, alongside two Parker Knoll chairs which had been given a new lease of life courtesy of the RSN Studio team and Jay Blades' company.

Our final exhibition for this special year was hosted to recognise the work of our students who graduated in 2020 and 2021; these students had missed the opportunity to have an end of year show because of the restrictions imposed during the pandemic. The RSN was very grateful to the Worshipful Company of Girdlers who made their hall available for a week so we could hold the show. Invitations were sent to people from the local area and the fashion world, as well as to parents and friends. The exhibition had been planned for late September but with the death of Her Majesty The Queen, as both organisations had strong links with the monarchy, it was decided to postpone the event, and it eventually took place in November. Despite train and tube strikes, a good audience attended each day and enjoyed seeing not only the students' work but also Girdlers' Hall, which is not usually open to visitors.

With the passing of Her Majesty The Queen there was, obviously, a coronation on the horizon, but before any such announcement was made, work needed to begin on the changing of the monarch's initial. The first such request came from the Royal Albert Hall for the Hammer Cloth, which is displayed whenever the monarch attends an event there. This would be the sixth change of initial. Originally made for Victoria, the V had been changed to E, G, E, G, E and now needed to be changed to C. One of the main events that the monarch attends at the Royal Albert Hall is the annual Festival of Remembrance, close to Armistice Day. This was only a few weeks away, so the RSN team got straight to work. The cloth was carefully conserved; cleaned of dirt and dust by surface cleaning. The letter E was removed and the area where it had been resting was carefully cleaned and the pile restored, especially where it would be visible in the change from E to C. Because of the stocks the RSN holds, the team were able to find a matching material in the stores which would give an authentic look. This was carefully worked to match the font of the R (now for Rex) which it would be seen alongside. All of this was completed and returned to the Royal Albert Hall in plenty of time for it to be hung at the festival in November.

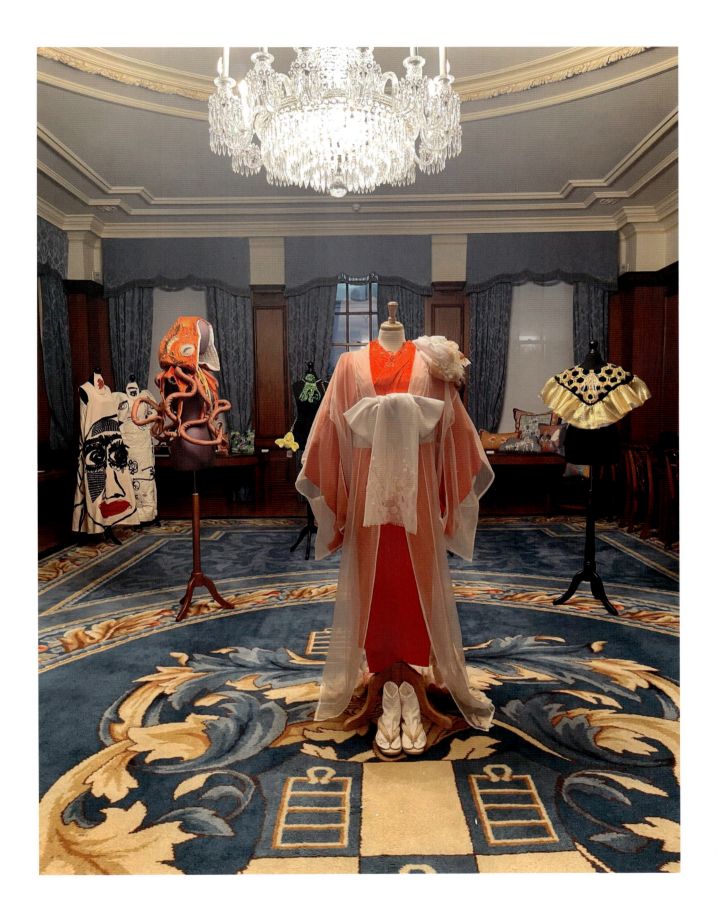

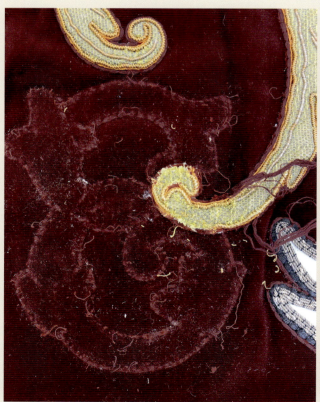

(top left) **The letter E on the Hammer Cloth**
[RSN Collection. Photograph: RSN Studio]

(top right) **Close-up of the letter E on the Hammer Cloth**
[RSN Collection. Photograph: RSN Studio]

(bottom left) **The marks on the velvet needed to be carefully removed**
[RSN Collection. Photograph: RSN Studio]

(bottom right) **The new letter C in place, with no trace of the E**
[RSN Collection. Photograph: RSN Studio]

The Coronation of Their Majesties King Charles III and Queen Camilla

As readers of this book will be aware, the RSN had worked on every coronation during the 20th century and, following the announcement of the coronation for May 2023, some supporters were quick to get in touch to ask what the RSN was working on. Contrary to popular assumption, nothing is worked on before the new monarch makes their own decisions, and while it had been seven decades since the last coronation, the King's interest in sustainability is well known; it was for the King to decide which of the chairs, thrones and vestments were to be reused and adapted. When the call came, the RSN was very happy to answer and also to keep quiet about it. The RSN has always been very good at keeping a secret. The first meeting was to discuss just one piece, and the RSN sent Head of Studio, Anne Butcher, and Studio Manager, Gemma Murray. Over time, the number of pieces upon which the RSN team was asked to work increased. In total we worked on nine elements, conserving some and creating others. They are presented below in the order in which they were worn or seen during the ceremony.

To achieve all the work to the required deadline, the RSN offered the opportunity to participate to graduates of the Apprenticeship and Future Tutor programmes, on condition that each person dedicated a certain amount of time to the project, because continuity was important. Notwithstanding the stitching ability to pick up where another has left off, it was also important to have an overview of each project so that time was not wasted in briefing more people.

In order to keep everything else working 'as normal' we were grateful to Historic Royal Palaces for loaning us a room where much of the work could be done in secret, especially while tour groups were being shown around the Studio.

The RSN began by working on one item, and as the list of items grew, the team were glad they had taken the care to assess how much time would be needed for each one so that they could ensure the whole – and growing – project would remain on schedule.

Private Visit by Their Majesties to the RSN

The Head of Studio was keeping in regular touch with the Palace about the progress of each of the items and on Tuesday 21 March the RSN was honoured to receive a visit from the King and Queen to see the work in progress, and to talk to and thank our professional embroiderers. This was a very special day for those involved although alas, we could not involve all the team due to space constraints. The King and Queen were both highly interested in seeing the work, especially on the Queen's Robe of Estate. They spent some time looking at it and asking questions as they spotted the different flowers and especially the insects on it. They examined the Anointing Screen, which looked rather large in the limited space at the RSN, and observed the work on the cyphers and for the Throne Chairs. Then they were talked through the plans for

the Stole Royal which was the final piece to be started. We had also brought out a number of items from the Collection and Archive as His Majesty appreciates the historical continuity with his own forebears and was interested to see the RSN's connections, confirming with the Chief Executive that he had reverted to the Tudor crown of George VI in preference to St Edward's crown which was on the cypher for his mother.

The visit was a great boost to the team and ensured everyone was even more focused on ensuring the work was achieved to the RSN standard and to time.

The King's Robe of State and the Chairs of Estate

The King arrived at the Abbey wearing the red Robe of State. This had certainly been worn by King George VI in 1937 and may be even older. In order for it to be used again, the RSN conserved the velvet while Ede & Ravenscroft conserved the ermine and gold lace so that it was all ready for the start of the coronation.

On their arrival at Westminster Abbey the King and Queen sat on chairs bearing their cyphers. These chairs were the ones which had been worked by the RSN with the cyphers of Her Majesty Queen Elizabeth II and the Duke of Edinburgh in 1953. The worked fabric was removed from the chairs, conserved and laid up, and the chairs were re-upholstered with new damask bearing the new cyphers which had been worked by the RSN. One of the challenges was ensuring the size of the cyphers was appropriate to the pattern of the damask ground fabric, as well as to the scale of the chair. One departure from 1953 is that the new cyphers do not include the garter which had been part of the cypher of Queen Elizabeth II.

(above left) **The King and Queen paid a private visit to the RSN to see the work in progress and were particularly captivated by the embroidery on the Queen's Robe of Estate**
[RSN Collection. Photograph: Andy Newbold]

(above right) **The King and Queen chatting with the RSN team in front of the Wall of Wool.**
[RSN Collection. Photograph: Andy Newbold]

(below) **Conserving the Robe of State last worn by George VI in 1937**
[RSN Collection. Photograph: John Chase]

The Anointing Screen

Designed and created to be used at the most sacred moment of the coronation, the Anointing of His Majesty The King, the screen combines traditional and contemporary sustainable embroidery practices to produce a design which recognises His Majesty The King's deep affection for the Commonwealth.

The screen was a gift to His Majesty from the City of London Corporation and the City Livery Companies. The design was selected personally by the King and created by iconographer Aidan Hart based on the window in the private chapel at St James's Palace, which had been donated to the late Queen for her Golden Jubilee by the City Livery Companies. The screen was realised by the RSN, this time with the help of Digitek Embroidery using Madeira Sensa thread made from 100 per cent lyocell fibres which are sustainable. As there was a large amount of work that was needed, it was decided that the base of the tree design, the branches and the outer rim of leaves would be worked in digital embroidery with the centre containing hand-worked leaves bearing the names of all 56 Commonwealth countries. The individual leaves were worked in gold thread, while

(top left) **The stained-glass Sanctuary Window in the Chapel Royal at St James's Palace, which was the inspiration for the Anointing Screen**
[Royal Collection Trust/All Rights Reserved]

(bottom left) **Embroidering the leaves, birds and flowers**
[RSN Collection. Photograph: John Chase]

(bottom right) **Working on the sun for the top of the screen**
[RSN Collection. Photograph: John Chase]

The cypher worked for the base of the tree represents the King supporting the Commonwealth
[RSN Collection. Photograph: John Chase]

The Anointing Screen at the coronation being flanked by Guardsmen
[PA News/Alamy]

the rest of the panel incorporated threads we already had in our famous store of old threads and the Wall of Wool. The leaves were worked by the RSN Degree students, Future Tutor students, representatives of the Trustees, Certificate and Diploma students, staff and tutors. In addition, representatives of the Worshipful Companies of Broderers, Drapers and Weavers also participated. In total some 150 people played a part in the creation of this piece.

The leaves were worked individually and then padded before being applied; the flowers and birds which also appear in the tree were worked by the RSN's professional embroiderers. The screen is three sided, each side being supported on a wooden frame. The poles and frame were worked by Nick Gutfreund of the Worshipful Company of Carpenters from a windblown tree in Windsor Great Park which had been planted by the Duke of Northumberland in 1765.

Apart from the 'tree' panel the other five sides of the screen (inside and out) feature a cross on a base of maroon fabric. The cross is worked in cloth of gold, blue and red fabric to represent the colours of the Cosmati pavement which is the floor in Westminster Abbey where the anointing takes place. This piece reflects His Majesty's well-known and longstanding commitment to heritage craft skills.

(left) **The Stole Royal**
[Worshipful Company of Girdlers.
Photograph: Prudence Cuming Fine Art
Photography]

(top) **Detail of the Stole Royal**
[Worshipful Company of Girdlers.
Photograph: Prudence Cuming Fine Art
Photography]

(above) **Detail of the roundel
inspired by the Cosmati
pavement in Westminster
Abbey**
[Worshipful Company of Girdlers.
Photograph: Prudence Cuming Fine Art
Photography]

(top) **Detail of the Stole
Royal, showing the leek in
silk shading**
[Worshipful Company of Girdlers.
Photograph: Prudence Cuming Fine Art
Photography]

(centre) **The rose to
represent England**
[Worshipful Company of Girdlers.
Photograph: Prudence Cuming Fine Art
Photography]

(above) **The Gridiron is
the symbol of the Girdlers
and their patron saint, St
Lawrence**
[Worshipful Company of Girdlers.
Photograph: Prudence Cuming Fine Art
Photography]

The Stole Royal and Girdle

The Stole Royal is part of the vestments for the coronation that His Majesty wore for the crowning and was placed over the Supertunica, the Girdle or Sword Belt, and the Imperial Mantle. The Stole Royal for the Coronation of His Majesty The King was newly created and embroidered by the RSN, from a design created by the College of Arms.

Inspired by the Stole worn by Queen Elizabeth II in 1953, the design features a series of roundels set in a gold chain framework and applied to cloth of gold. Each roundel features an embroidered image which has been created using silk shading, also known as 'painting with a needle'.

Designs in the roundels include the four national flowers of the United Kingdom – the rose, the thistle, the leek and the shamrock; a Dove of Peace (representing the Holy Spirit); a Tudor Crown (which features on His Majesty's cypher); the Crossed Keys of St Peter; the four Apostles, and a pattern inspired by the Cosmati pavement in Westminster Abbey.

His Majesty The King attired in the Supertunica, Girdle, Stole Royal and Imperial Mantle

[PA News]

At the nape of the neck is an icon representing St Lawrence, the patron saint of the Girdlers' Company, who gifted the Stole Royal to His Majesty. The grid iron is the symbol for the Girdlers and the palm leaves are for St Lawrence. The Girdlers have presented succeeding monarchs with a new Stole Royal for the past four coronations. The RSN also worked the Stole for George V in 1911.

The embroidered illustrations have been worked in different colours, using fine twisted silk threads, and the framework has been edged with Gold Grecian and Pearl Purl threads. The Stole has a gold-coloured lining and a gold twisted fringe.

The Girdle or Sword Belt was worn by Queen Elizabeth II in 1953. A small extension needed to be added for His Majesty The King, and the whole was conserved by the RSN team in readiness for the King to wear. The Mantle is the oldest piece of attire, originally made for George IV in 1812, it has been worn by George V, George VI (when it came to the RSN for a little TLC as witnessed by the list of everything we worked on for the 1937 coronation), Queen Elizabeth II and now King Charles III, with only the smallest amount of conservation this was able to be reused again.

Silk shading in progress on the Queen's crest
[RSN Collection. Photograph: John Chase]

The Throne Chairs

As with the Chairs of Estate (or Cypher chairs) the throne chairs had previously been used for another coronation – that of George VI in 1937. Once again, the original crests for the King and Queen were worked by the RSN. The fabric and coat of arms for the Queen Consort, Queen Elizabeth was removed, conserved and laid up. The fabric bearing the crest for George VI was given to the RSN for conservation and then to be cut from the original ground fabric and reapplied to new velvet ground because the King's crest remains the same from monarch to monarch. Each Queen Consort has her own lineage, so it is always necessary to create a new consort's crest. For the throne chairs the crest appears on the front and the back so the RSN worked two crests for The Queen. These were worked on two frames placed side by side, with two people working on each frame at any time. They were worked as slips and then transferred to the

velvet fabric before all being handed to the royal upholsterers who had completely stripped the chairs to the frames and then rebuilt them with the new upholstery.

The roses at the lower centre of each chair are the York Roses from 1937 which were transferred and sit front and back of each chair.

Her Majesty's Robe of Estate

The RSN Studio was absolutely thrilled to receive the call from the Palace inviting them to go and meet with Their Majesties to discuss the Robe of Estate, the train the Queen would wear to leave the Abbey. The RSN of course made this piece for both Queen Elizabeth, consort of George VI in 1937, and Queen Elizabeth II in 1953.

The brief was quite open within the theme of flowers and nature, so the team got together to undertake a great deal of research to find flowers that would be meaningful to the King and Queen. They also undertook a large amount of sampling as they wanted to make the effect of the whole less heavy than traditional coronation goldwork

which is deeply padded and looks very solid. They sampled various
approaches to ensure the goldwork looked lighter and more modern
and sent these back to Her Majesty for approval. Under Anne
Butcher and Gemma Murray's leadership, the Studio team took
the research and then also decided to add wild flowers to represent
the diversity of nature and insects, highlighting the King's long
held interest in organic farming and biodiversity. The embroidery
incorporates 24 flowers as well as dragonfly, butterfly, bee, snail,
beetle, ladybird and caterpillar.

The inclusion of small creatures in embroidery has been practised
since the 16th century at least, but not previously on coronation
regalia. However, it seemed completely appropriate to marry this
long-standing embroidery tradition with His Majesty's passion for
the environment.

The flowers include delphinium (one of the King's favourite
flowers, it is also the flower for July, the month of the Queen's
birthday), primrose and lily of the valley (which formed part
of the Queen's wedding bouquet and was a favourite flower of
Queen Elizabeth II). To these the RSN added *Scabiosa* (which
is appropriately known as the pincushion flower given that Her
Majesty is Patron of the RSN) and perhaps most surprising of all,

(top) **Detail of a section of the Queen's Robe of Estate featuring a rose and a thistle**
[RSN Collection. Photograph: John Chase]

(centre) **Detail of a section of the Queen's Robe of Estate featuring a thistle, a shamrock and some oak leaves**
[RSN Collection. Photograph: John Chase]

(bottom) **The lower section of the Queen's Robe of Estate**
[RSN Collection. Photograph: John Chase]

Working on the Queen's
Robe of Estate (see pages
84 and 106 for the same
scenes from 1937 and 1953)
[RSN Collection. Photograph: John
Chase]

dandelion (here to represent the Passion but indicative of all wild flowers). It has been brought to life by showing the dandelion clock beginning to blow away and each seed is represented by a tiny pearl. The rendition of the dandelion has made it the most popular of the flowers, from the appreciation of Their Majesties when they saw the work in progress to later commentators; *Hello* magazine singled it out as their favourite motif of the whole coronation regalia.

'So many of the pieces ... wouldn't have existed without the skills of the RSN. The dandelion seeds realistically worked to appear as if they're blowing across the silk velvet are, perhaps, a favourite.' *Hello* magazine, Monday 24 July 2023

In the typical way of RSN working, a team of people worked on the Robe and when one got up, another would carry on, yet it still looks like the work of just one person. This remains the hallmark of the RSN professional embroiderers.

(top left) **Working on the Queen's Robe of Estate**
[RSN Collection. Photograph: John Chase]

(top right) **Detail of the Queen's Robe of Estate, showing the rose**
[RSN Collection. Photograph: John Chase]

(right) **The Queen's cypher**
[RSN Collection. Photograph: John Chase]

Gemma Murray (left) and Anne Butcher
(right) were able to add a few stitches to
the robe

[RSN Collection. Photograph: John Chase]

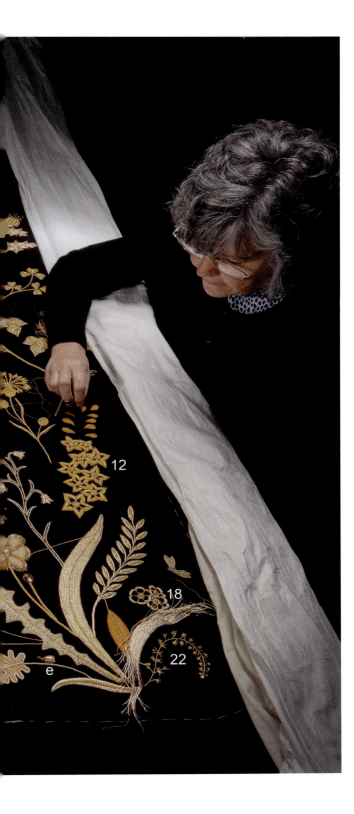

1. **daffodil** – national flower of Wales
2. **olive** – peace
3. **clematis** – mental acuity and wisdom
4. **rose** – national flower of England
5. **hawthorn** – birth flower of May, the Coronation month
6. **thistle** – national flower of Scotland
7. **shamrock** – national flower of Ireland
8. **oak leaves and acorn** – strength and longevity
9. **ivy leaves and berries** – undying affection
10. **apple blossom** – long life
11. **cornflower** – love and tenderness; adored by butterflies and bees
12. **delphinium** – one of The King's favourite flowers and the birth flower of July, the birth month of Queen Camilla
13. **lily of the valley** – love, purity and humility, featured in Queen Camilla's wedding bouquet and a favourite flower of Queen Elizabeth II
14. **myrtle** – hope, featured in Queen Camilla's wedding bouquet
15. **dandelion** – symbolic of the Passion
16. **maidenhair fern** – purity
17. **fern**
18. **auricula** – understood to be one of Queen Camilla's favourite flowers
19. **primrose** – fresh beginnings; featured in Queen Camilla's wedding bouquet
20. *Scabiosa* – pincushion flower (linking the Royal School of Needlework with our Patron)
21. *Alchemilla mollis* – known as lady's mantle, love and comfort
22. **bell heather** – Scottish wild flower

a   **dragonfly**
b   **butterfly**
c   **bees**
d   **snail**
e   **ladybird**

Not shown: **barley** (to represent the countryside of East Sussex where Queen Camilla grew up) and **forget me not** (loyalty and true love)

In addition to the flowers, the robe needed to include Her Majesty's crown and cypher. As for previous robes, these were worked separately and we chose to give this work to our most senior tutor, assessor and moderator, Debra Jackson. Debra started as an apprentice in 1979 and graduated in 1981; she led the work on this piece but in true RSN style, she was assisted by several others.

Her Majesty loved the Robe of Estate and was only sad she could not wear it the entire time. She sent the RSN a very warm personal note of thanks after the coronation.

Altogether the List for 2023 would certainly rival that of 1937 with the conservation of three items and the creation of six. This was an immense amount of work, especially as only one was in production by Christmas 2022, but it was a task the RSN professional embroiderers were able and willing to rise to. Watching the coronation, work by the RSN was visible during almost every moment of the ceremony.

While all the coronation work was going on in secret behind the scenes, normal day-to-day life was continuing, even tours in the Studio (while carefully ensuring visitors did not see anything they should not), and the teaching on all courses continued. In our tried and tested way, anyone asking questions about items we might be working on for the coronation were met with polite but firm silence, even when challenged by someone who, as an RSN student at the time, had put a stitch into the 1953 Robe. The answer was a firm 'no comment'.

However, when from a short while before the event, the Royal Communications team began to release information we could at last begin to say something and the team could reveal to family and friends that they had been working on items for the coronation. But, in the RSN tradition, we do not generally declare who worked what, where or when. This is always the work of a team, and, publicly, we leave it at that, but this time we have documented the names of all those involved which will be archived for the future.

The days following the coronation were a time to reflect on the immense amount of work the RSN had undertaken in a remarkably short space of time and the satisfaction that it all came together at Westminster Abbey. Head of Studio, Anne Butcher, reflected: 'From time to time, we wondered if and hoped the Studio would be involved with the Coronation of King Charles III, I never thought we would ever have as much to do as we did. Working with Studio Manager, Gemma Murray and the amazing team of Studio Embroiderers and Tutors, has been a tremendous experience, one that I will treasure as the pinnacle of my career.'

The Ongoing Cycle

No sooner had the coronation taken place than it was time for our degree students to hand in their work for assessment, and the cycle of exhibitions and graduations began once again. Each year the students are taught the same techniques but what we love to see is the variety in the work that they produce. Bringing this chapter on the RSN's activities in 2022–23 to a conclusion, a selection of our students' work is presented here.

Top student award from the Worshipful Company of Broderers went to Jenna Riddell who dedicated herself and her time to her final major project. She recycled, reused and made her thread from old plastic bags and other recyclable materials, highlighting the plight of endangered species in the process. Her final pieces are placards protesting the degradation of the Earth and its natural habitats. The thread is plastic, and each piece is hand worked using a variety of stitches and techniques.

The RSN is already looking forward, beyond its 150th anniversary, aiming to develop new courses, new programmes and create a wider impact as we recognise the positive benefit embroidery can have on people's mental health and wellbeing at any age. There is a lot more to come.

(top left) **Final major project by Anfaal Hussein**
[RSN Collection. Photograph: TAS]

(top right) **Final major project by Fiza Shahid**
[RSN Collection. Photograph: TAS]

(bottom left) **Final major project by Chloe Rogers**
[RSN Collection. Photograph: TAS]

(bottom right) **Final major project by Chloe Rogers (detail)**
[RSN Collection. Photograph: TAS]

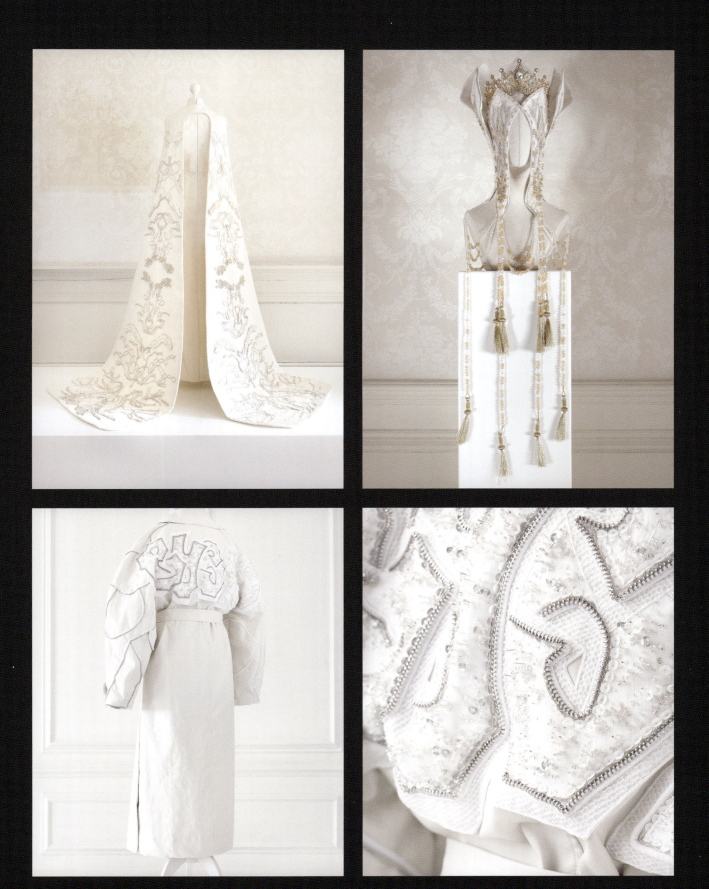

First published by ACC Art Books 2022
Revised and extended edition 2024

ISBN: 978 1 78884 260 0

British Library Cataloguing-in-Publication Data
A catalogue record for this book is available from the British Library

Page 8: Her Majesty Queen Camilla [Chris Jackson/Getty Images ©]

Endpapers: The Wall of Wool, Hampton Court Palace

Design: Ocky Murray

Printed in China by C&C Offset Printing Co., Ltd.
for ACC Art Books Ltd, Woodbridge, Suffolk, England

www.accartbooks.com

ACC
ART
BOOKS

(above left) **Final major project by Jenna Riddell**
[RSN Collection. Photograph: TAS]

(above right) **Final major project by Elizabeth Gray (detail)**
[RSN Collection. Photograph: TAS]

(bottom left) **Final major project by Tomas Asmelash**
[RSN Collection. Photograph: TAS]

(bottom right) **Final major project by Imogen Marmont**
[RSN Collection. Photograph: TAS]

Notes

Additional to those sources cited below, much of the information contained in this book is drawn from the RSN Archives, especially: RSN Archive Box 19, RSN Archive Box 216, RSN Archive Box 11, Managing Committee Minutes, RSN Archive, Minutes of the Art Committee, Minutes of the Executive Committee, Minutes of the Council.

Chapter 1

1   The school has had three names over its 150 years: School of Art Needlework 1872–1874, Royal School of Art Needlework 1875–1922 and Royal School of Needlework from mid-1922. For ease of reading, the acronym RSN will be used throughout.
2   Lady Welby's home is still in the Welby family, Lady Marian's home, Belton House, is now owned by the National Trust.
3   When Princess Helena married Prince Christian of Schleswig-Holstein, press references to her used her formal title of Princess Christian, but to the RSN she was known as Princess Helena and mostly signed her correspondence as such, so throughout this book she will be called Princess Helena unless using a direct quote from elsewhere.
4   Angela Georgina Burdett-Coutts, *Woman's Mission*, pp. 224–27.
5   Angela Georgina Burdett-Coutts, *Woman's Mission*, p. 224.
6   Anastasia Dolby, *Church Embroidery*; Anastasia Dolby, *Church Vestments*.
7   Letter from Lady Welby to Sister Winifred of St Katherine's school of embroidery in Hulse (2010).
8   As described in a published sheet about the school, almost as an annual report October 1873.
9   Over the 150 years, Council changed its name a number of times (for example, Executive Committee with a sub-Committee of Management). The name of the governing body returned to Council in 1961 although the sub-Committee of Management continued until 1976. There has always been a separate Finance Committee in addition.
10   Miss Wade is variously referred to as Superintendent, Manager and Principal over the next 40 years up to her retirement in 1915.
11   The fee had originally been set at 3 gns but in the Minutes of the Council meeting of 7 June 1873 it is increased to £5. If a student was removed, initially they were only given back two-thirds of the fee but later it was returned in its entirety.
12   This remains the standard teaching day at the RSN.
13   The Victoria and Albert Museum since 1899.
14   Bradshaw's was the railway timetable published annually.
15   *The Times*, 10 April 1874.
16   The 1851 Great Exhibition had made money. It was the 1851 Commissioners who were then charged with using this money for further exhibitions and subsequently for developing what became known as Albertopolis.
17   *The Globe*, 4 June 1875.
18   *Windsor and Eton Express*, 5 June 1875.
19   Built 1871.
20   Founded 1882. One of the reasons behind the RSN's move to its own premises was the 1851 Commissioners wanting to give the Royal College of Music the space the RSN occupied.
21   The committee's first meeting was 3 June 1875.
22   G.F. Bodley was an architect, especially involved in designing churches for the new urban towns. At this time architects frequently designed the interiors of their buildings too. He was also responsible for establishing Watts & Co. ecclesiastical embroiderers.
23   There is no further information on this. William Morris does not appear at any of the minuted meetings.
24   Madeline Wyndham was an artist and designer in her own right and was responsible for several designs interpreted by the RSN. Her support for the school continued to her death in March 1920 and was then continued through her daughters Lady Wemyss and Lady Glennconner.
25   The committee petered out by mid-1883 with their last recorded action being to approve items to go to the exhibition/sale at Mansion House.
26   Originally the Rev. Selwyn Image, he put aside the Church to concentrate on design.
27   The front cover of the 1880 *Handbook of Embroidery* was attributed to Crane until the original pencil drawing was acquired in 2015, which is signed by Selwyn Image.
28   An embroidered version of *The Musicians* is at the V&A and was for many years attributed to Burne-Jones, but the original design is in the RSN Archive and clearly signed by Image.
29   Third annual report of the Women's Centennial Executive Committee, 31 March 1876, pp. 7–8. The invitation was sent by Mrs E.D. Gillespie (president of the aforementioned committee) to Lady Marian Alford.
30   *John Bull*, 11 March 1876.
31   Candace Wheeler (1827–1923) was a major influence on textile and interior design in late 19th-century America and was a driving force behind the professionalisation of women in the design field. Inspired by the embroideries produced by the Royal School of Art Needlework, which she saw at the 1876 Centennial International Exhibition, her organisation offered instruction in the applied arts to women, and helped them sell their work, providing some measure of economic independence. See: Amelia Peck and Carol Irish, *Candace Wheeler*.
32   Candace Wheeler, *The Development of Embroidery in America*.
33   George Titus Ferris, *Gems of the Centennial Exhibition*; *Masterpieces of the Centennial Exhibition*; *The Great Centennial Exhibition Illustrated*.
34   The *North British Daily Mail*, of 22 September 1874 reports that 'The Princess Christian and the ladies who form her committee at the School of Art Needlework have agreed that the word antimacassar must henceforth be banished from all refined society. How a word which is so decidedly vulgar, and borders on slang, ever gained currency, no explanation can be

given, for it we must question the last generation; the present and the future, the Princess requests [we] are to speak simply of "chair backs".'

35 *London Daily News,* 14 March 1877.

36 This was also to be secured by a debenture which might give interest up to 5 per cent to provide a fund against the school not breaking even.

37 HRH The Princess Christian of Schleswig-Holstein, 'The Royal School of Art Needlework', in Angela Georgina Burdett-Coutts, *Woman's Mission,* pp. 224–25.

38 *Morning Post,* 7 March 1889.

39 *The Truth,* 8 June 1905.

40 *Sheffield Daily Telegraph,* 12 March 1902.

41 *The Queen,* 4 January 1996.

42 Memorandum of Conditions to be subscribed by persons desirous of becoming Agents for Sale of Needlework of the School 1878.

43 Subsequent to the awarding of royal patronage, the RSN developed a logo which it used on designs as well as on completed objects. We know that the earliest that this can have been used was 1875 and we see it printed in the *Handbook of Modern Embroidery* in 1880. However, we do not know when it stopped being used. By the turn of the century the RSN had had woven labels produced. These usually had to be produced in quite large numbers so the thrifty RSN continued to use them long after the death of Queen Victoria.

44 *Shipping and Mercantile Gazette,* 20 May 1874.

45 *Illustrated London News,* 18 March 1876.

46 *Dublin Evening Telegraph,* 22 February 1877.

47 *Belfast News Letter,* 28 March 1878.

48 *Manchester Courier and Lancashire General,* 30 August 1880. The *Livadia* was a one-off 'yacht' made to a prototype hull design for the Russian Czar. Built on Clydeside, and with one room designed by William De Morgan, the drawing room layout was on display at the RSN. The unusual hull design proved impractical and the ship had to go in for repairs on its way to the Black Sea, and was only formally used once.

49 See also Cathryn Walton, *Hidden Lives.*

50 Council Minutes, 19 March 1881. Letter to the Royal Institute of British Architects, recognising architects' difficulties and offering for the RSN to carry out this work for them.

51 *Illustrated London News,* 31 May 1913.

52 Advert in the *Glasgow Herald,* 19 December 1884.

53 Canvaswork is more frequently referred to as tapestry in the UK and needlepoint in the US. The RSN uses canvaswork to emphasise that this is embroidery as opposed to tapestry weaving. Canvaswork is the technique for heavy-duty items such as chair seats, stools and bell pulls.

54 Crewelwork is wool embroidery on linen twill fabric. Prick and pounce is the method by which the design is transferred to the fabric. Crewelwork had a resurgence in the late 19th century especially for art embroidery.

55 Goldwork is the name for embroidery with metal threads. These are most commonly gold, but silver and copper can also be used. There are many different types of metal threads to help create different effects.

56 Gertrude Jekyll is known for her garden-planting designs but started by designing for interiors until her sight deteriorated, after which she moved to larger outdoor spaces and the concept of drift planting – a concept readily understandable by anyone who is short-sighted.

57 The *Morning Post,* 6 December 1880, announced the dates for the first two lectures on art as applied to needlework. The *Morning Post,* 28 February, announced the repeat of the first

two lectures and the promise of two new lectures after that.

58 For a more detailed telling of this story see the facsimile edition of the book published by the RSN in 2010 with an introductory essay on the background by Lynn Hulse.

59 Lady Marian Alford died unexpectedly in February 1888 and, controlling until the end, demanded that no-one wear crepe at her funeral.

60 *Belfast News Letter,* 29 March 1877, p. 3.

61 *Leamington Spa Courier,* 30 July 1887.

62 *Manchester Courier,* 11 February 1891.

63 Today the Syon Cope is in the V&A Museum. The cope was saved from the convent cull of the Reformation and sent to the Continent, being returned in the 19th century after Catholic emancipation and given to what was then the South Kensington Museum.

64 As stated on the caption when exhibited at Tate Modern in 2018.

65 Executive Committee, letter from LCC.

66 W.G. Paulson Townsend, *Embroidery; or, the Craft of the Needle.* There is an advert for the RSN evening classes at the end of the book.

Chapter 2

1 *East Anglian Daily Times,* 29 January 1901.

2 *Nottingham Journal,* 30 January 1902.

3 *Globe,* 9 February 1901.

4 *The Sphere,* 30 November 1901.

5 *Pall Mall Gazette,* 12 February 1902.

6 *Daily Telegraph, and Courier,* 9 August 1902.

7 *Daily Chronicle,* 24 June 1902.

8 *London Daily News,* 21 June 1902.

9 *Brighton Gazette,* 15 November 1902.

10 *The Builder,* 12 August 1893 supplement and p. 122.

11 In 1910 the Training School rooms were designated the Pfeiffer Rooms.

12 *Northern Whig,* 13 April 1901.

13 RSN Archive 219/10. Princess Helena's speech at the foundation stone laying 23 June 1899.

14 RSN Archive 219/10 Princess Helena's speech at the building opening 1903.

15 *The Gentlewoman,* 25 April 1903, p. 580.

16 *Illustrated London News,* 20 January 1906.

17 Equivalent to more than £3million in 2021.

18 *East Anglian Daily Times,* 3 January 1906.

19 *St James's Gazette,* 10 June 1904.

20 *The Gentlewoman,* 21 March 1908.

21 *The Sketch,* 29 May 1907.

22 *Daily Telegraph & Courier,* 27 May 1908.

23 *The Scotsman,* 17 June 1908.

24 *Leeds Mercury,* 26 March 1915, p. 4.

25 See Stephen Barnard, *From the Hands of Heroes.*

26 *Kilmarnock Herald and North Ayrshire Gazette,* 13 March 1914.

27 *The Gentlewoman,* 14 April 1917.

28 *Sheffield Daily Telegraph,* 13 June 1917.

29 *The Gentlewoman,* 25 December 1915.

30 *Pall Mall Gazette,* 3 November 1915, p. 3.

31 *Mid Sussex Times,* 20 April 1915.

32 *Daily Record,* 14 March 1914; *Birmingham Daily Gazette,* 14 March 1914.

33 *Bradford Observer,* 19 May 1936, p. 8.

34 *Daily Mirror,* 14 May 1932, p. 11.

35 *Tatler,* 15 March 1916.

36 *The Gentlewoman,* 25 March 1916, p. 10.

37 *Sheffield Daily Telegraph*, 2 May 1916.
38 *The Truth*, 13 June 1923.
39 *The Yorkshire Post*, 15 June 1923, p. 6.
40 More than £70 was raised for the stone which was unveiled 1 June 1926.

Chapter 3
1 Miss Bradshaw was given a pension of £250 per annum.
2 *Western Morning News*, 4 June 1932, p. 8.
3 *Western Morning News*, 23 November 1931, p. 6.
4 *Sheffield Independent*, 11 May 1931.
5 *The Times*, 25 November 1931.
6 *Daily Mirror*, 8 June 1932, p. 7.
7 *Daily Mirror*, 22 November 1932, p. 21.
8 *Dundee Courier*, 23 November 1931, p. 12.
9 *Framlingham Weekly News*, 25 March 1933, p. 1.
10 *Newcastle Evening Chronicle*, 6 October 1926, p. 6.
11 By 1942 the RSN was defaulting on its lease with Imperial and was renegotiating the terms, in order to reduce rent liabilities during the war period they were prepared to accept a lower final payment.
12 *Shepton Mallet Journal*, 12 July 1935, p. 6.
13 14 December 1935.
14 The oldest surviving Lord Chancellor's Burse or Purse dates to the reign of Elizabeth I and is now in the collection of the Victoria and Albert Museum. The old tradition was for a new purse to be made for each Lord Chancellor and that he was entitled to keep it at the end of his term of office, as such there are a number still around, especially from the Victorian era. The RSN has one in its Collection and has conserved others.
15 *Belfast Telegraph*, 19 May 1937.
16 Ladies' column in the *Yorkshire Evening Post*, 2 September 1937.
17 As part of the fundraising, Briggs gave the RSN a double-page advertisement, free of charge for a year in their new publication, a combination of *Needlewoman* and *Needlecraft* magazines: *Needlewoman and Needlecraft* no. 1.
18 *Needlework in War-time*, volume 1: Lingerie, p. 2.
19 *Ellesmere Guardian* (New Zealand) 23 January 1942; *Illawarra Mercury* (Australia) 16 January 1942; *Cape Mercury* (South Africa) 6 January 1942; *Gatouma Mail* (Southern Rhodesia) 31 December 1941.
20 6 December 1941 (Twillingate, Newfoundland, Canada); *Your Health* (Vancouver, Canada) February 1942.
21 By the 1960s the RSN had no copies of the series. After asking for copies to be sent in, the RSN does now have one full set including one copy of the most rare, volume 1: Elementary Lingerie.
22 The carpet is now in the National Museum in Ottawa, Canada.

Chapter 4
1 Marguerite Randell, *Design and Needlework* from Women's Employment, n.d.
2 Personal correspondence from Jean Worker (née Millwood), 12 May 2005.
3 Letter 27 April 1949.
4 Princess Alice, Countess of Athlone was, like Princess Helena Victoria and Princess Marie Louise a grandchild of Queen Victoria as the daughter of the Duke and Duchess of Albany. They had been associated with the RSN back in the 1880s when the Duke of Albany opened the extension to the Glasgow branch. Princess Alice attended her first meeting 19 November 1948.
5 *Daily Mail*, 1 May 1951.

6 Completed framed version RSN Collection 288.
7 After graduating from the RSN, Beryl Dean began designing and making costumes for ballet and theatre. After her unhappy year back at the RSN she went on to teach at Hammersmith and West London College for many years. She also continued her practice, making many ecclesiastical pieces, and was especially known for a modern approach to goldwork embroidery. She is the author of several books on embroidery.
8 With thanks to Marion Scoular and Jill Du Plessis for this information. Both were students in the mid-1950s.
9 For example, *The Sphere*, 20 June 1953.
10 RSN Archive 68, *Nottingham Journal*, 20 November 1952.
11 Front cover, *Illustrated London News*, 21 February 1953.
12 This time the exhibition was open 10 am–10 pm and 3 pm–7 pm on Sundays with Tuesday as the special day with higher admission prices.
13 Constance Howard took an open approach to colour and design in embroidery. She taught at Goldsmiths College for many years, leaving behind an inspirational archive of embroidered pieces and collected ephemera as well as a series of books on design in embroidery.

Chapter 5
1 Broderers, Gold and Silver Wyre Drawers and Clothworkers continued their support right through the apprenticeship to 2009. Other livery companies also supported the programme: Dyers, Girdlers, Haberdashers and Needlemakers.
2 This was introduced by the Chief Executive who was somewhat surprised to see that there was no 'final' piece created to show their overall achievement.
3 Described at the time as a catering company.
4 Follow-up review of the Britain-France event hosted by the Franco-British Society, St James's Palace, 17 October 1966.
5 Sir Gordon Russell was a furniture maker and pioneer of modern design. He was the Director of the Council of Industrial Design, now the Design Council.
6 *Hastings Observer*, 5 November 1968.
7 The Inner London Education Authority replaced the London County Council.
8 Personal recollection from interview with Elizabeth Elvin on 15 March 2021.
9 Overlord Project, Miss Bartlett's private information, 1967.
10 Ibid., p. 3 verso.
11 Ibid., p. 6.
12 Ibid., p. 4.
13 Ibid., p. 6 verso.
14 Patron category was in effect Life Friend status but paid at a very low rate for this. Normally one would expect this to be around 15–20 times the annual fee. At £50 it was only seven times the annual fee.
15 2 July 1970.

Chapter 6
1 The name comes from the original motto on the 1880 *Handbook of Embroidery* a small bird may fly high.
2 The Youth Training Scheme was a 1980s government scheme to promote work skills for young people in a time of economic uncertainty.
3 Anthea Godfrey was then at the London College of Fashion, in 2021 she is the Artistic Director of the Embroiderers' Guild. She was also the first external examiner of the RSN foundation degree in 2010.
4 The last time the RSN sent items to Christie's was some large furniture items in 1998/99.

5   This was before Historic Royal Palaces was created, Hampton Court Palace was directly under the Queen and managed by civil servants.

6   The original apartment is not one of those occupied by the RSN today. We were moved again after arriving but then occupied apartments 11 and 12A consistently.

7   Mrs Field, supplementary note to the Minutes of the Finance Committee, 6 June 1986.

8   As a side note on the move, it is minuted that the first computer mailing list was compiled in 1987 because in the move all the 'old books might be destroyed' Council Minutes 6 May 1987.

9   A property was bought with money from the sale of Prince's Gate in King Street, Covent Garden. Well located, but rather like Prince's Gate had been, not an ideal set up. It was on six floors but lacked a fire escape from the top floor so while it had been planned and was used for the administration, eventually they were told to remove themselves while waiting for the fire escape to be built.

10 Jean Panter had been a senior police officer until retirement after which she developed her passion for hand embroidery, working on many commissions as well as teaching. She died in 2009 leaving her entire estate to the RSN, so helping to start the degree programme when government funding was not forthcoming.

11 The relative cost of print is today much less than it was in the 1980s.

12 I am grateful to apprenticeship graduate Helen Stevens for this story.

13 23 May 1988 at Liberty's.

14 Chairman's report to the Annual General Meeting, 20 October 1988, The Hon. Mrs Elizabeth Wallace.

Chapter 7

1   Alice in Wonderland by Rachel Doyle, 2009; Businessman and Shark by Lucy Reid, 2007; Icarus Ascending to the Sun by Kate Cross, 2009.

2   It was exhibited in 2017 at an event to commemorate 30 years of being at Hampton Court.

3   For example, during a ballet performance they are opened and closed for each solo or *pas de deux*; this could be 20 or more times in a single performance.

4   Elizabeth Elvin, Introduction to *Reflections* catalogue 2003, p. 9.

Chapter 8

1   Recruitment advert, 2007.

2   Formerly known as HDRA The Henry Doubleday Research Association, one of the things Susan had done at HDRA was to change its name to be more recognisable.

3   At the time it was the University College for the Creative Arts.

4   Most students choose one course or the other although there has been one who went from certificate and diploma to degree and one in the other direction.

5   Rachel Doyle, Kate Barlow and Alena Chenevix Trench supervised by studio manager Anne Butcher.

Chapter 9

1. In 2013, the exhibition *For Worship and Glory* was held at the RSN before touring to Ely, Chester and Exeter cathedrals. It featured ecclesiastical pieces in the Collection worked by and donated to the RSN.

2. *150 Years of the Royal School of Needlework: Crown to Catwalk.*

Bibliography

Barnard, Stephen, *From the Hands of Heroes: The St Paul's Cathedral First World War Altar Frontal and Memorial Book* (Romford: Memory Lane Media, 2016).

Burdett-Coutts, Angela Georgina, ed., *Woman's Mission: A series of Congress Papers on the philanthropic work of women by eminent writers* (London: Sampson Low, Marston & Co, 1893).

Dolby, Anastasia, *Church Embroidery: ancient and modern* (1867).

Dolby, Anastasia, *Church Vestments: their origin, use and ornament* (London: Chapman and Hall, 1868).

Ferris, George Titus, *Gems of the Centennial Exhibition* (1876).

Ferris, George Titus, *Masterpieces of the Centennial Exhibition*, 3 vols (1876).

Ferris, George Titus, *The Great Centennial Exhibition Illustrated* (1876).

Hulse, Lynn, Introductory essay to *Handbook of Embroidery* (reprint, London: Royal School of Needlework, 2010).

Jackson, Winefride and Elizabeth Pettifer, *Royal School of Needlework: yesterday and today 1872–1948 and 1948 onwards* (Leicester: Anderson Blaby, 1981).

Paulson Townsend, W.G., assisted by Louisa Pesel, *Embroidery; or, the Craft of the Needle* (New York: Truslove, Hanson & Comba Ltd, 1899).

Peck, Amelia and Carol Irish, *Candace Wheeler: the art and enterprise of American design, 1875–1900* (London: Yale University Press, 2001).

Randell, Marguerite, 'Design and Needlework', in *Women's Employment* (n.d. but probably 1946).

Walton, Cathryn, *Hidden Lives: Leek's extraordinary embroiderers* (Leek, Staffordshire: Churnet Valley Books, 2015).

Wheeler, Candace, *The Development of Embroidery in America* (location: publisher, 1921).

Acknowledgements

I must begin by thanking the RSN's Patron HM Queen Camilla for her kind words in the Foreword. Your support for the RSN is much appreciated.

I would also like to thank my colleagues at the RSN and former students for their information, examples of work and anecdotes from the past decades. Alas, there is not room for all of them in a book that covers more than 150 years. Also thanks for your forbearance while I was in writing mode.

From external sources I am very grateful to the British Newspaper Archive and all the many newspapers which have featured the RSN over the years. Due to a lack of primary archival materials on much of the first 30 years of the RSN, these have been a very valuable resource.

There is a tradition, at least in recent years, that when preparing an RSN exhibition some objects are sent or returned to the RSN which really add to the exhibition, and such has been the case with this book. I am grateful to Nina Guppy for donating the album of sketches she made of the RSN at Prince's Gate in the 1980s, two of which are included in the book, and thanks to Diana Springall for acting as courier.

I want to acknowledge and thank RSN volunteer Sue Lown for her sterling work in research, including finding the notes about the 1922 change of name in the National Archives. She was also active in the picture research, persuading various agencies to allow us use of their images. I also want to acknowledge Will@pressphotohistory.com for his immense help in tracking down some of the copyright holders of images that we hold in the RSN Archive. In turn I want to thank all those in the possession of works by the RSN who were generous with their photographs of pieces, including the Dean and Canon of St George's Chapel, Windsor, the Dean and Chapter of Westminster Abbey, the D-Day Story museum, Portsmouth, the William Morris Gallery in Walthamstow, the Royal Albert Hall, the Royal Opera House, the Royal Collection Trust, The Chapter of St Paul's Cathedral and the National Trust, and others who have helped with images, especially Matthew Lloyd, the Hathi Trust and the Library Company of Philadelphia.

I would like to thank Sue Bennett and all the team at ACC Art Books who have supported me through all the stages of production and dealt with all the challenges of photographs, especially from the pre-digital age.

One of the hardest parts of the book was making selections for the 'galleries' of work from the Apprenticeship, Certificate, Diploma, Future Tutor and Degree. Here there was far too much to choose from so I apologise that it will seem a small selection, but I also want to take this opportunity to thank all the tutors and lecturers at the RSN for encouraging the students to achieve more than they ever believed possible.

Thanks also to the Council and supporters of the RSN who have given their encouragement to myself and all the RSN team over the last 17 years.

I have endeavoured to give a fair overview of the trials, tribulations, triumphs and tenacity of the RSN, and illustrate the variety of people and organisations the RSN has worked with, based on press information, RSN minute books, archived papers and the objects in the Archive and the Collection. I have tried to ensure the accuracy of facts, but all errors and omissions are mine.

This book began as a labour of lockdown, and the last chapter was written after my cancer diagnosis and treatment so I cannot end without an enormous thank you to my husband who first put up with me working 24/7 and our house being filled with archive boxes for much of 2020–2021 and subsequently visited me daily in hospital in summer 2022. He then looked after me at home until I was physically stronger, while recognising that I needed to keep working for my sanity.

Index

Numbers in **bold** refer to illustrations

(top left) **Final major project by Freya Stanford**
[RSN Collection. Photograph: TAS]

(top right) **Final major project by Chloe Angrave**
[RSN Collection. Photograph: TAS]

(bottom left) **Final major project by Rebecca Ash**
[RSN Collection. Photograph: TAS]

(bottom right) **Final major project by Emily Barnett**
[RSN Collection. Photograph: TAS]